Disciplining Democracy

Disciplining Democracy: Development Discourse and Good Governance in Africa

Rita Abrahamsen

Zed Books

LONDON · NEW YORK

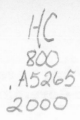
Disciplining Democracy: Development Discourse and Good Governance in Africa was first published by Zed Books Ltd, 7 Cynthia Street, London N1 9JF, UK and Room 400, 175 Fifth Avenue, New York, NY 10010, USA in 2000.

Distributed in the USA exclusively by Palgrave, a division of St Martin's Press, LLC, 175 Fifth Avenue, New York, NY 10010, USA.

Cover designed by Andrew Corbett
Set in Monotype Ehrhardt and Franklin Gothic by Ewan Smith
Printed and bound in the United Kingdom by Biddles Ltd, Guildford and King's Lynn

A catalogue record for this book is available from the British Library

Library of Congress Cataloging-in-Publication Data: available

ISBN 1 85649 858 1 cased
ISBN 1 85649 859 X limp

Contents

Acknowledgements /vii
Introduction /ix

1 Democratisation and Development Discourse　　　　　**1**

Conventional explanations /2
Fictitious dichotomies /6
A merely 'technical' adjustment /9
Power/knowledge and the invention of development /13
Conclusion /22

2 New World Order, New Development Discourse　　　　**25**

The changing fate of 'democracy' in development /26
The end of the Cold War /32
The failure of structural adjustment programmes /37
Power, hegemony and the good governance discourse /42

3 The Seductiveness of Good Governance　　　　　　　**47**

Alien state intervention, indigenous democratic capitalism /47
Liberating civil society /52
Empowerment through cost recovery /56
Good governance as modernisation theory /59
Conclusion /64

4 The Democratisation of Poverty　　　　　　　　　　**67**

Democratic theory and contemporary debates /68
Maintaining the status quo /76
Conclusion /82

5 Whose Democracy?　　　　　　　　　　　　　　　　**86**

The economic roots of democratic demands /87
Victory for the friends of adjustment /98
Conclusion /109

6 Economic Liberalisation and Democratic Erosion   **112**

No more 'cruel choices' /113
Two irreconcilable constituencies /117
'Kill me now' /121
Withering democracy? /125
Exclusionary democracies /132
Conclusion /135

7 The Success of the Good Governance Discourse   **138**

References   **148**
Index   **164**

Acknowledgements

This text has benefited from discussion with a number of friends and colleagues. I wish to thank in particular Abbas Vali, for his advice and inspiration over the years. Thanks also to Björn Beckman and Robert Bideleux for valuable comments on an earlier version of the text. I am immensely grateful to Michael C. Williams for his incisive and constructive criticisms. Finally, I wish to thank the Department of International Politics at the University of Wales, Aberystwyth, which awarded me the sabbatical leave that enabled me to complete the project.

Introduction

Once proclaimed as 'mankind's most ambitious collective enterprise' (Robertson 1984: 1), development has become a controversial and contested terrain. Not only is development widely perceived to have failed, most notably in its attempt to eradicate worldwide poverty, but development theory is also said to have reached an impasse, trapped within its own meta-narratives and unable to capture the diversity of the third world in any relevant and constructive manner (e.g. Booth 1985; Shuurman 1993). While the response of the 'development industry' itself to such criticism has been a continual attempt to refine and revise its theories and strategies so as finally to be able to resolve the problems of underdevelopment, a more wide-ranging critique has emerged that questions the project of development itself. Such critiques draw attention to the very assumptions that underpin development, and argue that the discourse of development is implicated in power relationships and serves to perpetuate international relations of dominance and subordination by constructing the third world as the first world's underdeveloped other.[1] This study of contemporary development discourse draws its inspiration from such insights. It aims to show how the so-called good governance agenda, which emerged as the Cold War came to an end, is an intrinsic part of the technologies of power employed in international politics and one of the ways in which the North maintains and legitimises its continued power and hegemony in the South.

The rebirth of political pluralism on the African continent in the early 1990s was heralded as a new beginning, a 'second independence', which would usher in freedom, welfare and prosperity for Africa's long-suffering peoples. But optimism soon gave way to a more sombre mood, as the democratic project was abandoned, aborted or subverted in country after country. This book provides a critical analysis of post-Cold War development discourse and its relationship to processes of democratisation in sub-Saharan Africa. It combines a theoretical and textual analysis of the good governance agenda with an empirical discussion of processes of

democratisation on the continent, and in this way it aims to render visible
the practical and political consequences of development discourse's current
narration of underdevelopment as an absence of democracy and good
governance. It also shows the historically contingent and culturally specific
nature of development discourse and its relationship to the changing
balance of power in the Cold War era, and makes the case for thinking
about the good governance agenda as legitimising certain forms of democratic politics while delegitimising and silencing alternative democratic
projects.

Almost any analysis of this nature runs the risk of representing discourse
as monolithic, unchanging and unchallenged, of constructing consensus
where diversity, discord and flexibility exist. While there are dissenting
voices within development and no complete uniformity and agreement can
be said to exist between various donor countries and aid organisations, it
is nevertheless the case that development discourse today is more homogeneous than perhaps ever before. The so-called 'Washington consensus'
(Williamson 1993) has been accepted by the vast majority of multilateral
and bilateral donors, and there is general agreement on the desirability of
both economic liberalism and liberal democracy. Disagreement is confined
to the more minor issues and details of what importance to assign to the
various aspects of 'good governance' and 'development', while the overarching tenets remain unchallenged. On this very basic level, then, it is
legitimate to speak of the existence of a development discourse that donors
and creditors in the North all subscribe to and advocate as the model to
be followed by the South. My main interest in this study concerns the
relationship between this development discourse and democracy, and I do
not purport to provide a full analysis of all the various proposals and
implications of the good governance agenda. In particular, I do not discuss
in any detail the more managerial and procedural aspects of the agenda and
its focus on institutional and bureaucratic efficiency and accountability.
Instead the focus is specifically on the way in which the good governance
discourse narrates democracy and its theoretical and practical implications
for African countries.

This book, then, is primarily a reflection and commentary on contemporary development discourse and practice, not a detailed account of
transitions to democracy in African countries. The empirical material is
intended to illustrate and complement the theoretical arguments of the
study, and may accordingly leave much to be desired for the 'country
expert' looking for a full exegesis of democratisation in individual countries.
The study uses examples primarily from four countries in sub-Saharan

Africa: Côte d'Ivoire, Ghana, Kenya and Zambia. All of these countries have in one way or another attempted the simultaneous economic and political liberalisation prescribed by the good governance agenda, and they have been chosen because they provide an opportunity to investigate empirically some of the practical effects of contemporary development discourse. While there is no claim that these countries are in any way representative of Africa, the analysis shows that across a huge geographical space, and in countries with widely different historical, cultural and political backgrounds, development discourse influenced the process of democratisation in particular directions. On this level, then, it is possible to generalise about democratisation in Africa, and some of the arguments may also have a wider application and relevance for countries in other parts of the world that are subjected to similar processes and pressures.

Summary of the Book

In order to set the scene for the ensuing analysis, the book starts with a review and critique of conventional explanations of democratisation in sub-Saharan Africa. These accounts maintain almost uniformly that the main causes of political change in the early 1990s were internal to Africa, and that international factors were merely inspirational and supportive. Chapter 1 challenges this relegation of external factors to such secondary importance. First, it is argued that these explanations do not take sufficient account of the interconnectedness of states and political forces in the global era, and that they maintain a strict internal/external dichotomy that is no longer an accurate or useful description of the world. Second, conventional explanations ignore the power of discourse and its role in the construction and maintenance of Western hegemony in the third world. The chapter shows how development discourse has constructed the third world as underdeveloped, and thereby normalised and legitimised the right of the North to intervene in, control and develop the South. The good governance discourse is merely the latest reproduction of the 'dream of development', and similarly entitles the North to develop and democratise the South in its image. In this way, the chapter shows both how the international is always present in domestic politics, and how many international interventions are sanctioned by development discourse's representation of the third world. Development discourse thus emerges as crucial to an understanding of recent transitions to multi-party politics in Africa.

In Chapters 2 and 3 the focus is on the good governance agenda itself. Historically, a neglect or even an outright dislike of democracy has been one of the few invariants of development discourse's changing vocabulary, and Chapter 2 contends that the discursive transformation represented by the good governance agenda is best understood with reference to the historical conjuncture at which it emerged. More specifically, it is argued that the end of the Cold War, the fall of Communism and also the failure of World Bank/IMF structural adjustment programmes to rekindle economic growth on the continent provided the conditions of possibility of the agenda. In this way, the chapter shows the intimate connection between development discourse and prevailing structures and relations of power, and how the institution of governance and democracy as the prime goals of development was rendered possible by changes in the global balance of power.

Centred on key World Bank documents, Chapter 3 provides a theoretical and textual analysis of the good governance discourse and aims to render visible its inconsistencies, evasions and silences. It argues that the discourse narrates governance in a manner that serves to blur the distinction between democratisation and the retreat of the state from the social and economic field, and thereby constructs a new legitimacy for economic liberalism in the form of structural adjustment programmes. This relegitimation is achieved by invoking images of an 'alien' interventionist state versus an 'indigenous' African capitalism, and through the reliance on a liberal conceptualisation of power, state and civil society. The key effect of the good governance discourse is accordingly the construction of structural adjustment, and the institutions and countries that promote it, as a force for democracy: the liberators of civil society from an oppressive African state. A closer analysis of the agenda's claim to 'empower ordinary people', however, reveals that the discourse deprives this term of its radical political connotations and gives it instead a highly instrumental meaning. Empowerment in the good governance parlance signals merely that people should 'pull their weight' and make development projects more cost-efficient, and again the near fusion of democracy and economic liberalism in the good governance discourse becomes apparent. Chapter 3 also challenges the good governance discourse's claim to cultural sensitivity and argues instead that it is not significantly different from the modernisation theories of the past in that it embodies an image of the good society that is largely constructed from European/US values and experiences.

Chapter 4 seeks to situate contemporary debates on good governance and democratisation in the South within the wider field of democratic theory. It traces the roots of current mainstream definitions of democracy to Weber, Schumpeter and other theorists of democratic elitism, and argues that such approaches lead to the valorisation of multi-party competition and elections as ends in themselves. The chapter contends that while electoral democracy is indeed important to Africa, in that it may offer protection from tyranny and provide the means of peaceful transfer of power, it provides only very limited opportunities for improved social justice. For the majority of poor people, democracy is not only about civil and political rights, but is intrinsically bound up with social and economic rights. Regarding democracy as a contested concept, the chapter shows how taken together the good governance discourse and mainstream literature on democratisation in the South serve to legitimise a particular form of liberal democracy, while delegitimising and marginalising alternative conceptualisations that are perhaps more in tune with the hopes and aspirations of the poor and more responsive to their needs. The detachment of democracy from the ideals of social and economic rights also amounts to an implicit endorsement of the existing social order, and in this way the discourse promotes a form of democracy that allows for the continuation of elite privileges and sanctions the persistence of suffering and deprivation among large sections of the population.

Chapters 5 and 6 provide a more empirical elaboration of the general theoretical issues raised thus far in the discussion. Drawing mainly on examples from Zambia, Côte d'Ivoire, Ghana and Kenya, Chapter 5 shows how externally imposed structural adjustment programmes contributed to democratisation in Africa not because they decentralised power away from the state (as the good governance discourse proposes), but primarily because people opposed the negative social and economic effects of these programmes. The chapter thus argues that popular calls for democracy in many countries were rooted in economic grievances, and as such they were protests against structural adjustment as much as they were demands for political pluralism. Posing the question 'Whose Democracy?', this chapter shows how external pressures and the governance discourse influenced democratic transitions, and argues that the form of democratisation that occurred on the continent in many ways represented a defeat for Africa's poor. Not only was their more social-democratic or welfarist vision of democracy rejected in favour of the governance discourse's minimalist version, but the return of political pluralism has also frequently signalled a renewed enthusiasm for economic liberalism and, by implication, further suffering for the poorer sections of society. The result has been a form of democracy characterised by an inability to incorporate the poorer sections of the citizenry into the political process in any meaningful way. This in turn is a key factor in explaining the social unrest and political instability that have plagued so many of the new democracies in sub-Saharan Africa.

Chapter 6 seeks to explain the rapid deterioration of democratic standards in many African countries by focusing on the relationship between external demands for continued economic adjustment and domestic political instability. The central argument is that economic adjustment has impeded rather than facilitated the institutionalisation and consolidation of democratic principles and procedures. Many newly elected governments on the continent had two irreconcilable constituencies: external donors and creditors and their poor domestic majorities. While governments were crucially dependent on each, for their financial survival and re-election respectively, they could not satisfy both at the same time. External sponsors demanded continued economic liberalisation, which was sure to create domestic dissatisfaction and unpopularity at the polls. Responding to popular demands for social improvements, on the other hand, was likely to result in loss of vital financial assistance. In many countries, the first casualty of this dilemma was the democratic process itself, as governments reverted to the tried and tested methods of the authoritarian past in order to contain civil disorder and silence critics. Nevertheless, in most countries the formal trappings of democracy have been maintained, partly as a consequence of aid dependency and the international isolation that would follow from a total collapse of democracy. In this way the effects of external pressures for simultaneous economic and political adjustment can be seen as paradoxical, in that they contribute both to the maintenance of (an imperfect) democracy and to the persistence of social and political unrest, which continues to pose a permanent threat to the survival of pluralism. The promotion of democracy and economic liberalism as two sides of the same coin has prevented the process of democratisation from progressing beyond the electoral stage, as it effectively rules out social reforms towards a more equitable social order. In this way, the good governance discourse has presided over the creation of what can be termed *exclusionary democracies*, which allow for political competition but cannot incorporate or respond to the demands of the majority in any meaningful way. Moreover, the linkage of democracy to continued economic liberalisation has narrowed the policy agenda in most African countries, and the influence of citizens have been severely curtailed by the power of donors and creditors. Hence, the good governance discourse has also presided over the creation of highly fragile democracies, where the voices of the poor are frequently overruled by the demands of external actors.

This study concludes that ten years on, the good governance agenda has been largely unsuccessful in promoting stable multi-party democracies on the African continent. Although most African countries have by now established democratic structures and procedures, the substance of civil and political rights has gradually been eroded and these democracies remain highly fragile and plagued by civil and political instability. This, however, does not mean that the good governance discourse as such has been a failure. Within the theoretical framework adopted in the study, success or failure should be judged by what development as a practice actually does rather than by its stated aims and objectives. Seen from this perspective the governance discourse has been eminently successful. The good governance discourse reproduces the hierarchies and unequal relationships that have characterised development ever since its inception, and seen as part of the multiple technologies of power in global politics it has helped legitimate the North's continued power and hegemony in the South. By constructing African countries as undemocratic and lacking in good governance it reconfirms the right of the North to intervene, set conditions and define the policy choices of the South. In this way, the good governance discourse is an intrinsic part of the governance of the African continent by the North, and one of the ways in which contemporary international structures and relations of power are maintained and reproduced. By constructing democracy as relevant only within countries, the governance discourse shields international organisations and relations from democratic scrutiny and serves to bestow legitimacy on a world order that is essentially undemocratic.

Note

1. Notable texts include Crush (1995); Escobar (1984–85, 1988, 1995); Ferguson (1994); and Sachs (1992). Texts within this perspective frequently place terms like development, underdeveloped, and third world in inverted commas in order to indicate their specific connotations and particularly contested meanings. I prefer to avoid this practice, which I find not only tiresome but also unnecessary as all terms, not only those related to development, are constructed and inscribed with meaning in discourse. The absence of inverted commas, however, does not indicate that I endorse the conventional meaning and values associated with these terms.

1

Democratisation and Development Discourse

The early 1990s witnessed both the emergence of the so-called good governance agenda and the return of multi-party democracy to the African continent. Despite this simultaneity, conventional explanations of democratisation assign relatively little causal importance to the new development paradigm. The good governance agenda may have placed democracy at the heart of development discourse, these explanations assert, but the real impetus for democratisation is nevertheless seen as internal to Africa, whereas external factors are regarded as only inspirational and supportive. Hence the introduction to a collection of case studies of democratisation claimed in no uncertain terms that the global political environment served merely to make 'things marginally less difficult for those in Africa seeking to democratise their political systems and marginally more difficult for those ... who sought to prevent them from doing so' (Wiseman 1995: 4).

This chapter challenges the relegation of external factors to such marginal importance. The argument is twofold. First, it is argued that conventional accounts disregard or underplay the interconnectedness of states and political forces in the global era. Second, it is argued that these accounts ignore the power of discourse and its role in the construction and maintenance of Western hegemony in the third world. The chapter aims to show how development discourse has produced and constructed the third world as underdeveloped, placing it in a hierarchical and unequal relationship to the first world, and how this discourse continues to justify and legitimise the right of the North to intervene in, control and develop the South. This is also the case with the good governance agenda, which promotes certain forms of intervention in order to democratise third world countries while simultaneously constructing the industrialised countries as implicitly democratic. In this way, the chapter seeks to show how the international is always present at the national and local levels, and how what are frequently perceived as 'domestic' causes of democratisation are

in fact profoundly shaped by international forces and interventions, which
in turn are sanctioned and legitimised by development discourse and its
representations of the third world. Development discourse cannot therefore
be treated as an innocent vehicle of neutral knowledge, disconnected from
the social relations and structures of power in which it is embedded.
Instead it is central to an understanding of contemporary North–South
relations and recent transitions to democracy.

Conventional Explanations

In order to appreciate the arguments of the chapter, it is necessary to
start with a review of conventional explanations of Africa's democratic
revival.[1] These accounts tend to centre on the domestic arena and involve
three closely connected factors: loss of legitimacy, economic decline and
popular protests. Inspired by post-Cold War triumphalism and with relatively little regard for theoretical discussions of legitimacy, many authors
maintain that present-day authoritarianism suffers from an intrinsic problem
of legitimation (e.g. Diamond 1989; Linz 1990). With more than faint
echoes of modernisation theory, it is argued that legitimacy based on
tradition, religion and custom is difficult to maintain with the spread of
education, communication and the democratic ethos (Diamond 1989). Due
to this lack of legitimating principles, authoritarian regimes around the
globe sought to justify their rule through promises of economic growth,
development, stability, or some other desired goal or state of affairs. But
most of these regimes failed miserably to deliver on their grandiose
promises, and consequently their popular support diminished and their
demise became inevitable. These accounts frequently draw a distinction
between poor economic performance by democratic and authoritarian
regimes. In the former, only the sitting government is discredited as a
result of economic mismanagement, whereas in the latter economic failure
is seen to threaten the legitimacy of the system as such. While the existence
of the Communist Eastern bloc lent some legitimacy to one-party states in
the South, the fall of Communism, combined with the disastrous economic
performance of most authoritarian regimes, is widely perceived to have
depleted the legitimating principles available to the world's dictators –
hence the claim that democracy is the 'only model of government with any
broad ideological legitimacy and appeal in the world today' (Diamond,
Linz and Lipset 1988: x).

The argument that democratic transitions occurred due to loss of regime
legitimacy is thus closely linked to the economic failure of authoritarian

rule. By the early 1990s, the gross domestic product of most countries in sub-Saharan Africa had been declining steadily for about a decade, and the states' capacity or willingness to meet the welfare needs of their citizens had deteriorated significantly or collapsed altogether. At the same time corruption, nepotism, mismanagement and human rights abuses persisted, earning African countries the label 'states without citizens': states that exist only for themselves and their own beneficiaries, excluding the vast majority of the population (Ayoade 1988). Most scholars accordingly argue that lack of legitimacy and state efficacy, combined with a general feeling of discontent and despair, stimulated mass demonstrations and contributed to the emergence of pro-democracy movements across the continent. These movements incorporated wide sections of the population, but especially prominent were urban workers, trade unions and the middle classes, including students, teachers and civil servants. It is with these broad-based popular protests against incumbents that many writers locate the real cause of Africa's democratic revival (Bratton and van de Walle 1992; Bratton 1994a; Wiseman 1995 and 1993; Clapham 1993). For others, focusing more on elite choices, the threefold explanation of lack of legitimacy, economic failure and popular discontent is seen to have occasioned a split between so-called hard- and soft-liners within authoritarian regimes, which in turn led to the return of political pluralism.[2] Despite their emphasis on different agents in the transition process, these various accounts are nevertheless united in the perception of democratisation as a result primarily of political pressures exerted in Africa, by Africans.

In addition to these internal developments, mainstream literature identifies two external factors that influenced political change, namely the end of the Cold War and so-called democratic diffusion. The collapse of Communism as an alternative development model rendered Western countries much more powerful *vis-à-vis* Africa and the South in general, and much more stringent conditions could now be attached to development assistance without fear of losing allies to Communist influence. It is at this juncture that we can locate the emergence of the good governance agenda, as will be discussed in more detail in the next chapter. At this point, we need merely to note that most authors regard political aid conditionality and donor pressures for democratisation as rather ineffectual and insignificant contributors to democratisation (Wiseman 1995; Bratton 1994a; Clapham 1993). What little influence is assigned to aid conditionality and donor pressures is confined to the early stages of the democratisation process, and in this context attention is frequently drawn to the case of Kenya. The withdrawal of aid funds is regarded as a crucial determinant of President

Daniel Arap Moi's decision to hold multi-party elections in 1992, but even so donors were unable to exert much influence over subsequent events (ODI 1992; Robinson 1993; Uvin 1993). The Kenyan elections were a far cry from being 'free and fair', albeit endorsed by international observers (*The Economist* 1993a: 47; Geisler 1993), and President Moi has continued his undemocratic style of government despite numerous protests by donors. It is also frequently argued that the good governance agenda has failed to live up to its stated aims, partly because the criteria are difficult to define and implement, and donors frequently disagree about the precise meaning of good governance. Moreover, as a foreign policy goal the 'promotion of democracy' is seen to be of second order importance, frequently sacrificed in the face of other foreign policy objectives such as national security and economic prosperity (see Sørensen 1993a; Hippler 1995). This is of course a main reason why the good governance agenda has been more strictly applied to marginalised African countries than to economically powerful states with poor human rights records, such as China.

Given the predominant scepticism regarding the effectiveness of political aid conditionality and direct foreign pressures, much of the existing literature pinpoints so-called democratic 'diffusion' as a more significant external contributor to political change. Variously referred to as 'snowballing' or the 'domino effect', the contagious nature of the process is also captured by Huntington's metaphor of the democratic wave, gathering strength and engulfing country after country, continent after continent.[3] Diffusion is explained in terms of extensive global communication networks, which not only make news of democratic change instantly available around the world, but also bring such distant events alive and make them seem close and relevant. This in turn can enable democratic movements in one part of the world to draw encouragement and inspiration from successful struggles elsewhere, to instil in them the belief that change is indeed possible (see Huntington 1991; Uvin 1993). Widespread knowledge of previous transitions may also convince incumbents of the need to instigate political liberalisation in order to pre-empt the opposition, escape the humiliation associated with large-scale popular protests and perhaps even avoid the loss of office.

Although democratic contagion is said to occur primarily on a regional level, the dramatic collapse of Communist regimes is believed to have influenced events in Africa and the South in general. The Communist states had served as a model of organisation and inspiration for many countries in the South, and, as already mentioned, their mere existence lent some political legitimacy to African one-party states. Almost by implication, the sudden and dramatic show of popular power in the Eastern bloc in 1989 and 1990 is thought to have dented the legitimacy of African regimes and encouraged political activists to voice their opposition to authoritarianism. For instance, the leader of the trade union movement in Zambia, now President Frederick Chiluba, is reported to have asked shortly after the Berlin Wall came down, 'if the owners of socialism have withdrawn from the one-party system, who are we to continue with it?' (*Times of Zambia*, 31 December 1989). Similarly, the founder of Tanzania's one-party state, the late President Julius Nyerere, conceded that Africa could learn a 'lesson or two' from Eastern Europe (in Huntington 1991: 288). On the regional level, some of the events that contributed to the diffusion of democratic ideas in the early 1990s included the release of Nelson Mandela, the emergence of independent Namibia, and Benin's much talked about national conference. These were all occasions that indicated that a new democratic ethos was taking hold on the continent, and each in turn further encouraged the demand for political change and renewal.

In the hierarchy of causal factors contributing to democratisation in Africa, however, the majority of contemporary scholars hold international factors to be subordinate. The *real* causes are regarded as internal to Africa, and international factors are merely supportive. The position is succinctly summed up by Wiseman, who argues that 'internal pressures ... have played the major role and ... external developments have, at most, contributed relatively modestly' (1995: 4). In the same vein, Bratton and van de Walle maintain in a frequently cited article that external factors served as precipitating conditions, rather than causal ones (1992: 420; see also Bratton 1994a; Schraeder 1995; Wiseman 1993). The consensus view is accordingly that in the absence of domestic pro-democracy movements, aid conditionality and changes in the global political environment would have had little or no impact on Africa's autocratic leaders.

This interpretation draws support from research on Latin America, and perhaps most importantly from the influential four-volume study *Transitions from Authoritarian Rule*, the most theoretical and wide-ranging comparative study of democratisation to date (O'Donnell, Schmitter and Whitehead 1986). In the concluding volume, O'Donnell and Schmitter state that 'it seems to us fruitless to search for some international factor or context which can reliably compel authoritarian rulers to experiment with liberalization, much less which can predictably cause their regimes to collapse'. They conclude that 'the reasons for launching a transition can be found predominantly in domestic, internal factors' (O'Donnell and Schmitter 1986: 18). Whitehead has, however, added a vital proviso to this generalisation: it holds only for a particular geographical area, in a specific historical period. It refers to countries in which 'local political forces operated with an untypically high degree of autonomy' (Whitehead 1986: 5). While this sounds a rather excessive claim even for Latin America, it is, as the next section will show, certainly not the case in contemporary Africa, where local political forces operate in a dependent relationship with international actors.

Fictitious Dichotomies

The insistence on the primacy of internal factors in recent processes of democratisation is both rather curious and somewhat perplexing, since it reverses a long-standing tendency in many discourses on the third world. A key characteristic of these discourses, whether produced by the political left or the right, journalists, academics or policy-makers, has been a denial of effective agency to the countries and peoples of the South. The terms first used to describe the study of these countries are in themselves telling examples; American political scientists in the 1950s and 1960s studied 'emerging areas' and 'emerging peoples'. This terminology indicates a people with no history, no civilisation, simply 'emerging' from nothingness to a future assigned to them by Western scientists.[4] While the study of 'emerging areas' has since mutated into 'area studies', 'third world studies', 'development studies' and so on, the denial of effective agency to these countries has continued more or less unabated. Seemingly unable to escape the legacy of imperialism and coloured by Eurocentrism, various discourses have perceived the third world primarily as an object of intervention and study, not an autonomous subject possessing political will. In many representations of Africa, it seems that the continent's history did not begin until the arrival of European explorers, traders, missionaries and settlers; and then the slave trade, colonisation and independence *happened* to Africa. In a similar vein, contemporary debates make much of the colonial origins of the modern state and its lack of roots in indigenous society – again the fact that Africa was acted upon becomes a defining feature of the continent, while the agency of Africa and Africans is obscured or ignored.

There is today an expressed desire among Africanists to give Africa back its own history, to excavate its historicity and place recent developments within the Braudelian *longue durée*.[5] While this is a laudable and long overdue development, little will be gained if the recognition of the history and agency of Africa and its peoples leads merely to the opposite extreme, namely the abstraction of the continent from its international setting, as seems to be the case in many contemporary accounts of democratisation. Instead a recognition of Africa's historicity should be a way of facilitating an understanding of history and politics that takes account of the manner in which the continent has been incorporated into the international system. The fact that Africa's integration into the world capitalist system has frequently been on unequal, dependent terms does not deny its agency. As Bayart has forcefully demonstrated, dependency does not negate historicity. On the contrary, Africa's 'unequal entry into the international system has been for several centuries a major and dynamic mode of the historicity of African societies, not the magical suspension of it' (Bayart 1993: 27). Throughout time, from the trans-Saharan caravan trade to the present, Africans have interacted with outsiders. They have not been passive puppets of world events, but have actively shaped their own history and politics in interaction with the external environment. The slave trade, for example, was not wholly forced upon an unwilling continent, but was voluntarily entered into by some elites who saw it as an opportunity to obtain luxury goods (Thornton 1992). Similarly, colonialism did not just happen to the continent – it was also used and given definition by Africans themselves. Various sections of the population used the colonial system to further their own ends and strengthen their position *vis-à-vis* others. Influential elites were formed through this relationship with the colonial powers and external capital, and still derive much of their income and status from their relationship with the international system.

In the same way, recent transitions to democracy are profoundly influenced by Africa's interaction with and place within the international system, and to explain these transitions with reference to domestic factors only is far too simplistic. The tendency to construct a dichotomy between the internal and the external and to examine the two in isolation, with little or no attention the way in which the two levels of politics overlap and intertwine, has a long history in the study of politics. Over two decades ago Gourevitch remarked that 'students of comparative politics treat domestic structure too much as an independent variable, underplaying the extent to which it and the international system are parts of an interactive system' (1978: 900). The foundations of this conventional, empiricist distinction are the national boundaries of the state system and the attempt by empiricist research to understand social reality in terms of methodological individualism and the real or perceived aims, intentions and functions of rational actors (conceived as states within the discipline of International Relations). But states do not exist in splendid isolation, and the state-centric approach is particularly inadequate in light of Africa's unequal entry into the global system and the more recent expansion of transnational relationships.

Perhaps more than any other historical period, ours is characterised by interdependence between states and their societies. Globalisation, defined here simply as the intensification of economic, political, social and cultural relations across borders, has gradually eroded or weakened the integrity of the nation-state as an autonomous, independent actor.[6] Governmental and non-governmental institutions, transnational corporations and markets continually cross borders, and the actions and decisions of one actor are likely to impinge on the choices and possibilities of others. In a world increasingly dominated by an international capitalist system, more and more decisions lie outside the direct control of individual states. The central agencies of the state, such as the finance ministries, the central banks and the prime ministerial and presidential offices, have become increasingly linked to each other and to international institutions such as the IMF. As a consequence, states are continually forced to adopt policies that reflect international as much as domestic imperatives (Cox 1987). An important function of the state today is accordingly to adjust domestic policies to the exigencies of the global market, and previously distinct national economies are increasingly incorporated into and subsumed by a larger global network of financial transactions and relations. Domestic decision-makers, whether politicians, public regulators or private business, can no longer consider only national conditions but must take account of the international situation, which may constrain certain plans and options and facilitate and encourage others.

Integration into the world economy also has profound effects on domestic state–society relations and class structures (Halliday 1987). It may enhance the position of some groups, reduce the influence of others and introduce international capital (in the form of transnational companies) as a significant actor in domestic politics. Moreover, the state and groups associated with the state frequently use their international role and recognition to consolidate their domestic positions of power. International resources can also be deployed to contain domestic challenges and threats, as exemplified by the financial and military aid extended to many African leaders lacking in domestic support, especially during the Cold War. In this way, much of international relations can be regarded as the 'internationalization of domestic conflicts' (ibid.: 222).

Both empirically and conceptually, then, the internal–external dichotomy is unsound and the neglect of the interplay of the internal and the external severely impoverishes contemporary explanations of democratisation in sub-Saharan Africa. The conventional methodological individualism and rational actor explanations of social change are wanting, and need to be combined with closer attention to historical context, structural relations and their political and cultural conditions of existence. National actors and structures have various international conditions of existence that ensure their functioning and reproduction, in the same way as the global system is conditioned by complex domestic configurations and circumstances. Furthermore, the conditions of existence of both the internal and the external are sustained and reproduced by the same capitalist world economy, which renders national boundaries highly porous and casts doubts on any argument for the structural or functional autonomy of the internal. Accordingly, the concept of causes of democratisation supersedes any given national borders. It is not sufficient simply to assess the effectiveness of political aid conditionality and direct foreign pressures, and then add a measure of 'democratic diffusion'. Instead any analysis of democratisation must take account of how the various countries are integrated into the international system of states, the world economy, the international division of labour and how international economic and political conjunctures condition the dynamics of domestic developments.

A Merely 'Technical' Adjustment

During the past fifteen years or so, the most notable articulation of Africa's interaction with the international environment has been the structural adjustment programmes imposed by the Bretton Woods institutions. These programmes represent the historical-specific expression of globalisation on the continent in the 1990s, and have vastly increased the speed of the continent's incorporation into the global economy. Inspired by neoliberalism, the adjustment package has served to open up African economies to transnational actors, while the leverage of indebtedness has been used to direct domestic production away from industry and towards further concentration on the production of primary commodities for export. Moreover, the required privatisation of public industries has frequently led to take-overs by foreign companies and multinationals, as sufficient national capital has rarely been available.

The economic crisis and lack of legitimacy that contemporary literature pinpoints as the internal causes of democratisation cannot be divorced from these externally imposed adjustment programmes. More than a decade of adjustment has yet to produce a definite success story on the African continent. Instead the programmes have generally worsened the living conditions of the already poor and resulted in deepening poverty, widening social polarisation and increasing unemployment across the continent.[7] The widespread feeling of disillusionment and discontent is intimately bound up with adjustment measures, and the mass demonstrations of the early 1990s were directed as much against these programmes as against authoritarian political systems. Adjustment programmes affected all sections of the population, and the emergence of pro-democracy movements must be placed in this context. While the urban poor swelled the ranks of street demonstrations in the early 1990s, the educated middle classes made up the backbone of the democracy movements. These groups had seen their purchasing power eroded by high inflation and devaluation had made luxury imports unaffordable, causing many to search for alternatives to the existing leadership. Economic crisis and adjustment measures are also likely to have affected the cohesion of the national elite, as patrimonial and clientelistic relationships may be more difficult to maintain in times of financial hardship. The ability of regimes to use patronage to stem opposition is reduced by imposed austerity measures, and the opportunities of the favoured few to collect the economic rents that their jobs previously gave them easy access to may dwindle in the face of adjustment policies. In some instances, then, economic decline may have pushed political elites to oppose incumbents in order to protect their own sources of income.[8] This effect of adjustment should not, however, be exaggerated, as state elites by virtue of their superior economic and political positions are often in the best position to benefit from adjustment policies like privatisation (see Galli 1990; Gibbon 1992; Hibou 1999; Zack-Williams 1990).

Structural adjustment has had profound effects on social, economic and political developments in Africa, and through these programmes the IMF, the World Bank and the donor countries that support their programmes have contributed to undermining the legitimacy of African rulers. This is not to say that external actors are singularly responsible for Africa's economic and political malaise, nor that the situation necessarily would have been any better or different without their intervention. It may well be that given the adverse political, economic, ecological, demographic and geopolitical trends on the continent in the 1980s and 1990s, the situation would have been equally desperate without structural adjustment. Such statements, however, can be nothing but guesswork and speculation, as the relevant counterfactual knowledge is wholly absent. The point here is not the extent to which adjustment caused or worsened the African crisis, but that through these policies external actors became active participants in the formulation of national policies. By actively shaping and directing the response to the crisis, the World Bank and the IMF in particular have become deeply involved in domestic politics. Adjustment policies have affected the power of the state *vis-à-vis* society and the international system, as well as the balance of power between classes and various sections of the population. The politics of adjustment have been played out in individual countries. Imposed measures have been implemented, manipulated, changed or altogether neglected by politicians. Various groups have responded in different ways, resorting to multiple survival strategies and coping mechanisms. Over time, the internal and the external have become interwoven in complex ways, so much so that we cannot with any degree of certainty say where one begins and the other ends. What remains clear is that the politics of democratisation cannot be reduced to the domestic level, rather the internal and the external are, in the phrase of Braudel (1985), inextricably linked.

The extent of this involvement in domestic politics is problematic both for the Bretton Woods institutions and for bilateral donors and creditors, in particular because it raises questions of national sovereignty and self-determination. With colonialism only a few decades away, donors have been eager to avoid allegations of undue interference in the domestic affairs of recipient countries. Part of the effort to avoid such accusations has been the representation of development as a neutral enterprise, driven by a humanitarian desire to universalise wealth rather than by any particular political or ideological objectives. This has become even more pressing with the emergence of the good governance agenda, which made development aid conditional on such overtly political issues as democracy, legitimacy and accountability. The launch of the good governance agenda was accompanied by an attempt by doners to define governance as both politically and culturally neutral, as calling simply for the efficient and optimal management of a nation's resources and not prescribing a particular system of rule (see e.g. World Bank 1992a; ODA 1993). Thus, Britain's minister for overseas development at the time, Lynda Chalker, characteristically claimed with reference to good governance that 'we have no ideological axe to grind' and on the issue of tying aid to political reforms she commented that 'Some may call this conditionality. I call it common sense' (1991: 8, 4).

For the World Bank the political overtones of the good governance agenda are particularly problematic, as the Bank's Articles of Agreement expressly forbid the institution to use non-economic and political criteria in its lending operations, and to interfere in the political affairs of its members.[9] The theme of neutrality has accordingly always occupied a central place in World Bank discourse. The authors of the early drafts of the Bank's Articles, including John Maynard Keynes, were eager to stress the impartiality of the institution with regard to political ideologies and interests. More recently, the Bank's General Council argued that '*Technical considerations of economy and efficiency, rather than ideological and political preferences, should guide the Bank's work at all times*' (Shihata 1991: 95, italics in original). To a significant extent, this claim to neutrality relies on the commonplace perception of economics as a value-free science. Economics is perceived as a 'realist', empirical discipline that can provide a neutral and true representation of the world. In this way correct economic policy becomes a question of objective facts and data, devoid of political and cultural preferences. Hence the Bank's Articles of Agreement permit economic judgements, which are merely 'technical', but deny the application of political criteria, which belong to the muddy waters of ideology and subjectivity. This statutory obligation to neutrality has in turn given the World Bank's good governance discourse a rather technocratic, managerial resonance, focusing on issues such as effective public sector management, legitimacy and accountability, rather than arguing explicitly for liberal democracy.[10]

Academics are of course well aware of the political nature of both the World Bank and the IMF, and have few illusions as to the neutrality of their programmes. The composition and distribution of power within the Bretton Woods institutions, and their close relationship to the richer countries, is well documented. Voting power in both the World Bank and the IMF is proportional to the amount of capital invested, and as the largest shareholder the USA holds the largest share of the votes. All in all the G7 states account for 40 per cent of the voting power in the World Bank, compared to just over 4 per cent for the whole of sub-Saharan Africa (Curtis 1998: 81). Needless to say, this gives the richer countries the power to define policy within the two institutions, and there is a close correlation between the policies of the major G7 countries and the aims and objectives of the Bretton Woods institutions. But despite this recognition, when it comes to transitions to democracy contemporary scholarship persists in regarding development discourse as largely irrelevant to these processes. Some authors even accept the World Bank claim to be concerned only with the 'technical' issues of the economy, the law and the bureaucracy. Accordingly, it has been argued that there are in fact two good governance agendas; an overtly political agenda of bilateral donors calling for multi-party elections and a purely managerial and administrative agenda of the World Bank, focusing on efficient and accountable government procedures (e.g. Bratton and Rothchild 1992; Moore 1993; Leftwich 1993).

In this sense, contemporary interpretations of democratisation continue to operate within an empiricist/positivist epistemology, whose hallmark is an ontological distinction between subject and object and which in turn produces the possibility of objective knowledge. In treating facts and evidence as objectively given and identical with the real signified by them, knowledge is separated from the conditions of its social production and stands in no relationship to contemporary structures and relations of power. Instead knowledge comes to represent the objective 'truth' that the World Bank and others concerned with development have discovered and accumulated about the third world and underdevelopment. Knowledge or discourses are of course not innocent in the manner assumed by such empiricist accounts. Rather they are intimately connected to historically specific structures of power, and their production cannot occur outside of these relations of power. The neglect of the power/knowledge nexus in conventional empiricist scholarship leads to an automatic acceptance of categories such as the third world and underdevelopment, and every time they are used their relevance as a way of understanding the social world is reinforced. But these categories are not an accurate reflection of some such entity in the 'realm of the real'. Instead they have been constructed and acquired meaning within specific discourses, which in turn have created a 'regime of truth', an accepted way of speaking about and acting towards these countries (see Escobar 1995). These particular ways of thinking and speaking about the third world have in turn made possible and legitimised certain practices and policies towards these parts of the globe, and in this way discourse has contributed to the production and maintenance of particular structures of power. The manner in which the third world and development are spoken about cannot therefore be ignored when discussing recent transitions to democracy in the South. Rather development discourse, and the good governance agenda in particular, is crucial to an understanding of democratisation in the contemporary world. It constructs democratisation in a particular way, it legitimises specific interventions and protects the Western democracies from scrutiny, while at the same time delegitimising and marginalising alternative representations of democracy and development.

Power/Knowledge and the Invention of Development

Edward Said argues in the introduction to *Orientalism* that there is 'no such thing as a delivered presence; there is only a *re-presence*, or a representation' (1979: 21). The study of development has traditionally paid little

attention to the politics of representation, as the practical challenges of
development have been perceived as far too urgent to allow for a 'purely
academic' or even esoteric concern with words and discourse. A focus on
representation, however, does not deny the existence of a material world
or the very real experience of poverty and suffering by millions of people.
Nor is an analysis that focuses on discourse by its nature any less motivated
by a desire to see a world free from human misery than the conventional
development text. Instead such analyses suggest that because objects and
subjects are constituted as such within discourse, an understanding of the
relevant discourses is a necessary part of any attempt to change prevailing
conditions and relations of power.

The approach of this study draws in particular on the insights of Michel
Foucault, whose forceful articulation of an intrinsic and irreversible
relationship between power and knowledge is of immense value to the
analysis of development and North–South relations.[11] According to
Foucault, power and knowledge are intimately connected and directly imply
one another, so that 'there is no power relation without the correlative
constitution of a field of knowledge, nor any knowledge that does not
presuppose and constitute at the same time power relations' (1991: 27).
This close relationship between power and knowledge alerts us to the fact
that the problematisation of a particular aspect of human life is not natural
or inevitable, but historically contingent and dependent on power relations
that have already rendered a particular topic a legitimate object of investigation. Underdevelopment and poverty, in other words, do not exist
as Platonic forms; they are discursive constructs and their constitution as
objects of scientific enquiry can be understood only in the context of the
prevailing balance of forces at the time of their formation. An analysis
informed by such insights does not accept at face value any particular
categorisation of the world, but seeks instead to establish how certain
representations became dominant and acquired the position to shape the
ways in which an aspect of social reality is imagined and acted upon. As
Escobar (1995) argues, thinking about development in terms of discourse
enables us to maintain a focus on power and domination, while at the same
time exploring the discourse's conditions of possibility as well as its effects.
It allows us to 'stand detached from [development], bracketing its famili-
arity, in order to analyse the theoretical and practical context with which
it has been associated' (Foucault 1986: 3). In other words, development
emerges as culturally and historically contingent, and the focus shifts from
'what is' to *how* subjects are formed within this discourse as developed and
underdeveloped. This conception of the relationship between power and

knowledge enables us to expose the political and strategic nature of discourses previously regarded as existing independently of power relations by virtue of their presumed scientific nature, and to ask instead 'whom does discourse serve?' (Foucault 1980: 115).

The study of development as discourse is a relatively new field, inspired in part by Said's *Orientalism*. Orientalism, Said writes, is a 'systematic discipline by which European culture was able to manage – and even produce – the Orient politically, sociologically, militarily, ideologically, scientifically, and imaginatively during the post-Enlightenment period' (1979: 3). This definition is instructive also for the study of development as a representational practice. By substituting the third world for the Orient and the West for Europe, the definition illustrates the productive power of development discourse. The third world and development are historical constructs, a particular way of seeing and acting upon the world that has less to do with the conditions it describes than with the constellation of social and political forces at the time of the emergence of the discourses. It does not indicate the discovery of something new or hitherto unknown, as the conditions of poverty (or underdevelopment) described in the new discourses have always been a feature of human history. Why then did development emerge? And what were its effects? The ensuing analysis aims to throw some light on these questions, and in the process, to show how such representational practices are an intrinsic part of hegemonic politics.

Development first emerged as a domain of knowledge and intervention in the early post-Second World War period, with President Harry Truman's inaugural address in January 1949 frequently identified as a landmark event.[12] The speech introduced the term 'underdeveloped areas' and marks the launch of the global effort to develop the world and eradicate poverty. It should, however, be noted that the notion of development has far deeper roots in Western civilisation and intellectual history than this interpretation may suggest. The modern idea of development is intrinsically bound up with notions of progress and evolution, which have had a marked effect on Western culture ever since the Renaissance (see Cowen and Shenton 1995 and 1996; Norgaard 1994; Rist 1997). With the growth of science and the rise of capitalism and industrialisation, the belief in progress gradually came to replace providence, and the perception that the future could be controlled and mastered through the advance of human knowledge became inseparable from Western culture. Thus, by the time Marx was writing his critiques of capitalist society, the belief in progress was so deeply ingrained in European culture that he regarded it as a law of history (Nørgaard 1994). But although the idea of development is intimately bound up with the rise of capitalism and modernity in nineteenth-century Europe, the institutionalisation of development really only started after the Second World War. This was the period that saw the birth of the development organisation, the development expert, the national development plan, and numerous university courses in development. The post-war period can therefore justifiably be termed and treated as 'the era of development'.

President Truman's inaugural address provides a revealing outline of the main development problems and the means of solution to them, and although over fifty years have passed since Truman launched his quest to eradicate poverty the central tropes of development remain largely unchanged. The famous 'Point Four' of Truman's speech called for a 'bold new programme for making the benefits of our scientific advances and industrial progress' available for 'underdeveloped areas'. The president described the situation in these areas in the following manner:

> More than half the people of the world live in conditions approaching misery. Their food is inadequate. They are victims of disease. Their economic life is primitive and stagnant. Their poverty is a handicap and a threat both to them and to more prosperous areas. (Truman 1949)

But according to the American president, there was now hope: 'For the first time in history humanity possesses the knowledge and the skill to relieve the suffering of these people' (ibid.). The hope stemmed primarily from the USA, which was 'pre-eminent among nations in the development of industrial and scientific techniques'. While the material resources available for 'underdeveloped areas' were limited, the 'technical knowledge' of the USA was, according to Truman, not only 'constantly growing', but also 'inexhaustible'. By making this technological expertise available, the USA could help the 'underdeveloped areas' to 'produce more food, more clothing, more materials for housing, and more mechanical power to lighten their burdens' (ibid.).

The order of discourse is telling. 'Underdeveloped areas' are portrayed as passive, as victims of diseases, poverty and stagnation. Their inertia stands in sharp contrast to the dynamism and vitality of the 'developed areas', and the USA in particular. These areas can embark upon 'bold programmes', and their technical knowledge and scientific advances are constantly expanding, always reaching new highs. This in turn enables them to rescue the 'underdeveloped areas' from their 'misery', to deliver them from their primitiveness to modernity; to the era of 'technical knowledge', 'scientific advances', 'greater production' and 'personal freedom and happiness for all mankind'.

Three aspects of this order of discourse deserve further elaboration here, primarily because they have continued to inform and underpin development discourse. These three can be summed up under the captions fear, absences, and hierarchies, and in one way or another they can be seen to have performed crucial functions in development ever since its inception. Fear may seem an odd category in this context. Development is always presented as a humanitarian and moral concern, an ethical obligation on behalf of the rich to help and care for those less fortunate. But behind this aura of humanitarianism lurks a certain fear of poverty and the poor. In the words of President Truman, 'Their poverty is ... a threat both to them and *to more prosperous areas*' (italics added).[13] The association of poverty with danger can be traced back at least to the eighteenth century, when rapid industrial improvements made the existence of widespread poverty appear as a threat to the wealth and 'civilised' way of life of the upper sections of the population. The 'dangerous classes' (Gordon 1991) therefore needed to be controlled, and in the West, the poor gradually appeared as a social problem, requiring new forms of intervention and management. 'Assisting the poor', Proccacci reminds us, 'is a means of government, a potent way of containing the most difficult sections of the population and improving all other sections' (1991: 151). This observation can be expanded to include not only domestic welfare arrangements, but also international development aid. In the post-war period, poor countries were associated with unrest and instability, and increasingly appeared as a threat to the liberal world order. This was particularly the case after the rise of Communism, as material deprivation was perceived to make people prone to irrational and extremist politics that could potentially upset the global balance of power.[14] Poverty, at both the domestic and international levels, therefore needed to be managed. In the words of Proccacci, poverty 'constitutes a development area for techniques designed to structure an organic social order which, whatever the concrete localization of the human subjects it deals with, is able to bring under its management those zones of social life which have hitherto remained formless' (1991: 164). Through the various techniques to combat poverty, the poor become observed and classified, managed and surveilled, they become visible objects of disciplinary power (Foucault 1991). In relations between North and South, development has facilitated such control and management of the 'third world' and its 'formless' population of poor and destitute (Doty 1996). Development allowed the North to gather 'facts' in order to define and improve the situation of the poor peoples of the South, and the third world became a category of intervention, a place to be managed and reformed. New forms of power and control that could be justified with reference to a humanitarian concern for development came into being, and in the process 'poor people's ability to define and take care of their own lives was eroded in a deeper manner than perhaps ever before' (Escobar 1995: 39).

Another central feature of development discourse, visible already in President Truman's speech, is the narration of underdevelopment as a series of absences. The third world is defined primarily by what *it is not*, rather than by what it is. Its central characteristics become what it lacks, not what it possesses. The essence of the third world is accordingly its lack of development, the absence of 'technical knowledge', 'scientific advances', prosperity, progress, and so on. As development discourse has changed and adapted to the changing circumstances of both donor and recipient countries, the specific nature of these absences has varied. Under-development has been variously described as the absence of 'growth', 'basic needs', 'integrated rural development', 'structural adjustment', 'sustainable development' and so forth, but the focus has remained firmly on what is wanting. The effect of this representation is twofold. First, it serves to erase differences within the third world. The essential characteristic of all third world countries is their lack of development; they are all poor, illiterate, primitive, and so forth. In this way, the street vendor in Rio, the South African miner, the Landak family in the Himalayas, and the Kikuyu in Kenya become one and the same: poor and underdeveloped. The third world emerges as a homogeneous whole, in need of the same development to be administered by development experts. Second, the structuring of discourse around a series of absences legitimises actions and interventions in the third world. Absences appear as deficiencies, or abnormalities, to be remedied and rectified through development. The third world consists of deficiencies, waiting to be improved, reformed and eradicated. Development becomes a means of rescuing the third world, a legitimate and necessary form of intervention to remedy the misery and suffering associated with underdevelopment. In this way, development promises not only an end to the deficiencies of the third world, but also to the third world itself as it becomes more like the first.

Notions of absences and deficiencies in turn establish a very clear hierarchy, where the first or developed world is placed above the third or underdeveloped world. There is a very strong evolutionary streak in dev-elopment discourse, most clearly articulated in the early development models of the 1950s and 1960s. Rostow's (1960) well-known 'stages of economic growth', where all countries would eventually reach the stage of 'high mass-consumption', is only one articulation of the normative expectation that the third world will follow in the footsteps of the first. Although the Eurocentric and teleological nature of development discourse has been much toned down since the 1960s, there can be little doubt that the industrialised countries of the West remain the model for third world development. At every turn, this discourse reinforces hierarchies. The very notion of development always invokes images of change for the better, from stagnation to dynamism, from simplicity to complexity, from scarcity to abundance. Before development, there is nothing but deficiencies. Underdeveloped areas have no history of their own, hardly any past worth recalling, and certainly none that's worth retaining. Everything before development can be abandoned, and third world countries emerge as empty vessels waiting to be filled with the development received from the first world. The superiority and dominance of the first world over the third is thus continually reinforced through this discourse.

The problematisation of development did not occur as a result of any natural progression of science, nor was underdevelopment suddenly dis-covered. Instead development is a historical construct, and its emergence must be seen in the context of the historical conjunction at which it emerged. The invention of development in the early post-war period was set against the background of rising nationalism in Latin America and growing demand for independence in Asia and Africa, which made it necessary to think in terms of new ways of managing and relating to these areas. But most importantly, development emerged at a time when Cold War hostilities came to define international relations.[15] The conflict between East and West was largely played out in the third world (Halliday 1989), and Western fear of Communism was one of the prime motivating forces behind the development effort. In the 1950s poverty was widely regarded as a breeding-ground for Communism, and Western policy-makers feared that the persistence of material deprivation would drive third world countries into the hands of Moscow. Development became a means of containing the spread of Communism, as is clearly evident in most early texts on development. A telling example is Packenham's observation that when American aid officials in the mid-1960s were asked what they under-stood by development, 'one of the most common responses was, in effect, that political development is anti-Communist, pro-American stability' (1966: 213). The Cold War then provided the main rationale for the war on poverty and legitimised the spending of vast resources on peoples in far-away places.[16]

Although the Cold War was by far the most important single factor contributing to the problematisation of development, other conditions also facilitated its emergence. Development was, for example, an efficient way of securing access to the primary products and the new markets of the third world. The USA in particular, which had emerged pre-eminent in the international economy after the Second World War, sought to expand its markets for goods and investment. By keeping third world countries within the Western sphere of influence, development ensured that access to their resources would not pass to the Communist enemy. Another factor that influenced the war on poverty was the increasing attention to the 'population problem' in this period. Bound up with profoundly racist views and attitudes, the expansion of the population in the South was feared to be spiralling out of control and hence threatening order and stability. In the industrialised countries, economic growth had reduced population growth and based on this experience development became a means of controlling the population explosion in the third world. Furthermore, an optimistic belief in science and technology fuelled the mission to develop the world. As articulated by President Truman, the technological capacity of the West was regarded as 'inexhaustible', capable of conquering poverty and solving the problems of underdevelopment. Progress was accordingly expected to follow more or less automatically from the transfer of technology, and development became largely a question of the right technology and the right form of intervention.

It was against this background, then, that President Truman launched the attack on poverty. On that day 'two billion people became underdeveloped. In a real sense, from that time on, they ceased being what they were, in all their diversity, and were transmogrified into an inverted mirror of others' reality' (Esteva 1992: 7). Within a short space of time social reality was ordered into new categories such as underdeveloped, the third world, malnourished, illiterate, etc., and in this way, development discourse established the third world as an object of intervention. Whole areas of the globe became constructed as objects to be reformed, rather than as subjects with a history and with their own power to transform the world and react to changing circumstances. This constitution of the third world as a subject of development legitimised intervention to remodel it according to Western norms of progress, growth and efficiency, and led to the emergence of a huge, global institutional apparatus seeking to manage these areas according to the dictates of development. The post-war period saw a spectacular proliferation of international, governmental and private development organisations and institutions – for example, the United Nations Development Programme, the World Food Programme, the World Health Organisation and the World Bank, which soon had thousands of development experts on their payrolls. These organisations constantly update and refine knowledge about how best to achieve development, and it is also through these myriad organisations that the decrees of development filter down from the various expert offices to the local settings in Africa, Asia and Latin America. Through these organisations knowledge about the third world becomes an active force, formulated in policy statements, implemented as rural and urban reforms, operationalised as growth strategies, and thus gradually reshaping the social world of underdevelopment.

Over the years development discourse has achieved the status of 'truth', effectively shaping and restricting the ways in which developing countries can be spoken about and acted upon. It is by now extremely difficult to speak or think about the third world in any other terms, as the words of development are the only ones available to us to describe these countries. Conditioned to look for the third world and underdevelopment, the images and hierarchies of development discourse are constantly reproduced and reaffirmed in the North's representations of the South. We see this almost on a daily basis in the media, where pictures of starving children and toiling peasants overshadow any alternative representation of Southern countries. So strong is this hegemony of development discourse that, as Escobar (1995: 5) points out, even those who are opposed to development as conventionally defined remained until recently trapped within its language and imagery. Unable to escape the terms of the hegemonic discourse, critiques often identified alternative forms of development, such as non-capitalist development or participatory development, and thus reproduced aspects of the discourse they sought to reject. The power of development discourse to define the social world and create a 'regime of truth' is also evident in that the governments and peoples of underdeveloped countries have on occasions and in certain contexts come to see themselves in these terms. On the one hand, these identities may at times have given under-developed countries a degree of leverage *vis-à-vis* developed countries, in that they provided the tools to argue for more assistance, more development experts, more rural extensions schemes, and so on. The Bandung Conference and the Non-Aligned Movement can be seen as examples of such collective demands by the third world *vis-à-vis* the North. On the other hand, the identities of development have instilled a degree of inferiority, a longing to escape the underdeveloped state of affairs, a hierarchy where underdeveloped countries and peoples are the perpetual losers, to be endlessly reformed, reshaped and improved. This is not to suggest that the production of subjectivities and identities by hegemonic discourses such as development is unmediated by or passively accepted by people in the

South.[17] Development, for all its power to control the manner in which the third world is spoken about and acted upon, is not immune to challenges and resistance. The objects of development are not passive receivers, wholly oppressed by power; they are active agents who may and frequently do contest, resist, divert and manipulate the activities carried out in the name of development. In this way, development can be seen as a contested field. Its constitution of subjects as underdeveloped, poor and illiterate enables the continuation of Western domination in the third world, while simultaneously opening up new avenues and strategies of resistance.

Conclusion

How, then, are we to understand the relationship between development discourse and recent transitions to democracy in sub-Saharan Africa? As we have seen, many scholars accord little influence to the good governance agenda, preferring instead to focus on what they regard as internal causes of democracy. I have argued that these accounts not only underplay the extent to which the international is present at the national and local levels, but also that development discourse has shaped and defined the ways in which the third world is seen and acted upon. Development discourse has created a 'regime of truth', and its representational practices inform contemporary relations between the North and the South. In the same way as Bhabha has observed that the objective of colonial discourses was 'to construe the colonized as a population of degenerate types ... in order to justify conquest and to establish systems of administration and instruction' (1990: 75), so development discourse can be seen to have produced a form of knowledge about the third world that has facilitated and legitimised certain forms of administration and intervention. Development discourse produced and constructed certain subjects, and put them in a hierarchical and unequal relationship to each other. It thereby normalised the right of the North to intervene and control, to adapt and reshape the structures, practices and ways of life of the South.

This is not to say that development is either necessarily wrong or ill-intended, nor that developing countries themselves do not have the capacity to influence and change their own destiny and historicity. Instead it draws attention to the constructed identities of the subjects engaged in the activity of development, and the way in which subjects so constructed have their agency constrained by their position within the discourse. In the process of promoting development, the relevance of categories such as the third world as ways of understanding the social world is reinforced, and at the same time alternative representations become ever more marginalised. The power relationship between these categories is also reconfirmed through its constant employment, and herein lies the link between presentational practices and international politics. Discourse legitimises and justifies particular forms of actions and interventions, and the first world has reserved for itself the right to categorise the third world and to devise new strategies for the eradication of its underdevelopment.

As Crush has observed, the 'texts of development have always been avowedly strategic and tactical – promoting, licensing and justifying certain interventions and practices, delegitimising and excluding others' (1995: 5). This is also the case with the good governance discourse, which, as Chapter 3 will argue in more detail, has constructed democracy in a particular way. At the same time, the good governance discourse sanctions the right of Western countries to intervene in the third world to promote their vision of development and democracy, while simultaneously marginalising alternative interpretations. As such, the good governance discourse also serves to shield the West from democratic scrutiny. The rich countries are automatically regarded as democratic and able to democratise the third world as part of the larger development effort. In this way, current development discourse reconfirms the unequal power relationship between the first and the third world, and by ignoring development discourse scholars ignore a whole realm of power that is crucial to an understanding of recent democratic transitions and North–South relations more generally.

Notes

1. This section draws on arguments previously developed in Abrahamsen (1997).

2. The notion of a split between hard- and soft-liners within the authoritarian regimes is associated in particular with the four-volume study edited by O'Donnell, Schmitter and Whitehead (1986), and is also taken up by Huntington (1991) and Di Palma (1990). In relation to Africa, many of the essays in Widner (1994) are supportive of this interpretation, arguing that the disruption of rent seeking opportunities weakened authoritarian regimes by undermining their internal discipline and causing divisions, defections and factionalism. This in turn made them more vulnerable to mass popular protest (see in particular van de Walle 1994).

3. Back in 1970 Rustow also recognised the contagious nature of democracy: 'Democratic ideas have proved infectious whether in the days of Rousseau or J.F. Kennedy. And the violent overthrow of one oligarchy (e.g., France in 1830, Germany in 1918) has often frightened another into peaceful surrender (e.g., Britain in 1832, Sweden in 1918)' (Rustow 1970: 348).

4. Doty makes a similar observation, arguing that 'human beings emerge as "a people" when they are recognised in the eyes of the West' (1996: 132).

5. Such intentions are expressed in Bayart (1993); Chabal (1986) and Manor (1991), amongst others. None of these authors, however, could be faulted for considering African politics in isolation from the international arena.

6. A lot has been written on the issue of globalisation lately; the following are particularly pertinent to the present argument: Holm and Sørensen (1995); Albrow (1996); Gill (1997) and Hoogvelt (1997).

7. Structural adjustment programmes will be discussed in greater detail in Chapter 2. For critiques of these policies see Mosley et al. (1991); Tarp (1993); Cornia et al. (1987); Choussudovsky (1997) and Caufield (1997).

8. This is the contention of many of the essays in Widner (1994).

9. World Bank's Articles of Agreement, III, Section 5(b), IV, Section 10, and V, Section 5(c).

10. The World Bank's construction of good governance is discussed in more detail in Chapter 3.

11. See in particular Foucault (1970; 1972; 1980; 1991). For analyses of development inspired by such insights, see Escobar (1995; 1984–85; 1988); Crush (1995); Doty (1996); Ferguson (1994); Manzo (1991) and Sachs (1992).

12. Truman's speech on 20 January 1949 is given as the date of birth of development by Escobar (1995), Rist (1997) as well as the contributors to Sachs (1992).

13. Similarly, Britain's minister for development, Clare Short, recently reminded the Labour Party Conference that if 'we don't make faster progress in reducing poverty, the consequences in growing population, environmental degradation, war and disease will damage the prospects of the next generation wherever they live' (Short 1999).

14. The political order literature is a good example of this fear; see for example Huntington (1968) and Pool (1967).

15. This paragraph and the next draw primarily on Escobar (1995: 31–9), who provides an excellent and more extensive discussion of the conditions of possibility of development.

16. Gendzier (1985) provides an interesting discussion of Cold War influences on development and modernisation theory.

17. The formation of subjectivities and identities under hegemonic discourses such as colonialism, post-colonialism and development has been explored by Fanon (1986); Memmi (1967); Nandy (1983); Bhabha (1990) and Shrestha (1995).

2

New World Order, New Development Discourse

Used for the first time by the World Bank in 1989, the term 'good governance' became the buzzword of development in the 1990s. Known as the good governance agenda, this new development doctrine identified 'poor governance' as the root cause of Africa's development predicament, and the prescribed remedy was of course good governance, or democracy. Democracy, the new development wisdom proclaimed, was not only desirable from a human rights perspective, but a necessary precondition for sustainable economic growth and prosperity. In this respect, the good governance agenda represented a significant break with previous development theories and models. These various past approaches, which were equally confident in their ability to solve the problems of development, were either indifferent to democracy or held that political freedoms and civil liberties would have to be deferred until other more pressing problems such as hunger and state-building were solved.

Conventionally, this change in development discourse might be accounted for in terms of a simple progression of knowledge: history has taught us that the previous models did not work, and they did not work because of a lack of attention to governance issues. Indeed, this is precisely how the World Bank justifies its focus on governance. 'History suggests', the World Bank argues in the report that first introduced the term, 'that political legitimacy and consensus are a precondition for sustainable development' (1989: 60). In other words, the time had come to take account of this historical lesson and to amend development prescriptions accordingly. Such explanations of discursive transformations, however, fail to recognise the relationship between power and knowledge, as set out in the previous chapter. The production and use of knowledge do not occur outside social relations of power, instead discourses are embedded within specific historical and political conditions and they change and are influenced by changes in this wider socio-political environment. This chapter regards the good governance agenda as a discursive formation, that is, a historically contingent form of knowledge intimately connected to contemporary relations of power. The analysis is not as such a search for origin or causality, but aims to explain some of the multiplicity of complex political, social, economic and theoretical factors and relations that made it possible to think about development as the absence of democracy. The chapter identifies the fall of Communism, the end of the Cold War and the failure of structural adjustment programmes in Africa as the main conditions of possibility of the agenda. The new development discourse is shown to be not only informed by, but also serving to sustain and reproduce specific forms of power and policies in the new world order.

The Changing Fate of 'Democracy' in Development

The constitutive interdependence of power and knowledge means that discourses should be understood with reference to extra-discursive relations, that is the historically specific social, economic and political conditions of its formation. Since its inception in the decade following the Second World War, development discourse has continually evolved and reproduced itself in interaction with changing domestic and international relations, giving rise to numerous new theories, strategies and practices for the eradication of underdevelopment. And as doctrines have come and gone, so the status of democracy as a constituent element of development discourse has varied. This historically changing position of democracy is important in seeking to understand the emergence of the good governance agenda and will therefore be reviewed before we turn to the conditions that made this recent discursive transformation possible.

Early theories and models perceived development as a relatively unproblematic process of transition from 'traditional' society to 'modernity'. History was seen as a linear progression, and the countries of the South were expected to follow the same development path as the already industrialised countries. Inspired by the structural functionalism of Talcott Parsons, these early development models were mainly concerned with stimulating economic growth, as all the essential features of modernity were expected to spring from economic prosperity. As societies developed, their various economic, social, cultural and political properties were expected to adjust to each other and eventually fit together like pieces in a jigsaw. Accordingly, liberal democracy was regarded as the almost inevitable outcome of the process of modernisation. Once the required stage of development had been reached, it was assumed that democracy would materialise across the third world in the same way as it had emerged in conjunction with capitalism and the process of industrialisation in the West. In the words of Gabriel Almond, 'in the new and modernizing nations of Asia, Africa and Latin America, the process of enlightenment and democratization will have their inevitable way' (1970: 232).[1]

The status of democracy as an unquestionable goal and inevitable outcome of the process of development was, however, short-lived and was soon sidelined by a new normative perspective that upheld political order and stability as its main values. This discursive transformation must be seen in the context of the intensification of Cold War rivalries in the mid-1960s, which were to provide the conditions of existence for discourse about developing countries in the following decades. In the light of Cold War competition, the realities of third world economic stagnation and social discontent were reinterpreted. What was previously regarded as a primarily economic challenge and an opportunity to test and experiment with various growth models now came to be seen as a potential breeding-ground for Communism. To allow political freedom to flourish in the 'third world' suddenly appeared as a hazardous strategy, and a fundamental reordering of development priorities occurred during this period.

This reorganisation of preferences proceeded from a rethinking of the relationship between modernisation and political development, whereby the view of democracy as an inevitable and desirable by-product of modernity was replaced by the perception of an essential conflict between the process of modernisation and political development. Urbanisation, the provision of education, increased social differentiation and other social transformations associated with rapid economic change were now seen to create new popular demands for the distribution of welfare and for political influence and participation. While such pressures were recognised as intrinsic features of the modern polity, in the Cold War climate they were feared as potentially destabilising and detrimental. In a classic contribution to this literature, Pool reasoned that 'in the Congo, in Vietnam, in the Dominican Republic, it is clear that order depends on somehow compelling newly mobilized strata to return to a measure of passivity and defeatism from which they have been aroused by the process of modernization. At least temporarily, the maintenance of order requires a lowering of newly acquired expectations and levels of political activity' (Pool 1967: 26).[2]

With such a high premium placed on order and stability, the central dilemma became how to achieve economic progress without creating the destabilising pressures intrinsic to the modernisation process. The result was some rather bizarre recommendations and viewpoints. Not only did personality traits like 'passivity' and 'defeatism', previously regarded as relics of 'traditional' society, become worthy of praise, the most inconspicuous aspects of development were also treated with suspicion. Education, for instance, became a potential danger in the sense that people with higher education were perceived as being more capable of expressing their discontent and organising the masses, and developing countries were therefore advised against expanding educational opportunities without the parallel increase in employment opportunities (Huntington 1968; Coleman 1965; Hoselitz 1965). In other words, the deliberate withholding of education could be justified in the name of political order and stability, a sentiment clearly expressed by Huntington in relation to India: 'political participation by illiterates ... may well ... be less dangerous to democratic political institutions than participation by literates' (1968: 49). During the Cold War, then, the criteria for judging the desirability of social reforms can be seen to change from their perceived socio-economic benefits to their capacity to enhance political stability.

The new emphasis on order and stability from the mid-1960s onwards was to a certain extent rooted in a realistic appraisal of the challenges that faced many countries in the South, but the reformulation of modernisation theory also brought discourse on developing countries in line with Communist containment, the main foreign policy objective of the West. It was, as Bernstein remarked, a reformulation that allowed for 'the classification of repressive regimes friendly to the West as authentic modernizers' worthy of financial support (1979: 82). Despite the powerful Cold War rhetoric of freedom and liberty, the promotion or defence of democracy was clearly subservient to the overarching foreign policy goal of containment and counter-insurgency.[3] This was openly acknowledged in an influential report by the Massachusetts Institute of Technology, which in 1968 recognised that increased participation may force third world regimes 'to adopt policies counter to US interests' (MIT 1968: 47). The report's authors recommended that if 'the political process brings to the threshold of power groups which are ideologically or for other reasons opposed to our continued presence, normally the United States should not encourage change' (ibid.: 55).

It is therefore not surprising to find that the six countries – Ethiopia, Kenya, Liberia, Somalia, Sudan, and Zaire – that received the bulk of US aid to Africa in the period from 1962 to 1988 were not only eminently friendly towards US interests, but also known for their blatant disregard for democratic principles and human rights. A deafening silence regarding 'good governance' was the order of the day, and the same applies to

Britain's relationship with repressive regimes like that of President Moi in Kenya and France's close links with authoritarian states like Chad, Djibouti and the Central African Republic. In short, during the Cold War the West supported and armed some of the world's most oppressive dictators, sponsored anti-socialist guerrilla movements as in Angola, Afghanistan and Nicaragua, and on occasions intervened militarily to defend dictators against popular opposition – all in the name of freedom and democracy.[4] It has thus been argued that the Cold War *Weltanschauung* 'justified the replacement of democracy by authoritarian rule as necessary in order to advance the common good of the free world by ensuring pro-American anti-Communist, political stability' (Müller 1985: 467).

Although the intensity of superpower rivalries gradually faded, democracy continued to occupy a subservient position within development discourse. Many donors, especially the Nordic countries, expressed their concern for the poor human rights records of recipient states, but liberal democracy was not a main priority of development aid. Rather it was treated as irrelevant to the development process, banished to the sideline by more immediate concerns like basic needs, famine, hunger, over-population, child mortality and illiteracy. Faced with such a plethora of development problems, the absence of civil and political freedoms seemed an unfortunate but necessary oversight, and an influential body of opinion held that strong, or perhaps even authoritarian, government was more important to these countries than 'adherence to the niceties of liberal democratic constitutionalism' (Emerson 1971: 250). African countries were accordingly expected to 'forgo the luxury of conventional democratic institutions and processes' for some time to come (Hodder 1978: 119).

With the arrival of neo-liberalism in the late 1980s, development discourse again took on a more explicitly undemocratic character. The shift to neo-liberalism followed the breakdown of the Keynesian consensus in the late 1970s, which saw an increasing disillusionment with the state as a promoter of economic growth and welfare in the West. In the industrialised countries, the retreat from Keynesian demand management was effected by the monetarist economic policies of leaders like Thatcher, Reagan and Kohl. Development organisations were not immune to these ideological currents, especially since it could be argued that the problems of third world countries had been exacerbated rather than eradicated by Keynesian development economics. State-led development was perceived to have failed conspicuously, and by the early 1980s the policies of the Bretton Woods institutions had been brought into line with the neo-liberal political climate in major donor countries.[5]

Neo-liberalism's scepticism of the state and its exaltation of the autonomous individual is intrinsically bound up with a disdain for pluralist and participatory ideals of politics. This disdain is also reflected in the structural adjustment programmes that have been imposed by the IMF and the World Bank throughout the South since the early 1980s. These programmes aim to create a free market and a minimal, technocratic and highly efficient state. In order to achieve this, the state not only needs to be extricated from the market, but it must also be shielded from the distributional demands of its citizens. Economic reforms accordingly take priority over political reforms and civil liberties. This order of priority was openly recognised by Deepak Lal, an influential figure in the Research Department of the World Bank. Writing on structural adjustment programmes, Lal argued that a 'courageous, ruthless and perhaps undemocratic government is required to ride roughshod over newly created interest groups' (Lal 1983: 33). As a result of this prioritisation, many reform-oriented but authoritarian third world governments were provided with financial support throughout the 1980s. This assistance may in turn have enabled regimes to overcome and suppress domestic protests against structural adjustment measures, and in this way development aid can be seen to have ensured the survival of authoritarianism (see Bangura 1986; Beckman 1992; Toye 1992). During the heyday of structural adjustment programmes, then, political participation was either relegated to a position of insignificance within development discourse or explicitly recognised as potentially harmful and detrimental to the overall aim of economic adjustment.

A neglect and even at times an outright dislike of democracy thus appears to be one of the few invariants of development discourse's changing vocabulary of 'basic needs', 'redistribution with growth', 'structural adjustment', and so on. But this was all to change with the publication of the World Bank's 1989 report *Sub-Saharan Africa: From Crisis to Sustainable Growth*. By proclaiming that a 'crisis of governance' underlies the 'litany of Africa's development problems', the report placed the concept of governance at the heart of the donor agenda for Africa (World Bank 1989: 60). Defining governance in rather general terms as 'the exercise of political power to manage a nation's affairs', the World Bank stressed the need not only for less, but also for better government in African states. Hence the solution to Africa's predicament was presented as greater openness and accountability, the rule of law, freedom of the press, increased grassroots participation, and the building of legitimate, pluralistic political structures (ibid.: 6, 61, 192). While refraining from using the term democracy itself, the message of the report was unequivocal: liberal democracy was not only a human right, but also conducive to and necessary for economic growth.

Economic reform, the World Bank argued, would be wasted if not accompanied by political reform, and accordingly the Bank urged bilateral donors to become far more selective and to direct their aid only to countries pursuing sound and sustained reform programmes (1989: 14, 183, 193). The request was quickly heeded, and the publication of the report was followed by a series of policy statements by most major donor countries. In February 1990 the USA declared that American aid would be used to promote democracy and would favour countries pursuing 'the interlinked and mutually reinforcing goals of political liberalization and market-oriented economic reforms' (in Clough 1992: 57, 59). Later the same year the *Democracy Initiative* of the US Agency for International Development was launched 'to help promote and consolidate democracy as the legitimate organizing principle for political systems throughout the world' (USAID 1990: i). The British position on aid and democracy was spelt out in no uncertain terms by Foreign Secretary Douglas Hurd in June 1990, when he announced that countries that 'tend toward pluralism, public account-ability, respect for the rule of law, human rights, market principles, should be encouraged'. Governments that 'persist with repressive policies', on the other hand, 'should not expect us to support them in their folly with scarce aid resources' (ODI 1992: 1). A couple of weeks later, at a Conference of Heads of State of Francophone Africa, President François Mitterrand of France followed suit. France, he said, expected 'true democracies with multi-partyism, free elections and respect for human rights' to be estab-lished, and promised that 'we will encourage the developments that lead to them' (in *IDS Bulletin* 1993: 7).

Not only bilateral donors but also international aid organisations and institutions were quick to endorse the new development doctrine. The Organisation for Economic Cooperation and Development (OECD), for instance, decided that aid should favour countries attempting democratic free market reform, while the European Council resolved that respect for human rights and the existence of political institutions which are effective, accountable and enjoy democratic legitimacy are the basis for equitable development (*IDS Bulletin* 1993: 8). To match this rhetorical commitment to good governance, most donors introduced political aid conditionality, which ties financial assistance to the implementation of reforms towards competitive, pluralist political systems in the recipient country. The good governance agenda thus marked a significant broadening of 'development', to include not only the traditional focus on economic reforms but also explicit political demands.

This new development discourse was unique in that it narrated under-development as an absence primarily of democracy. As we have seen, democracy has always been *part* of the official justifications for the main-tenance of aid budgets, but it has merely been one of many goals and it has also generally been given a low priority.[6] In the 1990s, however, democracy became the unifying theme of development discourse, an absolute necessity for a successful development process, and its main source of public legiti-macy in donor countries. Although presented by the World Bank and other proponents of good governance as a natural progression of knowledge about the underdeveloped world, the status of good governance/democracy as the foundational core of development discourse can be understood only with reference to the context in which it emerged. The remainder of this chapter explores the historical conjuncture that gave rise to the good governance agenda and aims to render visible the extra-discursive relations that provided its conditions of possibility. In particular, attention is drawn to the fall of Communism, the end of the Cold War and the failure of structural adjustment programmes to generate economic growth on the African continent.

The End of the Cold War

There is a definite and irrefutable simultaneity between the end of the Cold War and the emergence of the good governance agenda. The Com-munist development model collapsed in late 1989, and by mid-1990 the governance parlance and political aid conditionality had already made its mark on development theory and practice. It is not surprising that the end of superpower rivalry should engender a discursive transformation, given that the Cold War had provided the conditions of existence for develop-ment discourse during most of its lifetime. During this period aid policy was, as we have seen, to a significant extent shaped by strategic, geopolitical considerations, as East and West supported various African regimes as part of their ideological power struggle to secure allies and spheres of influence on the continent. To present African countries as merely victims of the Cold War would, however, be too simplistic, since superpower conflict also frequently enabled African leaders to play the two sides off against each other and to attract foreign assistance and increase the per-ceived international importance of their own countries.

However, during Mikhail Gorbachev's presidency, Cold War hostilities on the African continent gradually subsided. This was partly due to the Soviet Union's enormous domestic problems, and partly a reflection of a general rethinking of foreign policy inspired by *perestroika* and *glasnost*. According to Light (1992), Soviet policy-makers had long realised the high cost of involvement in some of the world's poorest countries, such as Ethiopia, Mozambique and Angola, and they also accepted that Soviet activism in the South had been a main cause of the deterioration in *détente* in the mid-1970s. Because the restoration of good relations with the West was of prime importance to the Gorbachev regime, the 1980s saw a rapid 'de-ideologisation' of Soviet foreign policy. Financial assistance was withdrawn from socialist client countries, and relations with capitalist countries such as South Africa, which offered the possibility of mutual economic advantage, were expanded. At the same time, 'national wars of liberation' were reclassified as 'regional conflicts', and accordingly no longer deserving of socialist support.

A milestone in the retreat from Cold War politics on the continent was reached in December 1988, with the signing of the tripartite agreement that enabled South African, Cuban and Soviet military disengagement from Angola as well as the independence of Namibia. The agreement was brokered by the Soviet Union and the USA, and marked the first attempt at superpower cooperation to end the Cold War in Africa (see O'Neill and Munslow 1995; Cohen 1995). The Soviet Union shortly afterwards informed President Mengistu that Ethiopia could expect no more arms shipments, and by 1990 the Soviet Union had extricated itself from military involvement on the African continent.[7]

The decline of superpower rivalry meant that Africa became of much less interest to the major world powers both strategically and economically. In the words of Decalo, 'African states were transformed from Cold War pawns, into irrelevant clutter' (1992: 17).[8] No longer fearful of losing allies to Communist expansion, the USA and other Western states gradually disengaged from Africa. Following the collapse of the Soviet Union, the USA reduced or eliminated military aid to long-term allies like Kenya, Somalia, Liberia, Chad and Zaire. The USA further reduced its presence in Africa by closing nine aid missions and 15 intelligence posts and redirecting aid personnel to new priority assignments in Eastern Europe and the former Soviet Union (Bratton 1994a). Similarly, Britain closed its embassies in Congo, Gabon and Liberia, while France's decision not to send troops to help stop an army and police mutiny in Côte d'Ivoire in 1990 brought further evidence of the continent's declining importance in the new world order.

Economically Africa has always been of limited importance to the industrialised countries. For example, only 1 per cent of US exports goes to the region, and between 1965 and 1992 Africa's total imports and exports as a percentage of world trade declined from 4 per cent to only 2 per cent (IMF 1965 and 1992). The dismal economic performance of the 1980s, characterised by increasing debt, falling GDP growth rates, capital flight and disinvestment, had inexorably defined the region as a humanitarian problem rather than a credible economic partner, and this economic marginalisation was further intensified by the end of the Cold War.[9] Almost overnight the former Communist states became not only successful competitors for Western aid, but also presented the West with new and lucrative opportunities for trade and investment. Not surprisingly, therefore, critics of the good governance agenda have seen it as a morally comfortable way of justifying a decline in Africa's share of scarce development resources (e.g. Barya 1993; Africa Recovery 1990). This interpretation gains some support from the fact that major donors appear to have been more active in cutting aid to authoritarian regimes than in showing significant generosity to those states that have made progress towards democracy (Moore 1993; Sørensen 1993b; Wiseman 1993). Donors have redirected their aid towards governance projects involving support for the electoral process and local government, as well as the training of journalists, parliamentary clerks, legislators, civil servants and the police, but total aid to reforming countries has not increased significantly (Robinson 1994). In fact, while average aid flows to the African continent expanded by 4 per cent a year in the 1980s, aid declined in the 1990s and from 1990 to 1996 official financial assistance to sub-Saharan Africa fell in real terms by 21 per cent, a contraction of $3 billion (Riddell 1999; Watkins 1995). The dispensability of Africa was thus a main corollary of the new world order, and without the continent's dwindling status the good governance agenda would not have been possible.

The end of the Cold War also had a significant influence on the intellectual climate, and the Western triumphalism that followed the collapse of Communism undoubtedly contributed to the formation of the good governance agenda. Following the disintegration of the Eastern bloc, Communism was once and for all identified with inefficiency, stagnation, corruption and mismanagement. Henceforth there could be no credible alternative to liberal democracy, no feasible non-capitalist development model. The fall of Communism was widely interpreted as a confirmation of the superiority of Western values, or in the celebratory idiom of Fukuyama (1989), mankind had reached the 'end of history' and liberal democracy had revealed itself as the final form of human government. The same victorious mood is evident in the introduction to an influential three-volume study of democracy in developing countries, which declares that 'democracy is the only model of government with any broad ideological legitimacy and appeal in the world today. [It is] the new global *zeitgeist*' (Diamond, Linz and Lipset 1988: x).

A more muted expression of this kind of triumphalism was perhaps evident in the renewed interest in liberal universalism and particularly in Kantian ideas, which emerged in American academic circles as Cold War hostilities gradually subsided. Kant's essay *Perpetual Peace*, first published in 1795, argued that the spread of liberal republics (or democracy in contemporary language) would usher in a 'pacific union' and ultimately mean the end of war. Such Kantian notions of lasting peace have been revived in the post-Cold War era and the global spread of democracy is seen as conducive to world peace.[10] Both President Bill Clinton and the former UN Secretary-General Boutros Boutros-Ghali have proclaimed their belief in the peace-building capacity of democracy, the latter stating unequivocally that 'Democratization supports the cause of peace' (UN 1995: 58).[11] The validity or otherwise of the neo-Kantian thesis is not the point at issue here; rather we need to note that at the end of the Cold War this kind of liberal universalism added further fervour to the belief in the pre-eminence of Western political values.

Post-Cold War triumphalism also enabled the USA to indulge in the more moralistic aspects of its foreign policy. It has been widely observed that the 'tradition of American foreign policy encompasses both moral idealism and raw self-interest' (Kegley and Wittkopf 1987: 78; see also Moss 1995). In short, this moral idealism is a particular kind of liberal universalism that holds that the American values of free enterprise and individual liberties are universal human aspirations. The notion of the 'chosen people' destined to bring liberty and civilisation to the world is central to the American self-image, and this American exceptionalism has given foreign policy a distinct evangelical flavour; it is the destiny of Americans to spread the American way. Augelli and Murphy (1988) have convincingly demonstrated how such popular American self-perceptions influence foreign policy and the rhetoric of aid. While national interests undoubtedly dominate foreign policy behaviour, American presidents will have foreign assistance available as a policy instrument only if they succeed in securing the support of the public, and frequently this necessitates an appeal to the chosen people's 'missionary' instinct. This has also been noted by Brown, who argues that the perception of a 'grand moral crusade or a clear and present danger to the nation' is needed to forge American consensus in support of altruistic acts like foreign assistance (Brown 1983: 25).[12]

The Cold War provided the American public with such a clear and present danger, and traditionally the containment of Communism served as one of the main justifications for development assistance. When this rationale disappeared, a new justification for large aid budgets was needed to satisfy an American public suffering from aid fatigue and saturated by a Fukuyama-like desire to liberate the world. In this context the good governance agenda can be regarded as the new 'grand moral crusade', which serves to re-create a domestic political constituency for US development aid.

The American missionary zeal may have no direct equivalent in post-war Europe, but a certain paternalism has always permeated the West's attitude to the third world. Traditionally, rich countries have presented their relationship with developing countries as a civilising mission. Colonialism, for example, was driven by economic and political self-interest, but it was also perceived and justified by those involved in it as a highly moral and religious undertaking. It was the 'white man's burden' to bring religion, culture and the benefits of civilisation to populations regarded as savage barbarians, or 'half devil and half child' to continue with Kipling's verse.[13] Notions of the civilising mission were even enshrined at the Berlin Conference of 1884–85, which declared that the colonial powers had an obligation to care for 'the moral and material well-being' of Africans and to bring them 'the blessings of civilization' (in Gann 1988: 329–30). The Berlin Conference concentrated on political, commercial and judicial questions, and lacked a specifically philanthropic agenda. Humanitarian principles were nevertheless invoked in order to justify the empire, and, needless to say, were grossly violated by the colonial powers. The point here, however, is that the need to rely on moral and ethical justifications has a long history in Europe's dealings with Africa, and it is not too far-fetched to regard the good governance agenda as a reformulation of these justifications, a continuation of Europe's 'civilising mission'. Freedom and democracy are among the most highly valued ideals of Western culture, intrinsic to both Western self-perception and the perception of others, and the good governance agenda is frequently couched in moralistic terms. Former British Foreign Secretary Douglas Hurd, for example, claimed that the promotion of good government is a 'moral imperative' (1990: 4), while the present Labour government makes frequent references to the 'moral duty' to spread democracy and human rights abroad.[14] The good governance agenda can thus be seen to contain an underlying belief in the superiority of Western values and political systems, and as such it reveals clear continuities with colonial discourses and practices and with past development theories.

The Failure of Structural Adjustment Programmes

During the 1980s, structural adjustment programmes were the defining feature of Western policies towards the countries in sub-Saharan Africa.[15] Inspired by neo-liberal economics and designed by the IMF and the World Bank, these programmes were devised to deal with Africa's unsustainable debt and economic decline, which had resulted in hyper-inflation, chronic balance of payment deficits, currency crises and deterioration of public services. The failure of these programmes to rekindle economic growth on the continent is closely linked to donors' and creditors' concern with issues of governance. Indeed, together with the end of the Cold War, the disappointing performance of structural adjustment provided the main conditions of possibility for the good governance agenda.

Broadly speaking, two types of adjustment programmes can be distinguished: stabilisation and structural adjustment policies. The former are advocated by the IMF and are generally short-term and designed to have an immediate effect on the economic balance-sheet of a country through measures such as devaluation, deflation, and fiscal and monetary restraints. These programmes, it is hoped, will reduce real incomes and hence suppress domestic demand both for imports and for goods that can be exported. The shrinking import bill and expanding export earnings will then enable the adjusting country to restore the balance of payments equilibrium. While stabilisation programmes focus on demand restraint, structural adjustment policies target the supply side of the economy. Structural adjustment measures are overseen by the World Bank and seek to tackle balance of payments problems by expanding the production of exports. The programmes are generally more long-term and attempt to increase productivity and efficiency and to shift resources towards more productive projects and from the non-tradable to the tradable sector.

Stabilisation and structural adjustment measures are not, however, mutually exclusive and actual programmes normally contain combinations of the two. Under the existing division of labour between the Bretton Woods institutions, advice on macro-economic policies from the IMF must be implemented before the World Bank agrees to support a country. In practice, therefore, the two types of adjustment are overlapping and virtually indistinguishable and in this study 'structural adjustment' is used as a generic term to describe the package of reform measures advocated by the two institutions.[16] The programmes share the same theoretical foundations in neo-liberal economics and their primary underlying assumption is that markets are intrinsically superior to planning and physical controls in the allocation of resources, and hence in dealing with development problems. Accordingly, 'the state should not intervene where markets can work even moderately well' (World Bank 1994a: 183). The result of structural adjustment programmes has been a general liberalisation of African economies, and the role of the state has been drastically scaled down through the reduction of public expenditure, the privatisation of public sector activities, and the removal of controls over imports, exports and foreign exchange.

Considerable disagreement exists about the effects of adjustment. The Bretton Woods institutions have struggled to defend the programmes against a barrage of criticism, but no amount of juggling or massaging of statistics has enabled adjustment to appear as an unqualified success. On the contrary, almost every positive evaluation of adjustment policies has been countered by an equally convincing condemnation of their negative repercussions. The World Bank's first major review of the adjustment effort, for example, concluded that adjustment programmes had a favourable impact on economic performance and that 'strongly' adjusting countries performed better than countries with 'weak' or no programmes (World Bank/UNDP 1989: 30). Adjustment, the Bank stated, 'helps raise living standards overall and especially for the poor. The agricultural reforms that many countries have adopted, for example, increase the earning of small farmers – who make up about 80 percent of the population of sub-Saharan Africa and include most of the poorest people' (ibid.: iii).

These sanguine conclusions were quickly challenged by the United Nations Economic Commission for Africa (UNECA), which accused the World Bank of faulty methodology and selectivity in the compilation, presentation and analysis of the data (UNECA 1989b). Using the same empirical data as the World Bank, UNECA arrived at the opposite result: countries with 'strong' adjustment programmes were found to have the most disastrous economic performance, with a negative annual growth of -0.53 per cent. 'Weak' adjusting countries, on the other hand, had a growth rate of +2.0 per cent, whereas non-adjusting countries grew by +3.5 per cent a year (UNECA 1989a). A similar controversy surrounds the World Bank's 1994 report *Adjustment in Africa: Reforms, Results and the Road Ahead*. Again the Bank claimed that the countries that had adopted its recommendations had improved their economic growth, and put forward the equation that the greater the degree of implementation, the better the results. Furthermore, the report argued that where some reforms had been implemented, 'the majority of the poor are probably better off and almost certainly no worse off' (World Bank 1994a: 6). Critics, however, have arrived at diametrically opposing conclusions. By relying solely on data presented in the World Bank report and by splitting the countries into four rather than three groups, Schatz (1994 and 1996) has demonstrated that structural adjustment programmes in most cases resulted in poorer economic performance. Ponte's analysis of the same statistics also determined that the claimed success of adjustment programmes was misleading and that the 1994 report revealed the World Bank's failure to adopt an adequate long-term strategy for Africa (Ponte 1994; see also Mosely and Weeks 1993).

Such disagreement is perhaps to be expected, both because neo-liberalism's attack on the developmental state is bound to meet political opposition and because the evaluation of structural adjustment programmes involves complicated calculations, which have to take account of not only a multitude of variables but also control for the effects of variations in initial conditions and external influences. In this sense, the controversy surrounding the impact of adjustment illustrates more than anything the possible uses and abuses of statistics and the variety of conclusions that can be supported by the same macro-economic data. Nevertheless, the evidence against structural adjustment is convincing, and the critique of the programmes is made even more powerful by the fact that the Bretton Woods institutions' own praise of the policies has become increasingly muted as their own appraisals have identified significant shortcomings.[17] A particularly damaging piece of evidence has been the failure of adjustment to stimulate investment. A World Bank publication that summarises three of the Bank's own reviews of adjustment concluded that although adjusting countries experienced higher GDP and export growth than non-adjusting countries, their level of investment was lower (Corbo, Fischer and Webb 1992).

The same result was reported by an influential study carried out by Mosely, Harrigan and Toye, which found that while structural adjustment had a favourable effect on export growth and the external account, it had not improved national income or financial flows from overseas and its effect on aggregate investment had been negative. In short, the result was 'disappointing' (Mosely et al. 1991: 308). Even where adjustment has achieved sustained economic transformation, as in Ghana under the authoritarian rule of Flight Lieutenant Jerry Rawlings, significant private investment has not occurred. In fact disinvestment has emerged as a trend in Africa, with foreign firms moving their business elsewhere and local companies closing down as a result of increased competition and poor credit facilities (see Lancaster 1993; Callaghy 1994). For the World Bank, the negative impact on private investment is of course of particular importance as without high rates of investment, growth will be restrained by existing capacities and remain dependent on foreign aid.

Structural adjustment programmes have also been severely criticised for their negative social and humanitarian effects. A frequent reproach is that adjustment tackles only the symptoms of the African crisis, not its root causes, and adjustment is accordingly regarded as detrimental to long-term development (see e.g. UNECA 1989a). The pioneering work on the social impact of adjustment was the UNICEF study *Adjustment with a Human Face* (Cornia et al. 1987). While sympathetic towards the overall aim of adjustment, UNICEF argued that the programmes 'tend to increase aggregate poverty, or in other words the number of people – and of children – living below the poverty line' (ibid.: 66). This finding has since been confirmed by numerous studies, and it is widely reported that those few countries that have achieved some macro-economic stability have done so at the expense of growth, investment and human welfare. Adjustment tends to worsen the living standards of the already poor by depressing employment and real incomes, and the introduction of user fees in order to cut the cost of public services has reduced access to health and education. In short, adjustment has been a recipe for deepening poverty, widening social polarisation and rising unemployment.[18] Following such damning evidence, safety-nets for the poor and vulnerable have been grafted on to otherwise largely unchanged adjustment programmes. This has not, however, silenced the critics, nor have the World Bank's own statistics been able to conceal the fact that after a decade of adjustment Africa's social and humanitarian situation is just as bleak as when the programmes were first introduced. Poverty and absolute poverty increased during the adjustment decade, both as a percentage of Africa's population and as a percentage of world totals. The proportion of the poor, i.e. that part of the population subsisting on about US$1 a day, increased from 47 per cent (184 million) in 1980 to 48 per cent (216 million) in 1990, and this trend is projected to continue in the twenty-first century (World Bank 1992b).

By the late 1980s it was an inescapable fact that the miracle of the market had failed to materialise as predicted. More than a decade of adjustment had yet to produce a single definite success story on the African continent, and it is in this context of the perceived failure of the reigning development paradigm that we must analyse the emergence of the good governance agenda. The development community, and in particular the World Bank, needed to explain why economic growth had not occurred in the manner so confidently predicted by its neo-liberal economists. The answer they came up with was 'poor governance'. Political factors, the World Bank report *Sub-Saharan Africa: From Crisis to Sustainable Growth* asserted, had prevented the implementation of the right economic policies and the 'root cause of weak economic performance in the past' was blamed on 'the failure of public institutions' (1989: xii). In other words, the reason for the failure of structural adjustment was not the programmes themselves, not imbalances in the global political economy, unfair markets, or adverse domestic conditions, but African governments themselves. Drawing attention to the lack of accountability, transparency and predictability the Bank concluded that a 'crisis of governance' was making it almost impossible for the right economic policies to work. Africa's uncertain and unpredictable political environments were also seen to discourage private investors from risking their money, due to fear that their property would be unprotected and their profits consumed by corruption. Successful adjustment thus came to be seen as a result of appropriate institutions, political skill and personal commitment, as well as of bureaucratic competence.

Compared with the neo-liberal development orthodoxy of the 1980s, which largely ignored the political sphere and concentrated on economic issues, the good governance agenda represents the rediscovery of politics and its relevance to development. The agenda is a recognition that merely 'rolling back the frontiers of the state' is not in itself enough to stimulate growth, and that closer attention has to be paid to politics. It is a realisation that economic reforms are implemented and affected by concrete social and political actors, and that these actors are important in explaining the success or failure of adjustment programmes. Such insights originated from studies showing the lack of implementation of adjustment measures. For example, one World Bank study of 15 developing countries (five of them African) showed that between 1980 and 1987 only 60 per cent of the policy changes agreed as conditions of adjustment loans were fully implemented and that the degree to which the conditions were met differed substantially between policy areas (McCleary 1989; see also Mosely et al. 1991). This poor implementation record was due in large part to the fact that many of those who had most to lose from adjustment programmes were located in or closely related to the state apparatus, and were therefore able to curtail and dilute the programmes. Adjustment, in other words, came to be concerned with not merely the size of the state, but also its quality.

But although the good governance agenda acknowledges the importance of the state in the development process, it would be a grave misconception to regard it as a complete break with neo-liberalism. The ideal 'good governance state' is still a minimal state; it is just more efficient and competent in carrying out economic reforms. Rather than marking a break with neo-liberalism, the governance agenda is best understood as a means of managing the adjustment effort. After being identified as the culprit of past reform failures, the patrimonial African state has become the subject of the new development project: only when the state is reformed and democratised will economic reforms succeed. As regards adjustment programmes, their overall shape remains largely unchanged and the central contention of the World Bank's 1994 report *Adjustment in Africa: Reforms, Results and the Road Ahead* is still that 'adjustment is the necessary first step on the road to sustainable, poverty-reducing growth' (World Bank 1994a: 15). Consequently, the recommendation is for more of the same; 'countries should continue with the current strategy: avoiding overvalued exchange rates and keeping inflation and budget deficits low' (ibid.: 10).

The failure of adjustment to stimulate growth led to a search for possible explanations, and rather than changing the programmes themselves the blame was directed at the poor governance of African governments. The important point to note is that in the context of structural adjustment programmes, democracy or good governance is not valued in its own right but is seen first and foremost as a means to the end of economic growth. Governance issues were grafted on to neo-liberal economic policies, giving them a more democratic and humanitarian facade and thereby constructing a new legitimacy for the severely criticised structural adjustment programmes.

Power, Hegemony and the Good Governance Discourse

'Theory', Robert Cox has argued, 'is always *for* someone and *for* some purpose' (1986: 207). The production and use of knowledge always stands in a relationship to power, and the problematisation of a particular aspect of human life, for example governance, is not 'natural' or the result of the inevitable advance of science. Rather it is historically contingent and dependent on power relations already having rendered the issue a potential object of investigation. The above exposition has shown the historical specificity of the good governance agenda, the way in which the institution of governance and democracy as the prime goals of development was rendered possible by the changes in the global balance of power that followed the fall of Communism and the end of the Cold War. The end of the bipolar world system signalled the arrival of the West's indisputable hegemony over the third world. Aid recipients had no alternative but to rely on the West for assistance, and the collapse of Communism as an alternative, non-capitalist development model made donor states more confident of the superiority of their own economic and political solutions.

Ironically, this coincided with the growing recognition of the failure of structural adjustment programmes to stimulate growth on the African continent. But at the moment of capitalism's victory over Marxism-Leninism, the neo-liberal development paradigm could not easily be abandoned. Instead the failure of adjustment policies was blamed on the 'poor governance' of African governments, a timely and popular explanation given the prevailing political mood in the West: neo-liberal solutions were not wrong, they were simply incorrectly and insufficiently implemented. Western triumphalism and the need to construct a new legitimacy for structural adjustment thus coalesced in the formation of the good governance agenda.

This interpretation differs both from the commonplace condemnation of the good governance agenda as a tool for Western domination and from its more charitable characterisation as an expression of the West's genuine developmental and moral concern. The latter view is frequently expressed by supporters of liberal development orthodoxy as well as by Western leaders and policy-makers. From this perspective, superpower rivalry prevented the West from realising the more ethical goals of its foreign policy, and the end of the Cold War is accordingly portrayed as a moral release for the West: finally it was 'freed from the perceived need to turn a blind eye to the domestic excesses of Cold War allies', or in the words of another commentator, the USA was 'free at last to develop a new relationship with Africa' (Wiseman 1995: 3; Clough 1992: 2). For writers of this persuasion, then, Western foreign policy was always essentially ethically motivated, but moral concerns were derailed by the Cold War. Once the battle against the East was won and cruel and corrupt dictators could be abandoned without fear of Communists filling the vacuum, the formulation of more principled foreign policies and the good governance agenda became possible.

While it is true that the promotion of democracy has always been part of Western foreign policy rhetoric and that the end of the Cold War allowed this ideal to be pursued more consistently, the good governance agenda is not an expression of pure altruism or idealism. As a discursive transformation we have seen how it is historically contingent, and how it also enables the West to maintain its hegemony over the third world, perhaps with even fewer resources and less resistance than in the past. The emergence of both the good governance agenda and pro-democracy movements in the South at about the same time makes it tempting to regard the two as part of a single, undifferentiated historical and political phenomenon. Certainly, the existence of domestic protests facilitated the representation of the good governance agenda as a 'moral imperative' (Hurd 1990: 4), a democratic effort on behalf of the oppressed peoples of the world. But the relationship between the good governance agenda and pro-democracy movements is much more complicated than such a repres-entation suggests. Although the large-scale popular demonstrations against authoritarian regimes in the South share some of the good governance agenda's conditions of possibility and some of its goals, the two must be kept analytically distinct. Not only are their aims and motivations different, their historical simultaneity is also more apparent than real. While issues of governance and political conditionality are relatively new and can be dated quite precisely to early 1990, there is no such sudden mass conversion to the democratic ideal on behalf of African people. Rather, perennial domestic demands for change could be realised only once external support for African dictators was withdrawn – that is, after the end of the Cold War.[19] At the same time, the Left had been pacified in most countries or could no longer rely on financial support from a powerful Communist bloc. In this new world order, the promotion of democracy no longer represented a fundamental threat to the established order. Instead democracy became a powerful tool that could be used both to appease African demands for change and to satisfy Western domestic constituents concerned with human rights in developing countries. In this context, it is perhaps pertinent to mention that in all democratising African countries moderate political forces committed to liberal market reforms have emerged as the victors in the process.

The good governance agenda can thus be regarded as a discursive transformation that, while claiming to liberate the poor, enables the West to continue its undisputed hegemony on the African continent under the changed conditions of the new world order. It reproduces the hierarchies of conventional development discourse, whereby the third world is still to be reformed and delivered from its current underdeveloped stage by the first world. Through such representational practices the rich, industrialised countries retain the moral high ground, the right to administer develop-ment and democracy to the South. The implication is of course that these countries themselves are already democratic, and their own domestic political structures as well as the practices of international institutions such as the World Bank and the IMF are shielded from the scrutiny to which African countries are subjected. The first world becomes the symbol of democracy, and the third world is to be made more like the first through the application of the good governance agenda. By placing the good governance discourse in the wider context of the changing global balance of power, we can see how it is informed by and serves to sustain and reproduce specific forms of power and policies. It is, in other words, not simply a humanitarian effort concerned to promote development, growth and democracy, but rather a development discourse intrinsically linked to larger discursive practices through which global power and domination are exercised.

Notes

1. Almond was one of the most influential, and also among the most theoretically sophisticated, advocates of the political development approach. See also Almond and Coleman (1960); Apter (1965) and Lipset (1960).

2. Notable contributors to the literature on political order and development include Huntington (1968); Pye (1966); Pool (1967) and Zolberg (1966). The views of these authors are by no means uniform, but all subscribe to the values of order and stability. The political order literature is reviewed by Gendzier (1985); O'Brien (1979) and Kesselman (1973).

3. The subjection of development aid to foreign policy interests during the Cold War has been well documented by, amongst others, Gendzier (1985); Chomsky (1992); Müller (1985) and Lowenthal (1991). Tellingly, Packenham reported that when aid officials in the mid-1960s were asked what they understood by development, 'one of the most common responses was, in effect, that political development is anti-Communist, pro-American stability' (1966: 213).

4. The most well-known examples of the West's involvement (through the CIA and other services) in the overthrow of democratic and elected governments in the South are Iran (1953), Guatemala (1954), Brazil (1964) and Chile (1973).

5. This so-called counter-revolution in development theory is eminently documented by Toye (1987), who argues that the common-sense criticism of the overgrown and inefficient third world state does not constitute a theoretically sound justification for unchecked market forces. According to Toye, the theoretical claims of neo-liberal development economics are largely unsubstantiated and lack empirical support. The recommendation to 'roll back the frontiers of the state' is thus rooted in a deep ideological hostility towards state intervention and market regulations rather than in a firm theoretical or empirical foundation.

6. Democracy was one of the goals mentioned by President Truman in his 1949 speech, which is said to have inaugurated the 'development age' (see Chapter 1). Whitehead (1986) shows how the promotion of democracy has been part of Western foreign policy rhetoric since the 1940s.

7. For a more detailed discussion of Soviet policy towards and disengagement from Africa see Light (1991 and 1992) and Shearman (1987).

8. The same sentiment was expressed by UNECA's Executive Secretary Adebayo Adedeji: 'Africa has moved from being at the periphery to the periphery of the periphery

of the global economy – the permanent political and economic underdog of the world, the world's basket case' (in Africa Leadership Forum 1990: 24).

9. Africa's growing economic marginalisation was vividly illustrated by a high-ranking French diplomat writing in *Le Monde*: 'Economically speaking, if the entire black Africa, with the exception of South Africa, were to disappear in a flood, the global cataclysm will be approximately nonexistent' (in Chege 1992: 148; see also Callaghy 1994).

10. Russett (1993) has been one of the most vocal proponents of the democratic peace thesis. See also Doyle (1983a and 1983b), and for a critique Latham (1993).

11. President Clinton argued in his 1994 State of the Union Address that 'democracies don't attack each other', and 'democratic enlargement' has been a centrepiece of Clinton's foreign policy (Doyle 1997: 285).

12. This sentiment is echoed by Cullen, who writes that 'Whatever the practioners of realpolitik might wish, a strong and bright moral component is essential to American foreign policy. Without it, public support for foreign engagement tends rapidly to erode' (Cullen 1992–93: 80).

13. Rudyard Kipling's poem *The White Man's Burden* was written in 1899, and in many ways epitomises the mix of paternalism and racism so characteristic of the Victorian age.

14. Hurd maintained that Britain should use aid as a lever for better government not only because it is right for developing countries, but also because 'we owe it to the taxpayer' (Hurd 1990: 4). Clearly, neo-conservative attacks on aid budgets are another driving force behind the good governance agenda. For New Labour's pronouncements on a more 'ethical' foreign policy, see Cook (1997a and 1997b).

15. Between 1980 and 1989 no less than 241 adjustment programmes were applied in sub-Saharan Africa (Jesperson 1993).

16. For a more detailed description of adjustment programmes see e.g. Mosely et al. (1991) and Tarp (1993).

17. In 1992, the World Bank is reported to have withdrawn a report entitled *Why Structural Adjustment has not Succeeded in Sub-Saharan Africa* (*The Economist* 1994a). The report was later published under another title and with an introduction that disclaimed the analysis as flawed because it failed to take account of the extent to which countries actually implemented and enforced the reforms they signed up to.

18. An extensive literature exists on the effects of adjustment programmes. The following are particularly instructive: Caufield (1997); Chossudovsky (1997); Cornia et al. (1987); Cornia (1991); Onimode (1989); Griffith-Jones and van der Hoeven (1990); Stewart (1991). The burden of adjustment has fallen disproportionately on women, and adjustment policies have been found to have a distinct gender bias against women. For further discussion on the gender aspects of adjustment policies, see Elson (1991); Gladwin (1991); Lockwood (1992) and Moser (1991).

19. The extent to which such domestic demands for democracy differed from the form of democracy advocated by the good governance agenda will be elaborated in Chapter 4.

3

The Seductiveness of Good Governance

The strength of development discourse, Gilbert Rist has written, comes from its power to seduce; 'to charm, to please, to fascinate, to set dreaming, but also to abuse, to turn away from the truth, to deceive' (1997: 1). The promise to eradicate poverty is so seductive that although the history of development is littered with failures, the *belief* in development survives. Past failures merely give rise to new theories, each claiming to have discovered the real solutions to the problems of development. The good governance agenda is simply the latest in a long series of such theories, the latest reproduction of the dream of development.

This chapter is not concerned with the implementation of the hotch-potch of policy recommendations contained within the good governance agenda, nor does it seek to rectify or to arrive at the 'correct' theory of development. Instead the focus is on the discourse itself, the way in which it narrates development as an absence of good governance. It seeks to expose not only the discourse's conceptualisation of democracy, but also what the discourse silences and evades, the ways in which its seductive power is used to deceive. This in turn should enable us to show what effects these ideas about development have on larger social processes, what interventions and practices they legitimise, and also what actions and policies they delegitimise and exclude.

Alien State Intervention, Indigenous Democratic Capitalism

As mentioned previously, the concept of good governance was first introduced to development discourse by the World Bank's 1989 report *Sub-Saharan Africa: From Crisis to Sustainable Growth*. This document was a major statement of the institution's intellectual leadership of the donor community (Gibbon 1993), and ever since the Bank has taken the lead in the articulation and ideological refinement of the new development doctrine. The 1989 report, together with the Bank's study *Governance and*

Development (1992a) still today represent the most rigorous and assertive official pronouncement of current development thinking, the *locus classicus* of the governance literature.[1] Accordingly, my analysis of the governance discourse centres on these two documents, but also draws on articles published by two senior members of the World Bank staff and the more summary Bank report entitled *Governance: The World Bank's Experience* (1994b). By and large, bilateral donors have fallen into line with the views expressed in these documents, and although contemporary development discourse cannot be seen as monolithic and unchanging there is nevertheless broad agreement on the fundamental elements of good governance as constructed by the World Bank.

The World Bank's construction of good governance starts from a rejection of the development models of the past. The 'postindependence development efforts failed', we are told, 'because the strategy was misconceived' (World Bank 1989: 3). According to the Bank, there is now 'a growing consensus' that these strategies 'pinned too much hope on rapid state-led industrialization' and mistakenly encouraged African governments to make 'a dash for "modernization", copying, but not adapting, Western models' (ibid.: 83, 3). Following independence, 'Africa's governments were grafted onto traditional societies and were often alien to the indigenous cultures' (ibid.: 38). The Bank's senior policy advisor makes the same point, asserting that 'state institutions based on Weberian bureaucratic principles … were not compatible with the beliefs and practices of African society' (Landell-Mills 1992: 543). The post-colonial state was, in short, 'the perfect example of an alien system imposed from the top' and because the underlying cultural premises of Western state institutions were foreign to the continent, these institutions 'started to crumble the moment the colonial administrators left' (ibid.: 545, 543). With hindsight, then, Africa's 'economic, political and social disaster' can be blamed on 'a fundamental flaw in the prevailing development paradigm (ibid.: 543).

The lesson has now been learned, however, and development theory has been amended accordingly. While previous state-led development efforts failed because they 'did not build on the strengths of traditional societies', the good governance agenda claims to be different (World Bank 1989: 60). Past development strategies made a rigid distinction between the modern and the traditional, discarded the traditional and made it abundantly clear that 'Modern societies meant "progress"' (ibid.: 60). The good governance agenda claims to have a greater degree of cultural awareness and appropriateness, as there are 'close links between governance, cultural relevance and the components of civil society' (Landell-Mills 1992:

567). The new development paradigm recognises, in the words of the World Bank, that 'far from impeding development, many indigenous African values and institutions can support it' (1989: 60). Good governance does not therefore advocate a 'dash for modernisation' but understands instead the need to 'progressively remodel its institutions to be more in tune with the traditions, beliefs, and structures of its component societies' (Landell-Mills 1992: 545). Accordingly 'each country has to devise institutions which are consonant with its social values' (World Bank 1989: 60). Change cannot be imposed from the outside by development agencies, but will be effective only if it is 'rooted firmly in the societies concerned' and World Bank programmes must therefore 'reflect national characteristics and be consistent with a country's cultural values' (World Bank 1992a: 12; 1989: 193).

On the face of it, these suggestions are very seductive and almost common-sensical. The expressed desire to build on a society's own values, rather than imported ones, would today be endorsed by both the political left and right. The recognition of the 'alien' nature of the modern state and its lack of roots in indigenous society also reflects current debates among Africanists. The World Bank's order of discourse, however, performs two important functions within the governance discourse. First, it serves to dissociate the good governance agenda and its proponents from the development failures of the past. Previous development strategies may have been misconceived, but these mistakes have now been rectified as donors have discovered the 'real' solution to Africa's problems. In this way, the development apparatus and the World Bank in particular remain untainted by previous mistakes and retain the moral right to continue the development effort. Second, the representation not only serves to construct an image of the modern Weberian state as alien to Africa, but delegitimises state-led development.[2] The state is constructed as a Western invention, a result of foreign ideologies and misguided development theory, imposed from above to modernise indigenous societies. Because the state is a foreign imposition, everything the state does is tainted and state intervention, whether the provision of welfare or the ownership of enterprises, is bound to fail as it is out of tune with local values and customs. In this representation the prevailing developmental or interventionist state becomes the enemy of the people, the reason for Africa's underdevelopment and misery. The good governance agenda, on the other hand, emerges as the liberator that will allow not only for development, but also for the release of society's true, indigenous values. At this point the good governance discourse takes a rather astonishing twist. While the state and *state-capitalism* are regarded as imported artefacts, *capitalism* is represented as an integral part of Africa's indigenous culture, perfectly attuned to local, traditional values.

The governance discourse portrays African societies as bursting with suppressed capitalist energy and entrepreneurial spirit. Under the headline *Africa's market tradition* the World Bank reminds us that 'Entrepreneurship has a long history in Sub-Saharan Africa. In parts of the continent long-distance trade on caravan routes dates back to the 11th century' (1989: 136). We are further asked to recall that in Great Zimbabwe mining activities were linked to Arab trading and export centres on the south-eastern coast, where a liberalised system of exchange operated and where mutual tolerance prevailed (ibid.). In contemporary Africa, by contrast, state-led development has stifled private sector activities. In their misguided 'dash for modernisation', governments 'greatly underestimated the depth and potential of African entrepreneurship' (ibid.: 136). Massive resources were directed to public enterprises, and these policies 'have driven entrepreneurs into the informal sector' and 'crowded local firms out of access to markets and financial resources' (ibid.: 136–7). But 'despite considerable hostility from central government, local entrepreneurs have shown remarkable vitality', and the Bank argues that in sharp contrast to the failure of public enterprises 'almost everywhere the informal sector has been a thriving success' (ibid.: 59, 38).

Not only has African capitalism triumphed against the odds, but it has done so in a manner that is consistent with Africa's indigenous culture. According to the World Bank, enterprises in 'the informal sector are organized around, and supported by, local values and traditions' (ibid.: 140). Traders and artisans carry out their activities 'according to long-established customs and rules administered through grassroots institutions' (ibid.: 136). Thus the good governance discourse speaks of financing in the informal sector in terms of savings clubs, rotating funds and other informal arrangements where 'interpersonal loyalties' are more important than formal guarantees and profit (ibid.: 140–1). There is no mention of moneylenders charging exorbitant interest rates. Instead, informal sector capitalism is given a caring and compassionate face, less concerned with profit because of its reliance on 'personal relationships' (ibid.: 140).

In this way the good governance discourse constructs a binary op-position between alien state intervention, which is associated with past development failures, and indigenous capitalism, which represents the basis for future development successes. While there is no denying the dismal performance of the African state, a clear consequence of this binary opposition is that it bestows legitimacy on the contraction of the state and its services in accordance with structural adjustment programmes. Because the state is an alien oppressor, the curtailment of state activities becomes a people-friendly, democratic venture, almost to the extent that state contraction or destatisation is presented as synonymous with democratisation. This conflation of destatisation with democratisation is an essential characteristic of the good governance discourse, and, as we shall see, it reverberates in various guises throughout the entire discourse.

The conflation of destatisation and democratisation has its roots in the perception of democracy and economic liberalism as the two sides of the same coin. Contemporary development thinking perceives of democratisation and economic liberalisation as interrelated and mutually reinforcing processes, an argument that can be synthesised as follows: economic liberalisation is expected to decentralise decision-making away from the state and multiply the centres of power. This in turn is assumed to lead to the development of a civil society capable of limiting the power of the state and providing the basis for liberal democratic politics. Democratic rights, on the other hand, are seen to safeguard property rights, which in turn creates the security and incentives necessary for economic growth. A positive synergy is thus perceived to exist between economic liberalisation and democracy, and the World Bank accordingly argues that 'political legitimacy' is a 'precondition for sustainable development' and growth, and that economic reform will be 'wasted if the political context is not favourable' (1989: 60, 192). This view has been repeated by numerous other development organisations and bilateral donors. Former British Foreign Secretary Douglas Hurd, for example, maintained that 'good government goes hand in hand with successful economic development. In the short term an authoritarian or corrupt government may achieve some economic progress. In the longer term, however, such governments prove inefficient, and are unable to deliver social goods as effectively as governments which are accountable' (1990: 4–5). The same view also informs the present Labour government's foreign policy, with Foreign Secretary Robin Cook stating that 'the past two decades have repeatedly demonstrated that political freedom and economic development are mutually reinforcing (1998).

In the good governance discourse, democracy emerges as the necessary political framework for successful economic development, and within the discourse democracy and economic liberalism are conceptually linked: bad governance equals state intervention, good governance equals democracy and economic liberalism. Or in the words of two senior World Bank officials, governance means competent and accountable government 'dedicated to liberal economic policies' (Landell-Mills and Serageldin 1991: 307). Because democracy and economic liberalism are conceptually linked in the one concept of 'governance', the possibility of conceiving of potential contradictions between the two is virtually impossible within the parameters of the discourse. To be in favour of democracy is simultaneously to be in favour of free market economics and structural adjustment. The fact that the two may at times conflict, so that for instance economic inequalities generated by capitalist competition may undermine political equality and the functioning of democracy, is rendered inconceivable by the fusion of the concepts. It also follows from the above definition of governance that democracy will lead to good governance only if the electorate chooses governments that adhere to a free market ideology. This is of course an inherently undemocratic stipulation, in that it attempts to restrict the scope of political choice. It entails, in short, an *a priori* determination of economic model and a relegation of constituents' preferences to second-order importance.[3] The possibility that large sections of the electorate in poor countries may favour economic and political solutions that conflict with the good governance agenda's vision is passed over in silence by the discourse.[4]

Instead the good governance agenda claims to speak on behalf of the 'ordinary people' of Africa, and states that its primary aim is to 'empower' them and enable them to resist the alien and oppressive state (World Bank 1989: 54). In this way an essential unity of purpose is constructed between the development apparatus and the 'ordinary people', in that they all oppose the state and seek to reduce it. The good governance agenda's strategy for supporting the people against the state is to strengthen civil society, a strategy that is also intimately bound up with economic liberalism.

Liberating Civil Society

In the good governance discourse, civil society emerges as the key link between economic liberalisation and democratisation; it is both the locus of economic growth and vitality and the seedbed of democracy. The weakness of civil society on the African continent is blamed on the statism of past development strategies. The dominance of the state is seen to have prevented the growth of autonomous organisations, which in turn enabled state officials in many countries to serve 'their own interests without fear of being called to account' (World Bank 1989: 60). Civil society is regarded as a 'countervailing power' to the state, a way of curbing authoritarian practices and corruption, hence the concern for strengthening or nurturing civil society. The World Bank states that good governance 'requires a systematic effort to build a pluralistic institutional structure' (ibid.: 61), and intermediary organisations are seen to have an especially important role to play. They 'can create links both upward and downward in society and voice local concerns more effectively than grassroots institutions. In doing this, they can bring a broader spectrum of ideas and values to bear on policy making' (ibid.). Intermediate organisations are also expected to exert pressure on public officials for better performance and greater accountability. In short, it is believed that by 'deliberately supporting the development of plural institutional structures, external agencies can help create an environment that will tend to constrain the abuse of political power' (Landell–Mills and Serageldin 1991: 313).

According to the good governance discourse, the best way to strengthen civil society is to reduce the role of the state and expand the scope of market forces as suggested by structural adjustment programmes. This is expected to decentralise decision-making away from the state and open up new spaces for grassroots organisations and private initiatives. In this context, attention is drawn to the flourishing of informal, voluntary organisations such as credit unions, farming associations, women's groups and professional associations on the continent over the past decade (World Bank 1989: 61; 1992: 25; Landell–Mills 1992). The growth of such voluntary associations is in large part a reflection of the state's curtailment of services in accordance with structural adjustment programmes. As the African state has become unable or unwilling to deliver basic services and infrastructure to its citizens, more and more people have come to rely on private initiatives, frequently centred around traditional, ethnic associations, but also involving new, voluntary self-help groups. The vacuum left by the retreating state has thus been filled by private initiatives, and given the good governance discourse's representation of the state as an alien oppressor this development is regarded as enhancing the prospects of democracy. In the words of Landell–Mills, the 'proliferation of associations at all levels' supports the trend towards 'more participatory politics, greater public accountability, and hence basic democracy' (1992: 563).[5]

While the mushrooming of associational life on the continent in recent years is indisputable, the good governance discourse's representation of this development as inherently democratic is far from unproblematic. This representation is intimately bound up with the conceptualisation of civil society within the governance discourse. A notoriously vague and ambiguous concept, civil society is at no point defined in the World Bank discourse.[6] In fact, the two main documents under consideration do not use the concept at all, but refer instead to institutional pluralism as well as intermediate and grassroots organisations. It is only in the 1994 report *Governance. The World Bank's Experience* that the concept emerges, but here its meaning is taken as too obvious and familiar to require any definition or further discussion. This treatment of civil society as an unproblematic concept has become commonplace in much contemporary literature on Africa, where civil society is used as an all-encompassing term referring to a wide range of voluntary cultural, economic, social and political associations, institutions and relations outside the state. This is also the World Bank's usage and in effect the references to institutions and intermediate and grassroots organisations in the two main documents are simultaneously the Bank's definition of civil society. In the governance discourse then, civil society equals associational life.

The agenda's conceptualisation of civil society proceeds from a particular conception of state and society, where the state is associated with power and civil society belongs to the realm of freedom and liberty.[7] In this interpretation, power and exploitation become the exclusive property of the state and the public/formal sector, and any reduction of the state and its economic and social services can accordingly be represented as an expansion of democracy and freedom. Such a narrow sovereign conception of power gives rise to the rather romantic representation of civil society as implicitly democratic, and the mere existence of organisations outside the state is assumed to be sufficient to limit the power of the state and enforce a transition to democracy. This representation is reductionist in the extreme. The emergence of various voluntary groups and associations cannot automatically be expected to constitute the basis of an active, well-informed, articulate civil society, nor can it be taken for granted that political activities with a strategic dimension will be generated by societal organisations and movements. Many associations in civil society do not involve any self-conscious political intention or action, and do not seek to limit the reach of the state or influence its policies. Other groups, in turn, may espouse authoritarian ideologies and pursue undemocratic strategies and goals. Civil society cannot therefore be seen as either inherently democratic or undemocratic; rather, its character may vary across time and space.

Such observations are of particular relevance in the African setting, where the blossoming of informal associations is largely a result of the inability of the state to deliver basic services. People have withdrawn from an increasingly oppressive and exploitative state, and turned instead to community networks for their social welfare. In the same way, the black or parallel market has provided an effective way of avoiding high taxes and the artificially low prices paid for farm products by state marketing boards. Such exit or coping strategies may well have weakened the state, but the ability to avoid the state should not be conflated with an ability to support democratisation in any constructive and significant way as it does not necessarily imply any political alignment or relation to political parties or activities.[8] Instead, these strategies generally signal a deep distrust of the state and a perception of its institutions as irrelevant to everyday life and struggles. If anything, such attitudes may have negative implications for democratisation, which requires the associations of civil society to engage with state institutions in order to achieve their aims and improve their conditions of existence.

The heterogeneous and segmented nature of civil society also cautions against definitions that treat it as inherently democratic. Civil society in Africa (as elsewhere) embodies a diverse set of traditional, ethnic, professional, class, local, regional and national interests. While heterogeneity does not in itself prevent voluntary associations from mobilising for democracy, it increases the likelihood that some may become agents of ethnic or parochial interests, especially where state boundaries are still in dispute and nation-building an incomplete process. This is arguably the case in most African countries, and the atrocities of the Liberian civil war in the post-Doe era, the brutality of Somalia's warlords, and the killing fields of Rwanda are sufficient reminders of the potential dangers contained within heterogeneous societies. And while the vacuum created by the retreating state may well allow voluntary organisations to mobilise for democracy, it also raises the spectre of intensified particularism and fragmentation.[9] Indeed, one view holds that 'Africa seems too condemned to harsh nation-building as to rule out many hopes for civil society' (Hall 1995: 25).

While such interpretations may be too pessimistic, it seems equally clear that the good governance discourse's representation of civil society as inherently democratic is too romantic and optimistic. The mere existence (or absence) of civil society, important as it is, is not sufficient to explain the success or failure of democracy. Civil society and its relationship to democratisation cannot be understood in abstract terms, but requires instead a specific analysis of the various groups and interests involved in these struggles. The point here, however, is not merely to note that the highly differentiated nature of African societies both in terms of ethnicity and wealth must be taken into account when considering the democratic potential contained in the emergence of their civil societies. Rather the important question relates to the effects of an order of discourse that ignores such cautionary observations about the heterogeneous and potentially undemocratic qualities of civil society. What actions and practices are legitimised by this discourse, and what types of power does it underwrite? The short answer is that the good governance discourse serves to construct economic liberalism as a force for democracy. The equation is simple: coercive power is perceived to reside exclusively in the state and public institutions, and any reduction in the size or reach of the state is therefore regarded as conducive to democratisation. Structural adjustment curtails state activity and is associated with the growth of voluntary groups and organisations, and hence adjustment becomes a democratic enterprise for the liberation of civil society.

Empowerment through Cost Recovery

What, then, remains of the good governance discourse's claim to empower the 'ordinary people' of Africa? one may legitimately ask. The governance discourse has the effect of valorising everything outside the institutions of the state and bestowing democratic legitimacy on all organisations and practices in civil society. Civil society emerges as undifferentiated and harmonious, and there are no classes, no races, no genders, ethnic groups or oppressors in the civil society of the good governance discourse. Instead the various groups and associations of civil society are implicitly expected to further the cause of 'the people', that is to serve the interests of all groups equally and democratically, and we are repeatedly reminded of Africa's 'rich traditions of community and group welfare' and the 'widespread practice of sharing among people' (World Bank 1989: 60, 168).

Reality, unfortunately, is somewhat different. Structures of power and hierarchies of wealth and influence permeate all civil societies, and African societies are no exception. The governance discourse, however, builds on an essentially ahistorical notion of civil society, where tradition is regarded as part of human nature, unchanging and set apart from power and authority. Organisations are abstracted from the socio-economic structures in which they are embedded, and become instead part of Africa's eternal tradition of sharing. Not only does this representation render inequalities of power between individuals, classes and groups invisible, but it also conceals the possibility that various traditional associations and practices may be hierarchically organised and form part of structures that privilege certain individuals and groups and enable them to serve their own particularistic economic and political ends. Accordingly Landell-Mills discusses the Harambee movement in rural Kenya only in terms of co-operative effort and mutual benefit for all, neglecting alternative views that the self-help activities of the movement rely heavily on women's labour, and that 'some communities, some groups and some national elites benefit far more than others' (Thomas 1988: 23).

The good governance discourse not only obscures such relations of power and domination, but its declared intention to build on traditional, indigenous structures in the effort to improve governance implies a continuation of the forms of oppression entailed within primordial relationships. This position is of course not compatible with the new development paradigm's democratic message, but it is nevertheless the inescapable corollary of its rather romanticised conceptualisation of tradition and civil society.

The conception of power that underpins the good governance discourse also has the effect of obscuring the coercive and oppressive relationships associated with capitalism. By locating power exclusively in the state, the marketplace becomes a realm of freedom and liberty. Such a conceptualisation of civil society cannot take account of the possibility that economic liberalisation may reinforce existing socio-economic inequalities, as it does not recognise the organisational and institutional structure of power in social relations in the first place. Similarly, there is no room for a critique of the threat that capitalist market forces may pose to systems of social solidarity and justice, and thus to some structures of civil society itself, nor is it recognised that state action at times may be necessary or desirable to overcome or reduce inequalities in civil society.[10] Instead the confinement of power to the state and the portrayal of the market as a place of liberty reinforce the image of structural adjustment as conducive to the expansion of democracy, and yet again we see how democratisation becomes almost synonymous with destatisation.

The governance agenda's overall aim to 'release the energies of ordinary people' and to 'empower ordinary people to take charge of their own lives, to make communities more responsible for their development, and to make governments listen to their people' is also intrinsically bound up with economic liberalism (World Bank 1989: 54). The seductive power of development is clearly demonstrated in the intention to empower; it draws on emotive and forceful imagery and appeals to notions of rights and justice. If taken literally this call for empowerment has far-reaching political consequences, in that it implies a challenge to local as well as national power structures. If people were enabled to hold those in power more accountable, they might demand more services and a more just distribution of income, and thus put into question the whole gamut of existing socio-economic arrangements.[11] Needless to say, this is not the intention of the development apparatus, and when analysed within the overall context of the economic policies of the good governance agenda empowerment takes on quite a different meaning.

One of the central tropes of the good governance discourse is *cost recovery*, which the World Bank introduces as one of a few 'watchwords for the future' (ibid.: 7). The Bank advocates the introduction of user charges for secondary (possibly also primary) education and primary health care, whereas full cost recovery is recommended for 'nonbasic services such as university education and nonessential health services' (ibid.: 6–7, 86). Water supply and sanitation are other services for which 'much of the cost could be recovered through user charges' (ibid.: 7). The World Bank maintains that 'Whatever the merits of free social services, the reality in Africa is that it means inadequate provision or no provision at all to many people and particularly to the poorest and most vulnerable' (ibid.: 86). It is in this context that the emphasis on empowerment, as well as the need to build on 'indigenous African values and institutions', emerges. The World Bank suggests that 'Communal culture, the participation of women in the economy, respect for nature … can be used in constructive ways' (ibid.: 60). By placing the management of basic social services in local hands two purposes can be achieved: programmes become more responsive to users, who then in turn 'become more willing to contribute to their cost' (ibid.: 7). There is, according to the World Bank, little or no resistance to user charges in Africa and 'even very poor people willingly pay for health care if they demonstrably get value for their money' (ibid.: 6). All in all, cost sharing is a means of 'empowering the beneficiaries to demand improved services and of fostering a sense of individual and community responsibility for their delivery' (ibid.: 86).

It is this form of consumer sovereignty that the World Bank tries to dress up as empowerment and, by implication, as democracy. The incorporation of words like 'empowerment', 'self-help' and 'participation' into the Bank's otherwise monetarist vocabulary serves primarily to justify the curtailment of state responsibility. Adjustment programmes necessarily mean fewer state services, especially to the poor, and as a result of the economic crisis in the last decade the burden of caring for the sick, feeding the poor and so on has been increasingly transferred from paid state officials to unpaid local labour (mostly women). There is absolutely nothing democratic or empowering about this. By contrast, local people, and women in particular, are expected to make up for the shortfall in public services, to be able to put in more working hours to compensate for the withdrawal of state provisions. While this may register in national budgets and World Bank statistics as cost saving and a sign of increased efficiency, it entails increased burdens for many local people. Terms like 'empowerment' and 'community responsibility', however, serve to give this development an aura of democratic freedom. Within the good governance discourse, then, empowerment is deprived of its radical, political implications, and becomes instead a highly instrumental term; the objective is to 'capitalize on the energies and resources of the local people', who should pull their weight and thereby make development projects more cost-efficient (World Bank 1989: 58). Only in this context does it make sense for Landell-Mills to describe local, voluntary self-help groups as 'cost-sharing moves' (1992: 567). Local initiatives are expected to fill the gaps left by the retreating state, to provide social services like health care, water and sanitation. Self-help, participation and empowerment become an intrinsic part of the effort to liberalise the economy, efforts that can be tapped into and used to reduce the cost of public provisions. Community involvement and empowerment are intended to function within the framework of economic liberalism, not to challenge existing power structures or question adjustment programmes through 'excess' demands. This kind of participation and empowerment has nothing to do with democracy, but again we see how the good governance discourse blurs the distinction between the retreat of the state and democratisation.[12]

Good Governance as Modernisation Theory

The good governance discourse presents its intention to build on local grassroots organisations as evidence of the cultural sensitivity of the new development paradigm. As we have seen, a sharp contrast is drawn between the 'modernisation' strategies of the past, which imposed alien systems on traditional societies, and the new strategy, which builds on the indigenous and listens to 'the people'. Grave concern is also expressed about the risk of 'ethnocentric and cultural bias', and it is acknowledged that development institutions must be 'very cautious in proposing specific solutions or advocating particular arrangements' and that 'there should be no question of imposing a particular democratic system on any country' (Landell-Mills and Serageldin 1991: 311). Unlike the misconceived policies of yesteryear, then, governance takes account of cultural differences and recognises that African values and institutions can support development and be used in constructive ways (World Bank 1992a: 8; 1989: 60). The emphasis is on the need for 'home-grown solutions' (Landell-Mills and Serageldin 1991: 311) and it is argued that each country 'has to devise institutions that are consonant with its social values' (World Bank 1989: 60).

On closer inspection, however, this appears a peculiar brand of 'pick and mix' cultural relativism, which recognises that indigenous African traditions are not uniformly favourable to democracy and economic liberalism. In *Governance and Development*, the World Bank points out that the spread of political legal systems modelled on Western traditions may lead to the existence of two sets of norms and institutions: 'Western notions of the rule of law, private property rights, and contracts' may be superimposed on 'ideas such as "consensus", "communal property", and "reciprocity"' (1992b: 8). The question of whether these 'different ways of anchoring social rights and obligations ... hamper the functioning of modern economic institutions' is raised, only to be left unanswered in the document. Landell-Mills, however, is more outspoken on these issues. He asserts that the 'challenge is to build on the elements [of African tradition] that are compatible with modernisation and development, *rejecting those that are not* and, where necessary and appropriate, borrowing wittingly from foreign models, western or eastern' (1992: 545, italics added).[13] The turn of phrase is important: the good governance agenda may advocate institutions that are consonant with indigenous social values, but then proceeds to narrow those values down to compatibility with modernisation.

One aspect of African tradition that must be discarded is the strong family and ethnic ties, which 'have no place in central government agencies, where staff must be selected on merit and where public and private monies must not be confused' (World Bank 1989: 60). In the context of seeking to establish honest, efficient and accountable administration, such statements make eminent sense, but they simultaneously reveal a deeper contradiction within the good governance discourse. On the one hand, the World Bank praises Africa's strong family and communal ties in relation to issues of empowerment and cost recovery, while on the other, it attacks these aspects of African culture and practices as detrimental to good governance. It seems that the World Bank wants to make use of communal bonds when they can serve to reduce the cost of basic state services, and abandon them as archaic and hostile to the project of development in other contexts. Rather than cultural sensitivity, such statements signal not only a degree of instrumentalism, but also a simplistic understanding of cultural practices and traditions as existing independently of social structures and as something that can simply be abandoned at will. While the persistence of patrimonial practices in Africa may well be an affront to good governance, one should not disregard the fact that these practices have particular historical and cultural roots and that they may also serve particular political purposes. Abandoning patrimonial practices may accordingly prove far from easy, and may also have wide-ranging consequences for the construction of viable political authority and structures of governance.[14] Another custom that must give way to good governance is communal land ownership and land use rights, as the World Bank claims that agricultural modernisation makes land titling necessary (ibid.: 104). This issue is presented as entirely 'technical' in nature, and there is no discussion of the political and cultural significance of communal land ownership and networks of patronage. Thus the fact that land titling would most likely exclude some people from access to land and make the survival of others highly precarious, while enriching a few, is passed over in silence.

The good governance discourse asserts that it seeks to create 'a modern sector that *supports* the traditional sector, rather than one that aims to *replace* it' (World Bank 1989: 60, italics in original). It is nevertheless difficult to see how the governance paradigm is qualitatively different from the 'modernisation' strategies of the past. Development within the good governance discourse is still perceived to imply 'a profound change in social culture' and a 'long-term process of changing mentalities' (Landell-Mills 1992: 564, 565). As we have seen, good governance is conceptually linked to economic liberalism, and the effort to strengthen civil society concentrates primarily on nurturing the bourgeoisie and creating an enabling environment for business. Apart from the token references to the 'empowerment of ordinary people', which ultimately boils down to an issue of cost recovery, the civil society of the good governance discourse consists primarily of modern, professional and contractual organisations. The discourse embodies a liberal conception of civil society as the equivalent of market, or bourgeois society. This is not only a conception that elevates the right to private property over all other rights, but it also draws on notions of the universal liberal subject and the philosophy of possessive individualism (see Williams and Young 1994). Accordingly, the World Bank can perceive of a 'common desire of individual Africans to be independent economic operators' (1989: 59), and its development mission thus appears as the liberation of the liberal subject from the oppressive structures of the state.[15]

In order to assist Africans in their struggle to become 'independent economic operators', the good governance discourse pays particular attention to strengthening the business community. A free economy is perceived as absolutely vital to civil society, and the focus is on creating an 'enabling environment' that can 'release private energies and encourage initiatives at every level' (ibid.: 59). 'Private enterprises' are regarded as 'a crucial component of civil society, acting effectively as its life support' (Landell-Mills 1992: 563). Accordingly, 'measures taken to favour private-sector activities, including the widespread attempts to privatise state enterprises, serve to reinforce civil society' (ibid.: 564). The good governance agenda here employs arguments that are commonplace in many liberal accounts of the rise of democracy in the West, where the bourgeoisie is regarded as the engine not only of economic growth, but also of democratisation.

In the conventional manner of modernisation theory, the good governance discourse can be seen to draw on the historical experience of the West in its construction of development. As Barrington Moore's famous dictum 'No bourgeois, no democracy' indicates, the emergence of civil society in the West is closely bound up with the pioneering role of this class in demanding and maintaining a sphere free from state intervention (Moore 1991: 418). The good governance discourse now expects the African bourgeoisie to perform the same function. This view also holds strong support among contemporary liberal academics, and Diamond in particular has been an eager proponent of the bourgeoisie as the agent of democracy (1988a and 1988b). Diamond argues that the intimate link between political power and dominant class formation in Africa has stunted the growth of an autonomous, indigenous bourgeoisie and that this has 'meant the absence of that class that pressed for the expansion of democratic rights and limitation of state power during the early development of democracy in the industrialized West' (1988a: 22). In Africa, the 'bourgeoisie that has developed ... has been bureaucratic or political, non-productive, and even parasitic' (ibid.). He thus argues that the increasing movement away from statist economic policies and structures represents the 'most significant boosts to the democratic prospects in Africa' (ibid.: 27), as it is expected to loosen the connection between state power and class formation.

It cannot, however, be categorically stated that the bourgeoisie in European history was always in opposition to the state, nor can the African bourgeoisie be trusted to act as the democratisers of their societies. In European history this class has frequently formed vertical links and alliances with the state, especially when it feared challenges from below.[16] The bourgeoisie in parts of nineteenth- and twentieth-century Europe sought to overthrow political absolutism in order to safeguard the sphere of liberty and private property, but it did not seek to inaugurate the rule of the majority. In other words, the bourgeoisie had liberal goals associated with economic freedom, but not political democratic objectives. The bourgeoisie and democracy cannot therefore be regarded as logically or historically linked. Instead democracy has, as Therborn argues, always and everywhere been established in struggles against the bourgeoisie and can be seen as 'grafted' on to liberal capitalism (Therborn 1983: 271; Macpherson 1977). In the same way as the European bourgeoisie resisted democratisation, the emerging business classes in Africa may have much to fear from democracy and universal suffrage. To identify this class as an agent of democracy in the manner of the good governance discourse is therefore highly contentious. It is one thing to assume that the bourgeoisie is/can be the agent of liberal capitalism, quite another to expect it automatically to promote democracy. The support of this class for democracy and majority rights cannot be taken for granted, but requires instead concrete empirical investigation.

The good governance discourse also contains another, related assumption that is equally problematic, namely that economic liberalisation will lead to the development of an *autonomous* bourgeoisie (democratic or otherwise). This expectation entails a view of civil society as separate from the state, but no such clear demarcation line can be drawn between the two. Instead the boundaries of state and society constantly overlap and intersect in complex ways, and this is especially the case in African countries. This feature of state–society relations is effectively captured in Bayart's image of 'the rhizome state', which is linked to society through a multiplicity of horizontal networks (1993: 218–27). While the World Bank and many liberal writers (like the prolific Larry Diamond) lament the near fusion of state elites and economic elites, they appear to exaggerate the fragility of this relationship, expecting it to disintegrate once liberalisation begins. However, clientelistic relations between the state and the various groups engaged in production and accumulation have evolved over time and may not be easily superseded by an ideal-type bourgeoisie capable of acting independently of the state.

First, groups closely associated with the state are most likely to benefit from liberalisation measures, and clientelistic relationships may be continued and reinforced rather than severed by adjustment programmes. Government officials may use their positions of authority to gain a disproportionate share of privatised resources and income-earning opportunities, and recent concerns by donors, including the World Bank, about the politicisation of economic reforms lend further support to such arguments (see e.g. *Africa Confidential* 39 (13) 1998).[17] Second, sections of the bourgeoisie may actively seek the continued protection of the state. The reaction of the Chinese business class during the pro-democracy protests in 1989 may serve as an illustration here. The nascent Chinese entrepreneurial class did not come out in favour of reform, as they were anxious not to jeopardise the stability of the bureaucratic support that provided profit and protection. They were particularly opposed to any crackdown on corruption, as this would target precisely the kind of personal ties with state officials that business depended on. And as many firms were run by relatives of high-ranking government officials, the students' call for an end to nepotism fell on deaf ears (Wank 1995). Similarly, the Zambian business community, represented by the Zambia Confederation of Chambers of Commerce and Industries, argued against the government's economic liberalisation programme. In the Confederation's argument that the programme 'kills domestic industries' (*Zambia Daily Mail*, 24 May 1993), an implicit preference for state protectionism and old-fashioned 'crony capitalism' can be detected.

In the good governance discourse, however, the bourgeoisie, by virtue of its place within civil society, is inherently and automatically democratic. It is also assumed to be willing to defend the rights of the 'ordinary people' against the alien and oppressive state. Such a representation is rendered possible only by the extraction of power and interests from civil society, so that all individuals and groups are perceived as equal and as sharing the same goals and motivations. Not only is this a rather naive representation, but it can also be seen to rely on a particular interpretation of the emergence of democracy on the West. In this respect, contemporary development discourse is not significantly different from the modernisation theory it so eagerly disclaims. Like modernisation theory, it theorises about African development on the basis of the historical experience of the West, and despite its claim to be 'culturally sensitive' it embodies a vision of the good society that is largely constructed from Western values. Prime among these are democracy and economic liberalism, which according to the good governance agenda are historically linked and constitute the two sides of the same coin. The discourse then proposes to reconstruct or develop African societies according to these values, to re-create Africa in its own image.

Conclusion

The power of development to 'seduce' (Rist 1997) is clearly evident in the good governance discourse. Its language and imagery are forceful and emotive, and its claims to 'empower', 'democratise', to 'release energies' and 'liberate civil society' are the stuff that dreams are made of. Analysis of the good governance agenda, however, seems to go around in circles, always leading back to one factor: economic liberalisation. Governance is conceptually linked to economic liberalisation, and civil society is regarded as emerging from the liberalisation of the economy and reduction of the state. 'Empowerment of the people' is reduced to cost-sharing, and becomes a tool in the hands of liberal economists. The bourgeoisie is regarded as both the source of economic growth and democracy, and cultural sensitivity entails only a commitment to build on the traditions that are compatible with capitalism and modern state structures.

Despite the discourse's effort to distance itself from past development failures, its endless repetition of the specificity of Africa and its respect for indigenous traditions and cultures, the agenda's recommendations amount to little more than a new gloss on age-old prescriptions. The main effect of the discourse is to construct structural adjustment as a force for democracy, and although the discourse does not go all the way towards reducing democracy to economic liberalism it is clear that 'good governance' is impossible without liberal economic policies. In this way the discourse legitimises continued structural adjustment, and gives it a more democratic face, while simultaneously delegitimising more interventionist and socialist strategies, which by implication become examples of 'poor governance'.

Notes

1. Both these documents represent major research efforts by the World Bank. *Governance and Development* (World Bank 1992a) is the product of twenty-two members of staff, while the 1989 long-term perspective study was partly a response to critiques of structural adjustment programmes and consulted numerous scholars outside the Bank, including Göran Hyden, Claude Ake, Janet MacGaffey and Paul Harrison.

2. A similar point is made by Beckman (1992).

3. This is indicative of a long-standing tension in liberalism, but this is an issue that lies beyond the purview of this study.

4. This possibility will be explored in more detail in later chapters.

5. This view of associational life as more or less automatically supporting democratisation also finds widespread support in academic writing; see for example Bratton (1989); Chazan (1982, 1988a, 1988b, 1993) and Diamond (1988a, 1988b).

6. Useful explorations of the concept of civil society can be found in Cohen and Arato (1992); Calhoun (1993); Keane (1988); Taylor (1990); Walzer (1991). The concept has only more recently been introduced to the analysis of African politics, notable contributions include Bayart (1986); Chabal (1994, Chapter 5); Fatton (1995); Harbeson, Rothchild and Chazan (1994) and White (1994 and 1995).

7. A similar observation is made by Bangura and Gibbon (1992).

8. Ekeh argues that civil society in Africa is highly apolitical and is 'largely indifferent to the affairs of the civil public realm over which the state presides' (1992: 197). While

this may be a rather heavy-handed generalisation, it nevertheless serves as a useful corrective to the uncritical interpretation of civil society as an automatic check on the powers of the state.

9. The ambiguity of civil society's relationship to democratisation has for example been noted by Lucy Davis (1995) in a case study of the popular organisation Mboscuda among the Mbororo in northwest Cameroon. Davis is doubtful whether the organisation will become an effective participant in a national democratic movement, or whether it will instead develop into a vehicle for ethnic chauvinism.

10. Whitehead (1993a) has convincingly argued that the maintenance of social communal values to curb unbridled individualism was a major concern of the early theorists of civil society, such as Ferguson, Hume and Smith. Such concerns seem all too easily forgotten in contemporary debates that associate democracy with capitalism and state minimalism.

11. A similar point is made by Beckman (1992).

12. The good governance discourse's appeal to grassroots and self-help organisations is perhaps analogous to the neo-conservative call for a return to family values, tradition and religion in the West as part of the attempt to revive self-restraint and unburden the state.

13. This brief reference to Eastern models appears to be nothing more than a token gesture, as the experience of Japan and the East Asian Tigers is conspicuously absent from discussions of good governance. This is the argument of Moore's (1993) article 'Declining to learn from the East?', which maintains that if Eastern development models had been considered good governance would have appeared very different and accorded a much greater role to selective state intervention.

14. In relation to the decline of patrimonial politics and the maintenance of political authority and social order, see for example Reno's book on the emergence of warlord politics (1998) and Zartman (1995) on state collapse.

15. It is interesting to note here how culture can be used to defend almost any argument. For a long time, many leaders promoting the idea of an African socialism rooted their ideas in precisely the opposite interpretation of African culture. The late President Julius Nyerere, for example, argued that 'whenever we try to help Africans become capitalist shopkeepers, capitalist farmers, industrialists, etc., we find that most of them fail because they cannot adopt the capitalist practices which are essential to commercial success ... Capitalism demands certain attributes among its practitioners which the majority of our people have never been forced to acquire' (1968: 18).

16. Marx argued that the French bourgeoisie in the mid-nineteenth century sacrificed the autonomy of civil society to protect their interests from the masses. The 'French bourgeoisie', he wrote, 'was compelled by its class position to annihilate ... the vital conditions of all parliamentary power and to render irresistible ... the executive power hostile to it' (Marx 1963: 63).

17. See also Gibbon (1992); Galli (1990); Hibou (1999) and Zack-Williams (1990).

4

The Democratisation of Poverty

Simply proclaimed as the 'new global *zeitgeist*' (Diamond et al. 1988: x), lengthy theoretical discussions of the meaning and values of democracy are virtually absent from most mainstream contemporary literature on governance and democratisation in the South. Instead democracy appears as an unproblematic concept, an unquestionable 'good' about which there is little or no difference of opinion. The corollary of this representation is an image of a worldwide democracy movement with shared goals and aspirations, where Western donors and creditors join forces with the 'people' of the South against an oppressive state. The fall of one-party dictatorships and the holding of multi-party elections then in turn appear as the great victory and empowerment of the 'people'.

This image of consensus is a fragile construct. Democracy is one of the most contested and controversial concepts in political theory, and despite the global spread of democracy it remains an ambiguous concept, open to diverse interpretations, uses and abuses – so much so that democracy can be classified as an essentially contested concept, in the sense that any neutral definition is impossible as rival definitions embody different and indeterminate social and political allegiances and operate within a particular moral and political perspective. Democracy is thus one of those concepts that 'inevitably involves endless disputes about their proper uses on the part of their users' (Gallie 1955–56: 169). This notion of contestability is largely expelled from contemporary mainstream scholarship on governance and democratisation, which displays a clear convergence towards a purely procedural or minimalist definition of democracy. Participatory models are excluded or dismissed in passing as unrealistic or outdated, and the democracy the South should strive for is presented as an institutional arrangement or political method, centred on the competitive struggle between political parties for people's votes.

This chapter seeks to situate contemporary literature on governance and democratisation in the South within the wider field of democratic theory. It traces the roots of current mainstream definitions of democracy to Weber, Schumpeter and other theorists of democratic elitism and argues that such approaches frequently lead to the valorisation of multi-party competition and elections as ends in themselves. The chapter contends that electoral democracy, while valuable, contains substantial limitations in terms of its ability to address issues of social justice in highly unequal societies such as those found in Africa. If democracy is to have meaning to the masses it must address questions not only of political rights, but also of concrete socio-economic rights. This, however, is ruled out by donor insistence on continued economic liberalisation. Regarding democracy as a contested concept, the chapter shows how, taken together, the good governance discourse and mainstream literature of democratisation in the South serve to legitimise a particular form of liberal democracy, while delegitimising and marginalising alternative conceptualisations that are perhaps more in tune with the aspirations of the majority of poor people. It also bestows democratic legitimacy on the existing social order, and the continued suffering and deprivation of the majority of people on the continent.

Democratic Theory and Contemporary Debates

The overwhelming predominance of procedural definitions of democracy in contemporary mainstream literature on governance and democratisation in the South is quite striking. Multi-party elections are presented as the essence of democracy, and electoral competition is placed at the heart of the effort to globalise democracy. This preoccupation with elections can be illustrated by Diamond, Linz and Lipset's oft-quoted definition of democracy as a system that meets the following three conditions:

- meaningful and extensive *competition* among individuals and organized groups (especially political parties) for all effective positions of government power, at regular intervals and excluding the use of force.

- a highly inclusive level of *political participation* in the selection of leaders and policies, at least through regular and fair elections, such that no major (adult) social group is excluded.

- a level of *civil and political liberties* – freedom of expression, freedom of the press, freedom to form and join organizations – sufficient to ensure the integrity of political competition and participation. (1988: xvi)

The same emphasis is evident in Huntington's definition, which classifies a political system as democratic 'to the extent that its most powerful collective decision-makers are selected through fair, honest, and periodic elections in which candidates freely compete for votes and in which virtually all the adult population is eligible to vote' (1991: 7). According to such definitions, then, the existence of free elections becomes the key criteria for describing a country as democratic, and, as the following analysis will show, this procedural approach gives rise to numerous considerations, especially when applied to poor societies.

The intellectual roots of contemporary definitions of democracy can be found above all in the writings of Max Weber, Joseph Schumpeter and more recent theories of democratic elitism. For Weber, democracy is primarily a means of producing an effective political leadership in conditions of a modern bureaucratic society, and apart from their ability to dismiss the ineffective from office, voters are assigned little or no influence over decision-making. In Weber's own memorable words, modern democracy entails the 'soullessness of the masses', and the division of citizens into 'politically active and politically passive elements' (1970: 113, 99). Universal suffrage, in other words, is valued not in its own right, but simply as a necessary means of legitimising leaders and providing them with mass support. This reduction of democracy to a mechanism for legitimising the authority of a political elite was further elaborated by Schumpeter, for whom the role of the people in democracy was merely to produce a government, not to choose politicians who execute their will (1976: 269). Democracy, he wrote,

> does not mean and cannot mean that the people actually rule in any obvious sense of the terms 'people' and 'rule'. Democracy means only that the people have the opportunity of accepting or refusing the men who are to rule them … Now one aspect of this may be expressed by saying that democracy is the rule of the politician. (ibid.: 284–5)

Importantly, neither Schumpeter nor Weber regarded the limited influence of the electorate as a regrettable state of affairs – they saw it as a welcomed and necessary restriction on a mass public regarded as irrational, ignorant and easily manipulated.

Many of those who followed in Schumpeter's footsteps in the 1950s and 1960s often went further in valorising voter passivity. The point of departure for most theories of democratic elitism in this period was the insights generated by large-scale studies of voting behaviour and political attitudes in Western societies, which revealed that the overwhelming majority of people were ill-informed or did not care about politics.[1] In other words, the democratic virtues described by theorists such as, for example, Jean-Jacques Rousseau and John Stuart Mill – involvement, participation, and the sharing of responsibility – were more or less absent from modern societies, whereas the vices – lack of interest and apathy – appeared to permeate the citizenry. Based on such observations it was argued that a more empirically accurate and realistic theory was needed, and that such a theory should take account of the lack of involvement and interest in politics not as a deficiency, but as part and parcel of actual functioning democracies.

Accordingly, democratic theory came to recognise that democracy can work perfectly well with only low levels of voter participation. What is more, apathy was no longer regarded as an intrinsically bad thing. Instead, it was argued that apathy could be an indication of a high degree of trust in political leaders (Almond and Verba 1963), and hence a sign of the electorate's basic satisfaction and a reflection of 'the health of a democracy' (Lipset 1960: 32). Some went even further than this and suggested that apathy was positively helpful and functional to the stability of democratic systems. Too much participation and high voter turn-out could be a sign of declining consensus, increasing social tension and extremism, and the existence of a large passive population was therefore considered beneficial to the survival of political pluralism (Berelson et al. 1954; Berelson 1956; Lipset 1960). The historical-political context of the 1950s and 1960s goes some way towards explaining such viewpoints. The recent experience of fascism in Europe had left a fear of mass politics and the Cold War had created a binary opposition between liberal democracy and totalitarianism, where participation came to be associated with extremism and the total politics of the Eastern bloc. Hence the argument in an article entitled 'In defense of apathy' that 'many of the ideas connected to the general theme of duty to vote belong properly to the totalitarian camp and are out of place in the vocabulary of liberal democracy' (Morris-Jones 1954: 25). In this climate, the freedom to be apathetic and inactive came to be regarded as not only an essential feature of democracy (Sartori 1962: 90), but also a 'sign of understanding and tolerance of human variety' (Morris-Jones 1954: 37). By implication, to advocate active participation was to invite intolerance and totalitarianism.

Such standpoints were of course not only determined by the fascist experience and the East/West binary, but were also rooted in other factors, most notably a particular view of the 'people' as not only ignorant, but also uncommitted to democratic values. A telling example is Lipset's book, which includes a chapter entitled 'Working Class Authoritarianism' in which he argues that the lower strata are relatively more authoritarian than the middle and upper classes, and that the working classes therefore constitute the major threat to freedom (1960: 101). Dahl similarly concludes that if an increase in political participation brings the authoritarian minded lower socio-economic sections of the population into the political arena, democracy could be endangered (1956: 89). In this way the 'people' or the 'masses', rather than the governing elites, become the main enemy of political freedom and voter apathy becomes conducive to the survival chances of democracy and liberal values such as tolerance, liberty and equality (see e.g. Sartori 1962).

The purpose of this admittedly brief and selective sojourn into democratic theory is to draw attention to a series of features of contemporary literature on democratisation in the South. As already mentioned, the intellectual roots of today's mainstream approaches stretch back to Weber, Schumpeter and theorists of democratic elitism, most notably in their shared focus on electoral competition as the defining feature of democracy. And while not endorsing voter apathy as a 'fact of life' or even functional to modern democracies in the manner of democratic elitism, the passivity of the majority also finds its place in much contemporary writing. Because so much recent scholarship on democratisation has been caught up with the post-Cold War desire to encourage the global spread of democratic political systems, relatively little attention has been paid to the deficiencies of existing democracies (see e.g. Huntington 1991; Di Palma 1990; O'Donnell and Schmitter 1986). Hence lack of participation in the established democracies of the West is not recognised, but instead these countries are treated as implicitly democratic and as models for the South. Similarly, there is relatively little discussion of how to expand democratic control beyond periodic elections, and in a manner reminiscent of Weber and Schumpeter, democracy becomes a method for selecting leaders and establishing efficient leadership. In this respect, the emergence of the term 'governance' (rather than democracy) as a central concept of development discourse is in itself an indication of the paramount importance assigned to leadership as opposed to democratic participation.

Another shared characteristic of democratic elitism and much contemporary literature is the claim to provide an empirically accurate description of modern political systems. In the case of democratic elitism this was bound up with a desire to avoid normative prescriptions for how best to organise society, or in the words of Dahl to describe how the contemporary democratic system works, not to 'determine ... whether it is a desirable system of government' (1956: 149). By making 'realism' and descriptive accurateness the measurement of success for democratic theory it was hoped that normative judgements could be avoided, and scientific objectivity achieved. But the distinction between a descriptive, explanatory account and a normative theory is, of course, a notoriously slippery slope, and time and time again authors within this school of thought end up endorsing that which they claim only to describe. As Held (1987) argues, this approach entails abstracting a definition from already existing political systems, rather than focusing on the ideals of democracy. Thus what *is* automatically becomes democratic, and the label itself endorses and bestows legitimacy on the existing system.[2] The most glaring example of this is undoubtedly the incorporation of voters' apathy and ignorance into democratic theory not merely as facts of life, but as conducive to the functioning and stability of the system.

The theme of descriptive accuracy also reverberates through contemporary literature on democracy in the South, albeit it in a slightly different guise. Present-day authors are concerned to define democracy in realistic and operational terms; that is, democracy must refer to something that is actually 'out there'. Normative definitions that include socio-economic criteria and active involvement by subordinate classes are deemed unworkable because such systems do not exist, or as Karl puts it, scholars who adopt normative definitions would be 'hard-pressed to find "actual" democratic regimes to study' (1990: 2). Definitions of democracy that include socio-economic factors are also denounced as useless because they cannot 'investigate empirically the hypothetical relationship between competitive political forms and progressive economic outcomes' (ibid.: 2; see also Diamond et al. 1988: xvi; Hadenius 1992: 8). Broad-based popular participation is further dismissed as a pipe-dream because it requires 'another citizen than those we daily encounter ... In short, it requires a 'humanity' which is characterized by a veritable passion for politics' (Hadenius 1992: 23). Once again then, we see how what already *exists* provides the basis for the definition of democracy, while ideals of participation and self-fulfilment are regarded as irrelevant because they do not refer to actually existing systems and are therefore not operational. To a certain extent, this neglect of more normative or participatory democratic theories in contemporary literature, combined with the strong focus on competitive elections, entails an implicit acceptance of Weber's 'soullessness of the masses' in the sense that an expansion of democratic control and participation is deemed unachievable and unrealistic.

In one important respect many contemporary writers on democracy in the South appear to go one step further than the democratic elitism of the past. While the latter aimed for a purely descriptive account and shied away from explicit normative endorsements of existing liberal democracies, much recent literature praises the lack of vision embodied in current definitions of democracy as a *virtue* (see e.g. Huntington 1991; Di Palma 1990; O'Donnell and Schmitter 1986). Before proceeding with the argument, a brief reminder of the values and principles that are being discarded by current approaches is in order.

From Athens to nineteenth-century England, democratic theory embodied a commitment to the ideals of participation, equality, tolerance and liberty, and today these ideals are kept alive by the democratic theories of the political left (see e.g. Held 1987 and 1995; Pateman 1970). Always situated more in the realm of the ideal and the possible than in the actual politics of existing democracies, these various theories regard democracy as much more than a method for selecting leaders and protecting the individual from the arbitrary power of government. Instead participation is valued in its own right and for the benefits it brings to the individual and the community. Ever since Jean-Jacques Rousseau set out his ideas in *The Social Contract*, participation has been regarded as crucial to the self-development and the self-fulfilment of citizens. Through participation, the individual becomes a public citizen, capable of distinguishing between her own private good and the good of the community.[3] This function of democracy was similarly emphasised by John Stuart Mill, who held that without participation most people would be consumed by self-interest and the satisfaction of their daily wants. While most participatory theories recognise that widespread political involvement is not currently a reality on the ground, they pose a direct challenge to the tendency to extol apathy to a democratic virtue. Voter apathy is treated not as an inescapable fact, but as a product of a particular social, economic and political arrangement. Similarly, human nature is not regarded as uniform or fixed, and it follows that given the right social and political conditions people will be both able and willing to take a much more active part in the governing of their societies. Democracy thus becomes a project to be realised, a constant striving for the expansion of democratic control and participation.

It is the abandonment of these ideals that is heralded as positive and beneficial by contemporary writers, but more than anything the literature welcomes the de-linking of democracy from notions of social progress and economic equality. Huntington, for example, celebrates the fact that US political scientists have made democracy 'less of a hurrah word and more of a common sense word' (1991: 7). The sentiment is echoed by Di Palma, who writes that democracy's 'disengagement from the idea of social progress is a silver lining ... which gives democracy more realistic, more sturdily conscious grounds for claiming superiority in the eyes of public opinion and political practioners' (1990: 23). In contemporary literature, then, democracy is dissociated from economic structures and strategies; it is, in the words of Diamond, Linz and Lipset 'a political system, separate and apart from the economic system to which it is joined' (1988: xvi). Again, we see how party competition and elections become very definite ends in themselves, with little or no regard to structures of power and domination within these polities. Elections are even on occasion dissociated from questions of social justice, as in O'Donnell and Schmitter's argument that 'Political democracy *per se* is a goal worthy of attainment, even at the expense of forgoing alternative paths that would seem to promise more immediate returns in terms of socialization' or social reform (1986: 13–14). The concern here is obviously to insulate structures of electoral democracy from claims of authoritarian efficiency. However, in the process democracy risks becoming wholly formalised and without connection to its substantive outcomes and their impact on the lives of citizens.

Worthy of attainment for whom? one may legitimately ask in response to O'Donnell and Schmitter's statement above, for is it not conceivable that for some social reform can be as important as the right to vote? A common (Schumpeterian) reply to this question would be that democracy enables people to organise and campaign for the implementation of reforms, but that democracy itself cannot contain a substantive commitment to social justice and welfare. Following this train of thought, Przeworski (1991) describes democracy as a system of organised uncertainty, where the rules of the game are known to us, but not the outcome of the game. Outcomes can be determined only by political competition between various political forces, and democracies may or may not end up having a social content, depending on the wishes of the voters. Any *a priori* commitment to substantive equality beyond voting, such as welfare or social justice, can easily be cast as unrelated to the question of democracy. According to such approaches, the main value of democracy arises from its ability to produce a bloodless change from one government to another. Because there is always the prospect of doing better in the next election, losers in the democratic game refrain from violence and concentrate instead on winning in the coming round (see e.g. Przeworski 1999).

In essence, such procedural or minimalist approaches to democracy are concerned with equal legal or formal rights, and tend to underplay the extent to which these rights can be realised. To use Schumpeter's comparison, democracy requires that everyone is, in principle, free to compete for political leadership in the same sense as everyone is free to start another textile mill (1976: 271–2). Such abstract notions of freedom do not accommodate the material reality that in the same way as everyone is clearly not free to start another mill, a great number of citizens lack the necessary resources in terms of money, education, time and skills to compete for political office. These concerns are particularly pertinent to many African countries, as I shall demonstrate subsequently. Briefly put, the *uncertainty* of the democratic game does not apply equally to all political forces, as the various participants in the competition have unequal economic, organisational and ideological resources and those with greater resources are more likely to win conflicts processed in a democratic way. Accordingly, even 'a procedurally perfect democracy may remain an oligarchy: the rule of the rich over the poor' (Przeworski 1991: 34).

It is therefore highly problematic to treat democracy as a political system 'separate and apart' from the socio-economic structures of society, in the manner of mainstream contemporary literature. As Beetham (1992) has argued, the problem with representative democracy is not so much that it restricts political activity to the vote, but rather that the opportunities it creates for more extensive involvement and influence over decision-making are dependent upon a variety of resources, most notably time, money and education, that are distributed unevenly between different sections of the population. In this way, the freedoms of speech and association may expand political activity beyond the vote, but at the same time these practices are also the means whereby the inequalities of civil society are transmitted to the political domain.

At issue here is the question of how we define the concept of the political. The narrow definition of conventional liberal discourse confines the political to the sphere of local and national government and decision-making. By contrast, the democratic theories of those on the left of the political spectrum build on a much broader notion of the political: it includes all relationships based on power. Politics is not confined to the affairs of state, but is seen to condition all aspects of our lives, and to be present in all relationships. In common with feminist political thought, the democratic theories of the left often challenge the conventional distinction between the private and the public, arguing that the state is part and parcel of the mechanisms that maintain and reinforce the inequalities of everyday life. If democratic rights and the liberal values of liberty and equality are to have any meaning they must be concrete, actually realised rights, not merely abstract or cancelled out by asymmetries of power in daily relations between men and women, blacks and whites, among working, middle and upper classes (Held 1987). To enjoy liberty is not only to enjoy equality before the law, but also to have the capacities, the material and cultural resources to be able to pursue desired courses of action. Political equality, then, cannot be attained without a measure of economic equality, and without it democracy is likely to become a vehicle for the maintenance of elite dominance.

Maintaining the Status Quo

The hegemonic position of procedural or minimalist definitions of democracy is undoubtedly related to the liberal mood of the post-Cold War era, when socialist ideals of equality and distributional justice became virtually impossible to disentangle or rescue from the practical experiences of oppression, stagnation and economic collapse in the Eastern bloc and in Africa's one-party states themselves. Democracy in the South is therefore, as discussed in previous chapters, to be introduced in tandem with economic liberalisation. This demand for simultaneous economic and political liberalisation is a key characteristic of contemporary development theory and practice, an insistence that is fuelled by the fact that more or less all fully fledged democracies are also capitalist economies. The notion of a close affinity between capitalism and democracy is almost as old as liberal theory itself, and it is a commonplace of Western political discourse to regard democracy as the characteristic political form of capitalism. As early as 1819 Benjamin Constant argued that the modern liberty of free commerce was politically most consistent with a representative system (see Hawthorn 1993), and more recently similar arguments have been presented by well-known authors like Friedman (1962) and Fukuyama (1992). But while it is obvious to all but the most dogmatic that capitalism and democracy do have a number of features in common, their relationship is far from straightforward.

In terms of compatibility, capitalism and democracy share the same anti-paternalistic thrust: the individual, whether as voter or consumer, is assumed to be the best judge of his or her own interests (Beetham 1994). A market economy can also be seen to act as a check on governmental power, in that it serves to disperse power away from the state. In this way it facilitates the development of a civil society, of independent centres of debate, information and decision-making. But it is equally easy to point to ways in which capitalism and democracy are incompatible and pull in opposite directions. Capitalism, with its emphasis on competition and initiative, inevitably creates elites, inequalities and concentrations of wealth.

Unconstrained market forces produce inequalities that restrict the freedom of those at the bottom of society and prevent them from entering the political competition on an equal footing with those at the top of the hierarchy. Put simply, the social and economic inequalities linked to capitalist competition prevent political equality in two different ways. First, those with superior economic resources have more influence over and more bargaining power *vis-à-vis* the holders of state power. Second, they are more capable of 'setting the agenda' because of their economic strength, higher education, more competent mastery of communication techniques, and so on. It is in this context that 'capitalist democracy' has been termed an oxymoron (Miliband 1992; Hoffman 1991).[4]

The ambiguous relationship between democracy and capitalism presents itself in all its starkness in African countries attempting simultaneous economic and political liberalisation under the instruction of the Bretton Woods institutions. On the one hand, the reduction of the state can be seen to have a positive influence on individual liberty, civil society and hence democracy. On the other, it is difficult to see the reduction in social welfare and the distributive role of the state as anything but negative for the survival chances of democracy. The extent to which the liberalisation of the economy in Europe in the 1980s was accompanied by increased social conflict and the rise of law and order issues to the top of the political agenda is well documented (e.g. Gamble 1988), and similar tensions are also evident in most adjusting African states. The stability of democratic capitalist polities everywhere is to a large extent contingent on social compensation to the poor and less privileged sections of society, and in sub-Saharan Africa such compensation is prevented by sluggish growth and continued economic adjustment. In this way external pressure for simultaneous economic and political reform exposes fragile democracies to the contradictions between the social costs that economic transformation inflicts upon subordinate classes and the electoral power the political system formally assigns them.[5]

The promotion of democracy and economic liberalism as one and the same thing may not only cause political instability and hence jeopardise the survival chances of democracy (as will be argued in more detail in Chapter 6), but may also lead to a form of democracy that has very little relevance to and implications for the majority of citizens. The conceptualisation of democracy in contemporary development discourse is incompatible with a strong commitment to the redistribution of resources, and mainstream literature on democratisation in the South similarly shows a striking disregard for more normative approaches to democracy. Nevertheless, the issues raised by participatory democratic theory are of particular relevance to poor societies characterised by extreme inequalities of wealth. The African poor, despite constituting the majority in many countries, may not be able to influence decision-making in a political system characterised by regular elections and universal adult franchise in any significant way. As discussed above, the uncertainty of the democratic game tends to be reduced by the power of entrenched elites, and what is acceptable to these elites frequently provides the boundaries of democratic politics. Thus, while electoral politics in principle empowers the poor to demand socio-economic reform, the redistribution of resources may in practice be prevented by the power of dominant interests. In this respect, electoral democracy may well turn out to be of limited relevance to the majority of Africans, who are poor, illiterate and alienated from the centres of power.[6] India, frequently heralded as one of the most stable democracies in the South, serves as a useful reminder in this context. After over fifty years of democratic politics, 40 per cent of India's population still persists in absolute poverty, a percentage that has remained unchanged since independence (Sørensen 1993b). While democracy seems to have been crucial in averting the acute situations of severe famine, every year millions of Indians die prematurely due to endemic undernutrition (Dreze and Sen 1989). In India, then, the ability to vote does not appear to have accorded the majority much political influence and their demands even for the means of survival, let alone welfare improvements, have been blocked by the elite, who have retained the power to resist any reform that may threaten their privileged status.[7]

This is not to dismiss electoral democracy as unimportant, far from it. Democracy may offer protection against oppression by a tyrannical state and this is of immeasurable importance in societies where fear, oppression and coercion have been people's everyday companions. Its potential ability to avert large-scale catastrophes such as famine, due to the mechanisms of democratic accountability and a freer flow of information, is also not to be dismissed lightly. My argument, then, is not directed against the desire to promote political liberties in the South, but rather against the easy disregard for socio-economic rights that accompanies this desire in much contemporary literature. The overarching concern in the post-Cold War era seems to have been to globalise democracy, which in turn has led to a certain disregard for the actual quality or substance of the ensuing democracy. Much contemporary literature is action- and process-oriented in that it seeks to provide social agents with the necessary knowledge to understand and transform oppressive political conditions. It is an expressed hope that an awareness of the problems intrinsic to democratic transitions will help political leaders make the right decisions, and at times these studies read like an 'A to Z for would-be-democratisers'. O'Donnell and Schmitter, for instance, describe the four-volume study *Transitions from Authoritarian Rule* as a 'useful instrument – pieces of a map – for those venturing, and tomorrow will be venturing, on the uncertain path toward the construction of democratic forms of political organization' (1986: 5). Huntington similarly concludes various sections of his book with what he calls 'Guidelines for Democratizers', taking on the role of a political consultant or what he prefers to call an 'aspiring democratic Machiavelli' (1991: xv).[8]

The desire to produce politically relevant research is in itself neither wrong nor particularly surprising, but the eagerness of contemporary literature to secure democratic transitions has led to a degree of conservatism, an almost inevitable endorsement of the status quo. One expression of this conservatism is the disregard for welfare rights. The vast majority of impoverished people value political and civil rights not only because they offer protection from an oppressive state, but also because they open up political space for demanding social and economic reforms. Political rights then are frequently a means to an end, a way of achieving a decent standard of living. But such a conceptualisation of democracy is incompatible with contemporary development discourse and the prevailing liberal mood, and hence the need for social and economic reforms is frequently glossed over or dismissed by contemporary literature. Instead it is argued that years of authoritarian misrule have increased people's willingness to accept economic hardship in return for democratic freedoms. Remmer, for instance, talks of the 'democracy of lowered expectations' in contrast to the 'revolution of rising expectations' (1995: 113). Whitehead (1993b) similarly discusses the need for governments to lower and stabilise public expectations in order to make economic liberalisation possible. While it may well be the case that decades of deprivation and authoritarian neglect have led people to expect less from their leaders, this does not mean that welfare reforms are no longer needed and arguments to this effect seem like little more than a sanitised way of allowing for the continued suffering and hunger of the poor majority.

The tendency to endorse the status quo can also be seen in discussions of so-called democratic pacts, which were a striking feature of transition processes particularly in Latin America. These pacts were explicit, but not always public, agreements that defined the rules of governance and that were negotiated among established, often highly oligarchical elites. In short, they aimed to reassure traditional dominant classes that their vital interests would not be jeopardised under democracy, as illustrated for instance by the well-known amnesty from prosecution obtained by the military in Chile. Clearly, such broad elite consensus on the rules of political governance may substantially increase security, stability and thereby the survival chances of democracy. But at the same time, such pacts may serve as a vehicle through which elements of the previous authoritarian regime continue to influence the new democracy. In this manner, pacts may entail the marginalisation of popular demands for improved living standards or allow only fairly minimal and gradual transformations in gross social and economic inequalities.

While such considerations are recognised in the literature (see e.g. O'Donnell and Schmitter 1986; Przeworski 1991), the disadvantages of pacts are generally seen to be far outweighed by their advantages. Because uncertainty of outcome is regarded as an essential feature of democracy, it is stressed that pacts are reversible and that the guarantees negotiated by the elite can be overturned by voters at a later stage. Ruling groups are also expected to become more inclined to accommodate pressures from below as they gain more experience with democracy (see Przeworski 1991; Karl 1990; O'Donnell and Schmitter 1986). Huntington offers yet another reason not to fear pacts: democracy, he asserts, has historically almost always come 'as much from the top down as from the bottom up; it is as likely to be the product of oligarchy as of protest against oligarchy' (1984: 212). These arguments are problematic for several reasons. First, they rely almost entirely on the beneficence of the elite and their willingness to sacrifice their own privileges and bestow democracy on the (undemanding) popular classes. Contrary to Huntington's claim, this is not the way in which democracy has historically developed (see Therborn 1983; Rueschemeyer et al. 1992). Second, these arguments appear to overestimate the effect of political equality in conditions of vast socio-economic disparity, where as discussed previously the entrenched power of elites can frequently prevent socio-economic reform. Third, nothing is said about how long the popular masses should have to wait before pacted democracies allow for their voice to be heard more effectively. Again, then, the eagerness to effect a transition from authoritarian rule appears to lead to a neglect of the quality of the resulting democracy and the extent to which it continues to silence the voices of the majority.

The same conservative outcome arises from O'Donnell and Schmitter's observation that in order to succeed all transitions must observe two fundamental restrictions. It must be recognised, first, that bourgeois property rights are inviolable, and second, that the institutional existence, assets and hierarchy of the armed forces cannot be seriously threatened (1986:

69; see also Di Palma 1990). The risk of an authoritarian reversal is perceived to leave democratic forces and those on the Left of the political spectrum with no option but to settle for a compromise whereby the traditional elite secures the continuation of their privileges. In the words of O'Donnell and Schmitter, the 'only realistic alternative for the Left seems to be to accept the above restrictions and to hope that in the future more attractive opportunities will open up' (1986: 69). The danger is of course that by showing responsibility and willingness to compromise, democratic forces risk bending so far backwards to please the outgoing authoritarian leaders that they themselves become permanently marginalised in the new electoral system. Such concerns seem all too often to be overruled by the desire to devise a swift path to liberal democracy, a desire so strong as to produce some rather undemocratic suggestions. While stating that founding elections must be free and fair, O'Donnell and Schmitter maintain that the 'results cannot be too accurate or representative of actual distribution of voter preference. Put in a nutshell, parties of the Right-Centre and Right must be 'helped' to do well, and parties of the Left-Centre and Left should not win by an overwhelming majority' (ibid.: 62).[9] This result can be achieved 'artificially' by rigging the rules, for example by making sure that conservative rural districts or small, peripheral constituencies are over-represented. Alternatively, an influential political position for the right–centre coalition can be achieved 'naturally' by fragmenting the partisan choices of the Left (ibid.).

It may well be (and probably is) the case that any realistic appraisal of actual democratic transitions would reveal this type of electoral manipulation and gerrymandering, but it is nevertheless quite different to present such practices as necessary restrictions that must be observed in order for a transition to succeed. Such statements may not entail an endorsement of unfair practices, but certainly seem to imply that different standards can be applied to democracies in the South and very little seems to be left even of minimal definitions of democracy. According to such standards, just how rigged and unfair must an election result be before it is declared 'undemocratic'?[10] The rationale behind such representations of both electoral manipulation and the deficiencies of pacted democracies is the conviction that the alternatives – a reversal to authoritarian rule or a revolution – would entail even higher costs. Again, that may well be the case, and these issues are far from black and white. Democratic practices are never perfect, and it would be foolish to expect them to be so in countries that are unaccustomed to political competition. It is of course also true that liberal democracy is much easier to sustain when the fears of the political right and the propertied classes are minimised, and this needs somehow to be factored in when attempting a transition from authoritarianism. From an ethical perspective, however, the position of much contemporary literature is highly problematic. By recommending the postponement of socio-economic reform, and hinting at the necessity to marginalise political parties representing the poor, this body of literature comes dangerously close to an active endorsement of the continued suffering of the masses (see O'Donnell and Schmitter 1986; Whitehead 1993b; Di Palma 1990). Such observations may well be crucial to the survival chances of electoral democracy, but they simultaneously convey a certain arrogance and elitism and are undoubtedly more easily accepted at a university campus than in the squalor of a shantytown. What is to the academic mind a purely theoretical detachment of democracy from the ideals of social and economic rights amounts in practice to an acceptance of continued human suffering and to an implicit endorsement of the existing social order and balance of forces.

Conclusion

The intention of this chapter is *not* to dismiss electoral democracy as unimportant. For all its deficiencies, it remains the case that democracy is the worst form of rule, except all others. Democracy's promise of political and judicial equality, its recognition of the legitimacy of political opposition, and its ability to secure the peaceful transfer of power from one government to another are features that make it superior to any known alternative. But this does not constitute an argument for adopting a purely procedural or minimalist approach to democracy. While we may not expect welfare and equality to emerge from democracy, and certainly not overnight, this does not mean that we have to endorse the status quo or accept that the functioning of political democracy will always be hampered by structural inequalities. It is possible to adopt a stance on democracy that is compatible with the improvement of living conditions for the poorer sections of society. This, however, would necessitate a loosening of the strict link between democracy and economic liberalism, and it would also mean that the success or failure of democratisation should be judged not only on procedural criteria, but also on the extent to which it allows for the realisation of the democratic principles of popular control and citizenship. This entails a less static conceptualisation of democracy – it is neither perfect nor absent, but it is always and everywhere an unfinished process with the possibility of extending democratic control to more and more areas of political, social and economic life (see Beetham 1992). Such a conceptualisation would also go some way towards eliminating the limitations inherent in defining a country as democratic purely on the basis of periodic elections and the existence of certain civil rights. Definitions of this nature bestow democratic legitimacy on a wide range of societies, and blind us to the possibility that their public institutions and private arrangements may still be organised along undemocratic, corporatist, elitist or hierarchical lines. This is also the effect of contemporary literature on governance and democratisation in the South, which shields Western countries from democratic scrutiny and sets them up as models for the South. By the same token, this approach lends legitimacy to African countries where very little has changed despite the acceptance of multi-party competition.

Much contemporary mainstream literature is, however, primarily concerned with effecting transitions to democracy, and very little attention is paid to the quality and substance of the resulting political systems. Both mainstream literature on democratisation in the South and current development discourse advocate an attenuated version of democracy compatible with economic liberalism and continued elite privileges. Democracy is largely reduced to electoral competition and is grafted on to economic liberalisation, which is assigned primacy in discourse and practice. Taken together these two bodies of literature serve to legitimise a particular form of democracy, while delegitimising and marginalising alternatives that are perhaps more in line with the dreams and aspirations of the poor majority.

The discussion has thus returned to the notion of democracy as a contested concept and the assumed demarcation in contemporary scholarship between the public and the private, and of democracy as a political system 'separate and apart' from the socio-economic structures of society. The form of democracy championed by the good governance discourse and liberal scholarship is one that centres on the selection of leaders and excludes socio-economic rights. It may award limited opportunities for the majority of the poor to influence national policy decisions and choices, as political equality can be rendered largely meaningless by the unequal distribution of wealth and resources. Importantly, the uncertainty of the democratic game in sub-Saharan Africa is reduced not only by the power of domestic elites, but also by the dictates of the Bretton Woods institutions and bilateral donors. By linking democracy to continued economic liberalisation and austerity measures, a redistribution of wealth is effectively prevented, at least in the short term, and this ensures that the victors of conflicts processed in a democratic way are those who already possess power and wealth.

Contrary to the image of a worldwide democracy movement with shared goals and aspirations, there is not one, but in fact many democratic discourses. Importantly, not all of these discourses equate democracy with state minimalism and economic liberalism, and in particular the majority of Africa's poor people may not share the same definition of democracy as that embodied in much contemporary literature and the good governance agenda.[11] It is likely that for the majority of poor people, democracy is valued not only because it offers the right to vote, but also because it opens up the political space for demanding social and economic rights. In this way, democracy can be the means towards different ends: for the poor it is a means to a more decent standard of living, while for Africa's donors and creditors it is a way of ensuring political stability and the continued promotion of economic liberalism. Democratisation can accordingly be perceived as a power struggle, a process involving numerous political agents with various social, economic and political ambitions. The end result of this struggle need not be the victory of the 'people', as so often alluded to in the governance literature. Rather, as the next chapter will show, democratisation frequently entails the victory of one section of society over others.

Notes

1. See in particular Berelson et al. (1954); Campbell et al. (1960); Benney et al. (1956) and Berelson (1956). A useful summary of the research on voting behaviour and political attitudes is provided by Lipset (1960).

2. This point is also made by Skinner (1973). Drawing on the philosophy of language, Skinner classifies democracy as an evaluative-descriptive term. Such terms are applicable if and only if a certain state of affairs obtains, and whenever the corresponding term is used it is not only to describe the state of affairs but also to perform the speech-act of commending it (ibid.: 298). Thus, the claim only to describe cannot be sustained, as to term a political system democratic is to perform a speech-act within the range of endorsing, commending or approving of it. According to Skinner, the modern democratic elitism produced 'an apologia for the workings of certain existing political systems' (ibid.: 301) and this amounted to 'an act of political conservatism: it served to commend the recently prevailing values and practices of political systems like that of the United States, and it constitutes a form of argument against those who have sought to question the democratic character of those values and practices'(ibid.: 304).

3. The 'she' here is of course a contemporary formulation, as Rousseau excluded women from the franchise.

4. Lest it should be concluded from this passage that liberal scholars ignore the tensions between capitalism and democracy: Fukuyama writes that 'the inequalities brought about by capitalism *ipso facto* implies unequal recognition' and that 'major social inequalities will remain even in the most perfect of liberal democracies' (1992: 292). But in the familiar discussion of liberty versus equality (or negative versus positive liberty),

present-day liberals choose individual freedom. The individual should be left free and uncoerced, and attempts to reduce inequality are regarded as a threat to individual liberty.

5. It should be noted that today's emerging democracies are in some ways more exposed to such contradictions than the democracies that developed in the nineteenth century. Historically the franchise was extended only gradually, and this restrained the severity of conflicts since only a small and relatively homogeneous elite were eligible to vote. The widespread fear that the universal franchise would undermine the sanctity of private property could thus be averted by a slow absorption of the lower classes and groups like women and blacks. Such a gradual inclusion is not an option available to today's emerging democracies, and this adds to their risks of failure as they try to work out what Dahl refers to as 'a system of mutual security' (Dahl 1979: 39).

6. This interpretation is shared by Owusu, who writes: 'Beyond the ritual exercise of their right to vote, which often has very little meaning, most poor and powerless Africans, especially illiterate women, have very little say in the formulation and implementation of policies which directly affect their welfare. The truth is, of course, that the electoral system benefits immediately only the members of the educated middle classes and the rich, because they are generally the "bosses" of any party apparatus' (1992: 384). Other, equally downbeat appreciations of the relevance of electoral democracy for Africa's poor are presented by Mamdani (1995), Sandbrook (1988), Saine (1995) and Mengisteab (1995).

7. For a damning indictment of India's democracy and how it continues to ride roughshod over the wishes and needs of the poor, see Arundhati Roy's recent polemic *The Cost of Living* (1999).

8. The role of the political advisor is also adopted by Di Palma (1990), as indicated by such chapter headings as 'Tactics: On how to sell one's craft' and 'Time as a tactical resource'.

9. Di Palma (1990) makes a similar point in Chapter 4.

10. In this context it is perhaps pertinent to recall the deliberations of the Commonwealth's international election observers after the Kenyan elections in December 1992. The team stated that although 'some aspects of the election were not fair' the result 'directly reflects, however imperfectly, the expression of the will of the people' (in *The Economist* 1993a: 47; see also Geisler 1993). President arap Moi and the existing political elite won the elections.

11. This is not to suggest that all poor people have the exact same conceptualisation of democracy, but it does assume that all human beings are to some extent motivated by the desire to satisfy their daily needs for food, water, shelter, and so forth. Przeworski notes that the first connotation of democracy among survey respondents in both Latin America and Eastern Europe is 'social and economic equality' (1999: 40), and this lends further support to the contention that for poor people democracy is valued as a route to social and economic justice.

5

Whose Democracy?

Two key assumptions inform and underpin contemporary development discourse: first, that structural adjustment is conducive to democratisation; second, that economic liberalisation and democratisation are mutually related and reinforcing processes. The following two chapters investigate these issues in more empirical detail. It will be argued that while there is indeed a relationship between structural adjustment and democratisation, the connection is quite different from the suppositions embodied in the governance discourse. Adjustment policies contributed to the emergence of democracy movements across the African continent, not primarily because they led to the emergence of civil society and decentralised power away from the state, but rather because people opposed the negative social and economic effects of these programmes. This chapter will show how popular movements for democracy in many African countries were rooted in economic grievances, and as such were protests against structural adjustment as much as they were demands for political pluralism. Chapter 6 will discuss the assumed mutually reinforcing nature of economic liberalism and democratisation, through an analysis of some of the difficulties encountered by countries attempting simultaneous economic and political liberalisation as prescribed by contemporary development orthodoxy. Contrary to the claims of the good governance discourse it will be argued that these two processes are frequently contradictory and the harbingers of complex political conflicts and social tensions that may ultimately threaten the survival of democracy.

The ensuing discussion draws mainly on material from Zambia, Ghana, Kenya and Côte d'Ivoire, but it should be noted at the outset that these two chapters are not intended as a full and detailed account or explanation of democratisation in the countries concerned. Instead the arguments presented serve to illustrate and complement the theoretical issues raised in previous chapters, and as such these are not case studies of democratisation, but intended more as a commentary and reflection on contemporary development discourse and practice. Moreover, there is no claim that the countries discussed are in any way representative of Africa – they merely show that across a huge geographical expanse and in countries with different historical and political backgrounds, structural adjustment and the involvement of donors and creditors influenced the process of democratisation in particular directions. In this way, the form of democracy that emerged across the African continent is shown to be intimately linked to prevailing development discourse.

The Economic Roots of Democratic Demands

In October 1991 Zambia became the first country in anglophone Africa to return to multi-party democracy and the first on the continent to oust a 'founding father' through the ballot-box. The historic occasion did not go unnoticed. Zambia's transition was hailed by international observers and political commentators as a 'model for democratic change' (Joseph 1992) and a 'triumph not only for Zambia, but for the African continent' (Novichi 1992: 17). According to an international team of election observers, Zambians had during the transition period displayed a 'profound sense of civic virtue, tolerance and commitment to democratic values' (Carter Center 1992: 69). On closer inspection, however, the popular demand for political change in Zambia as well as in many other African countries appears to have had as much to do with a widespread and profound dissatisfaction with deteriorating economic conditions as with a deep commitment to democratic values and principles. As this section will demonstrate, with reference to Zambia, Ghana, Côte d'Ivoire and Kenya, the large-scale protests that swept the continent in the early 1990s were as much demands for better standards of living as for democracy.

Zambia's post-independence history is one of almost continual economic decline. After gaining independence in 1964 as one of the world's largest producers of copper, President Kenneth Kaunda's government failed to diversify the economy and the country remained overly dependent on copper exports. Accordingly, when in the 1970s copper prices plummeted at the same time as oil prices soared, Zambia's fragile economy crumbled. Faced with a dramatic decline in its terms of trade, the government resorted to external borrowing. Customs levies and excise duties were also increased in order to raise revenue, but to no avail. In the three years from 1974 to 1977, GDP fell by 29 per cent, while in the six years from 1974 to 1980 most Zambians experienced a serious drop in the quality of life as GDP per head fell by a full 52 per cent (ILO 1981: 3). By 1978 Zambia had no choice but to approach the IMF for financial assistance, and this was the start of what was to become a long and tortuous relationship with the Bretton Woods institutions.

Zambia's various agreements with the IMF and the World Bank contained all the usual elements of the adjustment package, the overall aim being to reduce consumption and government expenditure while increasing savings and investments. The first programmes were relatively modest, involving wage freezes, devaluations of the Kwacha, and increased producer prices to farmers in an effort to stimulate agricultural production. Public spending was also cut, but vast areas of the patrimonial state apparatus – the parastatals, the subsidies, political control over imports, exports and foreign exchange – remained largely untouched. The programme failed to reverse the economic decline. By 1985 GNP per capita had fallen from $600 in 1980 to only $300 and growth rates had turned negative. Import levels also fell dramatically due to the scarcity of foreign exchange, and by 1982 import levels were 50 per cent below those of 1975. As a result infrastructure and equipment were in a state of disrepair, and lack of inputs and spare parts significantly reduced production in the manufacturing sector. Escalating inflation and unemployment undermined living standards, and real wages were down to one-third of their 1975 levels (World Bank 1993; Callaghy 1990; Mwanza 1992). Despite IMF programmes to reduce spending, this was also the period when Zambia's debt accelerated most rapidly, almost tripling from US$1.6 billion in 1978 to US$4.4 billion in 1987. In 1985 the debt service ratio reached 70 per cent of export earnings, making Zambia one of the most indebted countries in the world relative to the size of its economy (World Bank 1993).

To alleviate this situation, the adjustment measures became progressively more wide-ranging, and the 1985 programme in particular was to have significant political consequences. The programme was designed primarily to reduce state expenditure and involvement in the economy, and included measures to liberalise and decontrol bank interest rates, create a foreign exchange auction, and abolish import restrictions and in particular the import-licensing system, which had provided politicians and state officials with ample opportunities for rent seeking. In addition the programme entailed the removal of subsidies on maize meal (the staple food) and fertiliser, as well as the gradual elimination of subsidies on fifty other commodities. The impact of the adjustment package on the Zambian economy and society was nothing short of devastating. As a result of the foreign exchange auction, the Kwacha was depreciated from K2=US$1 to K7 within three weeks (Ncube et al. 1987: Appendix V), causing prices on imported goods such as fuel and locally produced goods with an imported component to soar. The price hikes were further exacerbated by other reform measures such as the removal of food subsidies. Throughout the independence period urban consumers had been assured access to cheap food thanks to fairly generous government subsidies, which by now had become a major drain on the national budget. The gradual removal of subsidies was therefore a key component of the adjustment package, and in December 1986 Kaunda raised the price on maize meal by 120 per cent. In an effort to protect the poor, the subsidy was retained for a lower-grade maize meal, but although well intended, this policy backfired badly. Because millers feared that they would lose money on the lower-grade variety, they switched production to the decontrolled maize. As a result shortages of the cheaper meal soon became acute, and severe riots erupted in urban areas where the poor looted shops filled with imported luxuries. On the Copperbelt fifteen people were killed during a weekend of fierce street fighting. The Lusaka disturbances were less violent, but still left Kaunda badly shaken. In a dramatic U-turn, he reinstated the full subsidy and nationalised the mills, blaming the price increases and riots on the millers.

Opposition to the adjustment programme seems to have pervaded almost all sections of Zambian society, from the party elite to the urban poor. The poor suffered because of the price increases, and thousands of workers were made redundant as a result of the economic decline. In 1986 over four thousand workers were dismissed from the mining industry alone (Cheru 1989), and frequent and prolonged industrial unrest was a key feature of the 1980s. Frederick Chiluba, then chairman of the Zambia Congress of Trade Unions (ZCTU) warned that a 'government gets into power by making promises to look after its people. Once it reneges on these, the people begin to question the legitimacy of it continuing' (in Alagiah 1987: 19). Structural adjustment not only hurt the already poor and the working class, but also undermined the living standards of the middle class and state officials, including elements of the political elite. The neo-liberal attack on the state was simultaneously an attack on the elite's main source of wealth, and in the face of liberalisation and state reduction their jobs and rent-seeking opportunities were under threat. At the same time, the depreciation of the Kwacha diminished the ability of the rich and the middle class to pursue foreign travels and luxury consumption. Only a few wealthy members of the relatively small Zambian business community were in a position to benefit from the liberalisation of the economy, and seen in this light, it is not surprising that the reforms were only reluctantly pursued by the government.

On May Day 1987 the government bowed to domestic pressure, abandoned the IMF programme and adopted its own New Economic Recovery Programme with the theme 'growth from our own resources'. The programme reversed the liberalisation process and reinstated some of the old policies, such as price controls, the import licensing system of allocating foreign exchange, and a fixed exchange rate. It also limited the debt service ratio to 10 per cent of foreign exchange earnings. Politically, the break with the Bretton Woods institutions was a success, at least in the short term. Zambia's population greeted the news with celebrations in the streets, and the move probably saved the United National Independence Party (UNIP) the embarrassment of a significantly reduced voter turn-out or a low 'Yes' vote for the president in the 1988 elections.[1] But economically, the homegrown adjustment programme was a failure. The abandonment of the IMF package antagonised the donor community, and as a result financial support from multilateral as well as many bilateral donors dried up. Starved of foreign exchange and credit, the economy continued to deteriorate and most people experienced a further drop in standards of living. Accordingly, Zambia was soon forced back to the negotiating table. Informal negotiations with the Bretton Woods institutions appear to have begun in the summer of 1987, and shortly after the 1988 elections elements of the previous adjustment programme re-emerged, including new devaluations of the Kwacha and the removal of some price controls. In September 1989, a humiliated Zambian government agreed yet another adjustment package with the IMF and the World Bank, and in 1990 another substantial reform programme started. By now, however, the government had shown itself incapable of managing the economy, its credibility and legitimacy had reached rock-bottom and political unrest was growing.

The growth of political protest in Zambia cannot be understood in isolation from the economic situation, and all through the 1980s structural adjustment programmes were at the centre of political debate. Between 1965 and 1990 the average annual percentage growth of GNP per capita was -2 per cent, and for the average Zambian this meant that standards of living had been falling for more than twenty years and that many post-independence welfare gains had been partially reversed (World Bank 1992b: 216 and 1993: 62). Life expectancy declined during the 1980s, while infant and child mortality increased. Child malnutrition is among the worst on the continent, and as a result the stunting of children below the age of five in rural areas jumped from 38 per cent in 1970/1 to 54 per cent in 1990, nearly twice the rate of, for example, Namibia, Zimbabwe and Lesotho (World Bank 1993: 66). Primary school enrolment started to decline after

1985, and access to basic health services deteriorated significantly. At the same time user charges were introduced at hospitals and clinics, further reducing poor people's access to health care. Poverty grew at an alarming rate, and by November 1991 81 per cent of rural households were found to live below the poverty line and 75 per cent were classified as extremely poor. In urban areas 47 per cent of households were characterised as poor and 36 per cent as extremely poor (World Bank 1993: 64). Although less pervasive, urban poverty posed a greater threat to political stability. Zambia has a large and well-organised working class, and by the early 1980s union membership was more than twice that of UNIP (Gertzel 1984). The economic importance of the mining sector had given the Mine Workers' Union in particular substantial political muscle, and the unions increasingly came to function as a *de facto* opposition in the one-party state, frequently holding the government to ransom through strikes or threats of industrial unrest. During the 1980s labour unrest spread from the mining sector and manual labourers to include public-sector workers, with middle-class professionals such as teachers, doctors, nurses and civil servants sharing the frustrations over an ever declining quality of life. By 1989, the country seemed to have become ungovernable. There had been an attempted coup, food riots, and strikes by mineworkers, teachers and postal workers had brought the economy to a virtual standstill. Hence when the new structural adjustment programme was implemented in June 1990, massive riots broke out in Lusaka and other urban centres. The protests were dominated by workers and the urban poor, but students, the churches and professionals were also prominent. At least thirty civilians and one policeman died in the riots. In many ways, this unrest can be regarded as the start of the democratisation process, as President Kaunda, after over a decade of adjustment, eventually lost control over the political situation and acceded to demands for multi-party elections.

In Ghana as well the demand for democracy can be traced to pervasive opposition to structural adjustment. But unlike Zambia, Ghana at the beginning of the 1990s was regarded as the Bretton Woods institutions' star pupil. This, however, had not always been the case. When Flight Lieutenant Jerry Rawlings seized power in a military coup in December 1981, his intervention was met with widespread popular support and strong international scepticism and reservations. Rawlings' populist policy, emphasising the moral rectitude of the poor majority and launching a campaign against elite corruption, earned the Provisional National Defence Council (PNDC) a wide domestic following, but did not endear it to donors and creditors. The PNDC's was guided by a 'people's socialism' and its declared aim was to create a vibrant community based on egalitarian values (Chazan 1988a). In line with this radical, populist rhetoric, Rawlings (or JJ as he was affectionately know by his supporters) established a network of so-called Defence Committees at community, workplace and army levels in order to link people with the government and thus create a loyal cadre of supporters across all layers of society. But in 1983, after only two years in office, Rawlings changed course dramatically. Having failed to obtain financial assistance from the Soviet Union, the PNDC abandoned its anti-imperialist language and turned to the Bretton Woods institutions for assistance (see Herbst 1993). Since then the country has pursued an unbroken chain of IMF/World Bank designed structural adjustment programmes.

By the time Ghana adopted the Economic Recovery Programme (ERP), the country was in dire straits. Food was scarce, infant mortality had risen, social services had broken down, and roads had fallen into disrepair. In the period from 1975 to 1983, the real minimum wage fell by an astounding 86 per cent, inflation was in excess of 100 per cent and real export earnings had halved since 1970 (Callaghy 1990; Konadu-Agyemang 1998). Drastic measures were needed and the ERP was based on an initial shock treatment, including a sharp devaluation of the Cedi, cuts in government expenditure and removal of price controls.[2] Throughout the 1980s, the government implemented numerous adjustment measures, which resulted in further devaluation, cuts in public services, privatisation of government owned enterprises, and removal of import and export controls. On the macro-economic level, the programme was a success. By 1986, food was again available in shops and markets, production levels had increased and the infrastructure was in the process of being improved as a result of generous foreign assistance. Between 1984 and 1991, Ghana's economy grew by an average of 5 per cent annually, while population growth stood at 2.6 per cent (Haynes 1995: 95). Industries, which in the 1980s were operating at about 25 per cent of installed capacity, currently perform at 35–40 per cent, and inflation has decreased substantially, averaging about 18 per cent since 1994 (Konadu-Agyemang 1998). But the success was not unqualified. This period also saw the depletion of local industries as a result of foreign competition, and foreign investment has been slow to materialise (see Yeebo 1991; Callaghy 1990; Jebuni and Oduro 1998). Nevertheless, during the 1980s Ghana had one of the best growth records on the African continent.

Relative macro-economic success, however, did not translate into better standards of living for the majority of the population. Indeed, the negative social impact of Ghana's economic policies caused one commentator to ask whether this was in fact 'Adjustment with an Inhuman Face – the presumptive mirror image of UNICEF's Adjustment with a Human Face' (Green 1988: 7). The dramatic currency devaluations had severe consequences in a country dependent on imported fuel, machinery, hospital supplies and so on, and many essential items became unaffordable to the average person. The health care system also became seriously under-funded, and the 1983 budget introduced user fees at all levels of health care. As a consequence, poor people's access to health care was dramatically reduced, and by 1986 it was reported that hospital treatment had become so expensive that the sick simply stayed – and died – at home (Yeebo 1991). Kraus (1991) has similarly demonstrated that outpatient attendance at government hospitals in Accra fell by 50 per cent following the introduction of full user fees. As the health system progressively deteriorated, Ghana's doctors and nurses left *en masse* to seek work in neighbouring countries. As a result the number of doctors serving in the public health system declined from 1,700 in 1982 to only 665 in 1992, and the ratio of doctors and nurses to the population was better in 1970 than it is today (Konadu-Agyemang 1998). The education system fared no better. Government expenditure on education has declined, all subsidies have been removed, and parents and guardians now have to meet the costs of textbooks as well as school and university fees. Fewer and fewer children received the benefit of a full education, and by 1987 fewer than 7 per cent of Ghana's children gained admission to secondary school (Yeebo 1991). Overall poverty levels also increased during the adjustment period, especially in urban areas. In the capital, poverty tripled from 7 per cent in 1988 to 21 per cent in 1992. Real wages declined, so that in 1993 the daily expenditure of an average low-income household in Accra was at least eight times more than the minimum wage (Konadu-Agyemang 1998: 135). Urban workers nicknamed their new hardships 'Rawlings' chain', alluding to the chain of bones that becomes visible around the collarbone in conditions of hunger and starvation (Yeebo 1991).

Another result of the adjustment package was a massive retrenchment of workers, especially in the public sector. Donor assistance was made conditional on the reduction of the government's wages and salary bills, which meant getting rid of surplus staff in the parastatals and the public sector. The Cocoa Marketing Board alone dismissed more than 77,000 workers over seven years, and further job losses resulted from the government's privatisation programme. By 1994, the opposition leader in Parliament estimated that about 200,000 public sector jobs had been lost, while only 50,000 new jobs had been created by the government (Konadu-Agyemang 1998: 136). While there can be no doubt that the public sector in Ghana was massively overstaffed and grossly inefficient – a Manpower

Utilisation Committee had found that a full 20 per cent of the workforce in the public sector were 'underemployed' (Yeebo 1991) – the speed with which the retrenchments were carried out and the lack of alternative employment opportunities caused widespread suffering and hardship among the population.

By 1987 the negative social consequences of adjustment in Ghana were plain for all to see, and the PNDC and the Bretton Woods institutions introduced another programme to mitigate the social effects. The Programme of Action to Mitigate the Social Costs of Adjustment (PAMS-CAD) was agreed at a donor conference attended by fourteen donor governments and a dozen multilateral agencies, and was to a significant extent an admission of the havoc and misery that adjustment had caused among Ghana's poor. The programme was to finance projects with a strong poverty focus, and aimed to create new jobs in rural and urban small-scale enterprises. It was also intended to encourage community-based initiatives and to provide basic services such as water and sanitation. But PAMSCAD was too little, too late. The years from 1983 to 1987 had seen a dramatic deterioration of living standards, and a report by the Ghana Living Standards Survey suggests a further worsening of poverty in the three years immediately after the introduction of PAMSCAD (Jebuni and Oduro 1998). By the early 1990s it appeared that the PNDC had lost most of its original support base, including workers, students and many radical civil society movements.

As in Zambia, structural adjustment was the major cause of political conflict in Ghana during the 1980s, in particular between the state and the well-organised labour movement. The trade unions, led by the Ghana Trade Union Congress (TUC), resisted the adjustment measures and responded to them by way of wildcat strikes, absenteeism, 'moonlighting' and running their own 'private businesses' during working hours (Akwetey 1994). Labour unrest and threats of national strikes were frequent and led to several clashes between the state and the unions. With the implementation of the adjustment programme increasingly under threat, the government's response to labour militancy became more repressive, including frequent arrests and detentions without trial. On several occasions the government called in the military to suppress large-scale labour demonstrations, as in 1986 when the TUC headquarters in Accra were surrounded by an estimated one thousand policemen and armoured cars in order to prevent a planned workers' rally. When the government the same year decided to abolish promised wage and benefit increases, the TUC spearheaded a campaign in which workers flew red flags (the traditional symbol of mourning) in a defiant display of opposition to the government's decision, and there were demonstrations in Accra and neighbouring Tema. On another occasion, after a massive devaluation of the Cedi had caused prices to rise yet again, well over twenty thousand workers took to the streets carrying placards with embittered slogans like 'JJ – We are aware of your deceit' and 'The IMF and its baby will be crushed' (see Akwety 1994; Callaghy 1990; Yeebo 1991).

Despite efforts to repress labour unrest and co-opt trade union leaders, the PNDC was unable to prevent the widening of the gulf between workers and the government. The government that had seized power in the name of the people was no longer regarded as an ally of the poor; instead it was referred to as the redeemer who turned killer (Yeebo 1991: 215). Gradually the TUC's protests turned from an economic focus to more explicitly political demands. In 1986 the TUC produced a document that not only criticised the adjustment programme and a development policy that placed too much emphasis on private capitalist enterprise, but also raised specific political concerns. The organisation questioned the PNDC's lack of regard for the role of the masses in social transformation, and called for a demo-cratically elected People's Assembly in order to counter the 'growing alienation of the people' (in Akwety 1994: 91).

The National Union of Ghana Students was another group that voiced its opposition to the economic adjustment measures imposed by the Rawlings' regime. Initially the students' protest focused on the PNDC's education policies, which entailed a removal of subsidies, thereby signi-ficantly increasing the cost of studying. In 1988, following the arrest of a student leader, students launched a boycott of lectures. In response, the PNDC ordered the closure of the University of Ghana. When other universities embarked on solidarity strikes, they too were closed down. The important point to note in this context is the economic focus of the protest, as for example in June–July 1988 when students demanded that their allowances be increased from 51 to 150 Cedis. Churches and profes-sional middle-class associations like the Bar Association also increasingly came to oppose the Rawlings regime. Many middle-class urban groups saw their quality of life eroded by adjustment measures and were resentful of the influx of expatriates in the form of IMF and World Bank consultants (Chazan 1992). The main beneficiaries of the economic measures appear to have been rural dwellers, as the reversal of the rural–urban terms of trade favoured producers in the countryside at the expense of consumers in the cities (Callaghy 1990). Support in the rural areas was not, however, sufficient to sustain the regime in power and as opposition continued to gather force, Rawlings eventually conceded to urban and international demands for democratisation.

Democratic protests in Côte d'Ivoire were also sparked off by economic austerity. Frequently referred to as the 'Ivoirian miracle', this West African state was until the late 1980s one of the most politically stable and economically prosperous countries in the region. Ruled uninterrupted since decolonisation by the strong but relatively benign Félix Houphouet-Boigny and a small closely knit elite, Côte d'Ivoire depended primarily on the export of cocoa, and to a lesser extent of coffee and timber. The country maintained a close relationship with its former colonial master, and its development model encouraged foreign investment in a system that the president referred to as 'state capitalism'. Houphouet-Boigny and a small patrimonial elite possessed an almost total monopoly on wealth and political power, controlling access to public-sector jobs, political careers, participation in the export crop marketing system and joint ventures with foreign companies (Crook 1995). But despite the hegemony of its elite and the country's apparent stability, political protest erupted when the export-based economy ran into difficulties in the late 1980s. External debt had been increasing steadily since the 1970s, and by the end of the 1980s debt-service repayments consumed an average of 35 per cent of export earnings. When at the same time commodity prices fell on the international market, the president was forced to seek assistance from the IMF and the World Bank. Whereas Houphouet-Boigny had been able to use previous adjustment programmes to reinforce his own power, the crisis of 1989 allowed for no such freedom of action. Instead, the country's creditors lay down strict conditions for the granting of new loans, including a halving of the producer price for cocoa and a radical restructuring of the machinery of government. This included reducing the number of ministries and the size of the Cabinet, and also the gradual dismantling of the parastatals that controlled the export crop marketing system. In addition, donors demanded that the budget deficit be rectified by cutting the public salary bill by up to 20 per cent and by improving revenue performance (ibid.).

It was the announcement and implementation of these measures that caused the protests that ultimately led to the reinstitution of pluralism in Côte d'Ivoire. The austerity policies were announced in February 1990 with 'almost unbelievable maladroitness' (Crook 1990: 666), when the government let it be known that parastatal and civil service wages would be cut by up to 40 per cent, and that those in the private sector would have to pay an extra 11 per cent tax. The impact was nothing short of devastating. Strikes broke out almost immediately, with the electricity supply to the capital being disrupted for prolonged periods as public utility workers signalled their opposition to the new policies. The power cuts occurred shortly before the mid-term examinations, and precipitated student riots. Abidjan's university population of 25,000 were squeezed into buildings designed to hold a mere 8,000, and were easily aroused by the news of further economic belt-tightening. The strikes and protests spread to include the transport sector, civil servants, university lecturers and professional associations, all voicing their opposition to salary cuts and the hardships imposed by the adjustment programme. The upheaval reached a dramatic peak in May 1990, with both police and customs service strikes and a brief takeover of the airport by army conscripts. In this precarious situation, Côte d'Ivoire's all-important business community lost faith in Houphouet-Boigny's ability to maintain stability and started transferring money out of the country through the fixed rate franc-zone system, thus threatening the viability of the Ivoirian banks.

Initially then, the protests in Côte d'Ivoire were rooted in economic grievances, but as in other countries the concerns of protesters gradually turned more explicitly political. In particular, attention was turned to the continuation of elite corruption in the midst of economic austerity and deprivation. The most outrageous example of such high-level corruption was the building of Notre Dame de la Paix, a gilded replica of St Peter's in Rome, in the president's home village of Yamoussoukro. Widely reported to cost at least $300 million, the basilica became a symbol of the corrupt practices of the state elite. Unable to repress the protests, and left in the cold by the country's long-term ally, France, Houphouet-Boigny eventually agreed to return to multi-party elections.

The experiences of Zambia, Ghana and Côte d'Ivoire were replicated in one way or another in numerous other African countries in the late 1980s and early 1990s. Prolonged economic recession, combined with continued elite decadence and corruption, stimulated public resentment that erupted in strikes, student protests, marches and large-scale demonstrations. Eventually these economically motivated actions coalesced around the demand for political change and democracy. This is also the conclusion reached by Bratton and van de Walle (1992) in their review of popular protest in sixteen African countries during the turbulent 'spring' of 1990. The two authors show how unrest usually began with corporate demands by interest groups seeking to improve or defend their material conditions within their own sector of the urban economy. Frequently students were the first to take to the streets in outrage against government attempts to impose austerity measures in the educational sector. As we have seen, students were central to demonstrations in Côte d'Ivoire, and similarly Gabon's students went on strike in January 1990 in protests against teaching shortages and poor study facilities (ibid.). Students also played an important role in the demonstrations in Kenya, while in Benin unrest started among civil servants reacting against accumulated arrears in their salaries. Although different depending on the specific circumstances of individual countries, bread-and-butter issues were at the very heart of the wave of protest that swept the African continent in the late 1980s and early 1990s. Gradually economic demands came to be linked to more explicitly political demands for constitutional change, and in sharp contrast to earlier periods of unrest African leaders were unable to contain the demonstrations of the early 1990s. There were no longer sufficient financial resources to buy off and co-opt the protesters through the traditional practices of patrimonialism, and unlike in the past Western allies were unwilling to support and sanction repressive measures or to send troops to suppress the rebellions. Instead the international community sent very clear signals that the time of the dictator was over, and one by one Africa's 'presidents for life' conceded to multi-party elections.

Victory for the Friends of Adjustment

On the surface it seems a paradox that across the African continent popular protests were driven by economic grievances, yet the ensuing elections invariably resulted in victory for the forces supportive of further economic adjustment. If democracy is the rule of the majority, then presumably the African poor by virtue of their large numbers would have the electoral power to block the implementation of further austerity policies. But in most African countries, the return of democracy resulted in renewed political enthusiasm for adjustment, and in many countries, including Ghana, Zambia and Kenya, virtually all political parties of any significance campaigned on an adjustment-friendly platform.[3] There are many reasons for this, most notably perhaps the fact that any realistic appraisal of the economic situation in African countries would conclude that state survival depends on continued international financial assistance. In 1990 official development assistance accounted for 10.7 per cent of GNP in sub-Saharan Africa, with several countries depending on aid for between 15 and 20 per cent of their GNP (World Bank 1999/2000). Without adherence to the dictates of the Bretton Woods institutions, hardly any of this assistance would be forthcoming. Aid dependency, as will be

discussed in greater detail below, is thus an important factor in understanding the outcome of African transitions to democracy.

Another reason why adjustment-friendly parties emerged victorious
from the elections is to be found in the composition of the democratic
movements and the majority's economic, rather than political, motivation.
Africa's food riots, the large-scale demonstrations, and the huge enthusiastic
crowds at opposition rallies were expressions of a profound discontent
with the present, but did not necessarily embody a coherent political agenda
or an ideologically uniform commitment to democracy. Instead mass
protests across the continent were first and foremost demands for better
standards of living, that is for *change* rather than for democracy *per se*.
Events in Zambia illustrate the point well. At the height of the democracy
campaign, a radio announcement that President Kaunda had been overthrown by the military was greeted with joyous street celebrations. The
vivacious response was a measure of the depth of disillusionment among
Zambians, not a demonstration of a commitment to democracy (democrats
don't dance in the streets when the generals announce their political arrival,
no matter how unpopular the previous regime).[4] Instead the incident shows
that change, whether democratic or not, was the overwhelming desire of
many Zambians. *Africa Confidential* made a similar observation during the
wave of protests in 1990: 'Many Africans are now so poor that they are
prepared to back virtually any demand as long as it implies change. More
political parties? Fine, as long as something changes' (27 July 1990). This
may not be a particularly sophisticated political calculation, the report
continued, but it is nevertheless 'natural that the poor should reason thus,
and that opposition politicians, hungry for power should exploit it'.

But even if mass demonstrations were not driven by a deep ideological
commitment to political pluralism, it is clear that the majority expected
things to improve with the coming of democracy. In the course of the
period of unrest, a link was drawn between economic failure, the experience
of material deprivation and the lack of political openness and accountability. Protesters did not so much blame the IMF, the World Bank, or
donor countries for their hardships, but instead placed the burden of
economic mismanagement on their own governments. The expectation
was accordingly that a change of political leadership and system would in
turn bring an end to economic austerity. The issue, then, is not so much
that the poor majority was not in favour of political freedom, but that for
them a meaningful democracy entailed economic as well as political rights.
This was not, however, a conceptualisation of democracy shared by the
leaders of most democracy movements. Democracy, as argued in the

previous chapter, is a contested concept and democratisation can be the means towards different ends for the various actors involved. The composition of the democracy movements and the extent to which they embodied different and conflicting conceptions of democracy are thus important factors in attempting to understand the outcome of recent transitions.

Although the urban poor, the unemployed and workers dominated the initial protests and the mass demonstrations in most countries, the leadership functions of the movements were occupied by the elite and middle-class professionals. In Zambia, for example, the economic protests found their political expression in the Movement for Multiparty Democracy (MMD), which went on to win a landslide victory in the 1991 elections.[5] The MMD can be characterised as an elite movement with a mass following, with former trade union leaders and the business community taking on the leading roles. The party's popular support stemmed largely from widespread discontent with deteriorating economic conditions. As we have seen, by the beginning of the 1990s standards of living in the country were at an all-time low, and poverty had engulfed nearly 70 per cent of all households (World Bank 1993). The spontaneous food riots in June 1990 were the most dramatic expression of the frustration felt by most Zambians, but bread-and-butter issues also dominated the election campaign. It was on such issues that the MMD appealed for support among the population. Blaming the deplorable state of the economy on the ruling party, the MMD promised improvements in housing, social welfare, health and education. Its *Manifesto* pledged to construct 'adequate and suitable housing for all with water and sewerage facilities' and to 'reconstruct and rejuvenate the whole education system' (MMD 1991). More than anything else it was such promises that drew ordinary Zambians to the MMD, the only real alternative to the totally discredited ruling party.

The inclusion of the trade unions in the MMD alliance was also important in securing the party a mass following. Workers and urban dwellers had always looked to the unions for support, and the unions had consistently argued for higher wages, better working conditions and lower prices on basic commodities. Historically the unions in Zambia had adopted a social-democratic but essentially pragmatic policy outlook. While vigorous in its defence of workers' rights, ZCTU had become deeply opposed to the interventionism of UNIP and over time the organisation came to embrace a more capitalist, free market ideology. In addition to the trade unions, the MMD leadership consisted of some of Zambia's most highly educated individuals, successful businessmen, academics, professionals and lawyers.

According to Baylies and Szeftel (1992), at least one-third of the MMD candidates in the election had significant business interests, legal practices or both, and some were involved in large-scale business ventures and had links with international capital. In other words, the MMD included some of the most prominent members of the Zambian bourgeoisie, who had come to regard UNIP's interventionist policies as an obstruction to their interests. Another conspicuous feature of the MMD was the inclusion of a large number of former politicians, schooled within the one-party state. No fewer than twenty MMD candidates were former or sitting UNIP MPs, twelve had been cabinet ministers or members of the Central Committee and a further six had backgrounds as district governors (ibid.). Some of these candidates had fallen out of favour with or been dismissed by President Kaunda, while others had jumped ship in the waning days of the one-party state when the strength of the opposition became apparent. The same happened in other African countries: where politics had been reduced to a competition for resources, multi-party democracy offered disaffected and estranged politicians an opportunity to regain access to the wealth and resources of the state. It is therefore fair to assume that at least some MMD politicians were motivated as much by their economic interests as by their commitment to democracy. The populist rhetoric of its mass rallies aside, then, the democracy espoused by the MMD had little in common with the redistributive aspirations of the majority of its impoverished followers. The party's dedication to democratic values is stressed repeatedly in its *Manifesto*, but this is a liberal or market democracy where the services of the state are scaled down and where the emphasis is on elections and political rights rather than socio-economic rights.

In Kenya as well the economic and political elite took up the leading positions in the democracy movement, and demands for redistribution of resources were marginalised in favour of a focus on 'democracy as procedure'. Although the umbrella organisation Forum for Restoration of Democracy (FORD) included veteran campaigners for political freedom and tolerance, such as Jaranogi Oginga Odinga, the demand for political pluralism came with time to be dominated by the elements of the traditional economic and political elite, who for a long time had been Moi 'loyalists' (Holmquist et al. 1994). The privileged Kikuyu elite in particular, who had been systematically disadvantaged and largely removed from the political arena since President Moi's ascent to office in 1978, saw in growing public discontent an opportunity to recapture positions of power and influence. While the bourgeoisie and the urban middle classes dominated the democracy movement, workers and peasants were notably absent from the coalition. This was primarily due to years of successful co-optation and repression of the trade unions and the political Left in Kenya, and as a result there was no major group arguing for a vision of democracy out of tune with the liberal orthodoxy.

The bourgeoisie and the urban middle classes had much to gain from the reinstitution of political competition, and equally much to lose from economic redistribution. Kenya is a highly unequal society (World Bank 1999/2000), and with the erosion of living standards in recent years a focus on political rights rather than social and economic rights made sense from the point of view of the economically privileged sectors of the population. In order to win an election, however, the democracy movement needed to appeal to the masses and FORD's *Manifesto*, written in 1992, contained a number of ideas designed for this purpose, including promises of universal primary education, preventive health care, expanded low-income housing, affordable transportation and enhanced local-level democracy (Holmquist et al. 1994). Despite such popular pledges, the overall message of the *Manifesto* was in line with continued structural adjustment and called for liberating markets, reducing state control, abandoning price regulations, privatisation and fiscal reforms. In this sense, many democratic movements can be seen to have embodied two different conceptualisations of democracy. While for the poor, the demand for political change was a demand for an end to poverty and suffering, the political elite and the middle classes supported democracy primarily as a route back to power and as a way of protecting their own lifestyles. Unlike the poor, these sections of the population have little to gain but everything to lose from policies that enable a redistribution of resources in favour of the less privileged.

Unlike in Zambia, however, in Kenya the opposition lost the election, despite its clear support among the population. A number of factors explain the victory of unpopular incumbents in countries such as Kenya, Ghana and Côte d'Ivoire. One important reason in all the three countries was the failure of the opposition to maintain unity and to fight the president on a single platform. In Kenya and Ghana the multiplicity of interests contained within the umbrella organisations FORD and the Movement for Freedom and Justice (MFJ) caused them to fragment in advance of the elections. In Kenya, the opposition candidates, taken together, collected more votes than President Moi (well over 60 per cent), who was re-elected with only 36 per cent of the vote. Had the opposition managed to agree on only one candidate, President Moi would probably have been voted out of power.[6] A fragmented opposition divided into multiple small parties that are not only poorly funded, but also often lacking a clear political agenda, is ill-equipped to compete with the formidable economic and political resources at the disposal of incumbents, and the ability of the governing party to exploit the benefits of political office may reduce its opponents to an insignificant force within the new democracy. The power to set the date of the election, choose the electoral system, control the registration of voters, combined with privileged access to state resources such as the media and control over the law enforcement agencies, have influenced the electoral results in most countries. This was, for example, clearly the case with Houphouet-Boigny's overwhelming 1990 victory.[7] Closely connected to, and sometimes difficult to distinguish from, the ability to exploit the benefits of incumbency are electoral fraud, gerrymandering and miscon-duct. Many elections in Africa, including those in Kenya, Ghana and Côte d'Ivoire, were marred by allegations of intimidation, fraud and various 'strong-arm' tactics on the part of the ruling parties. In all these cases, however, international observers maintained that the elections were largely free and fair.

To the extent that they were committed to democracy, however, the various parties that emerged victorious from the African elections can be seen, by and large, to share the same conceptualisation of democracy as donors and creditors. This is no coincidence, nor can it be explained merely by reference to the economic self-interest of the elite to avoid the politics of redistribution. Instead the explanation involves a consideration of the power of discourse and the politics of representation. At the end of the Cold War, the West had captured the language of democracy. Emerging triumphant from the fight against Communism, the 'right' to define democracy resided with the West. In relation to the third world this was expressed in the good governance discourse, which as we have seen linked democracy to values of individualism and economic liberalism. Importantly, development aid at this conjuncture was made conditional not only on political liberalisation, but also on further economic liberalisation. Recipient countries, if they wanted to continue as such, had to play by these rules. Indeed, the signals coming from donors and creditors concerning their definitions of an aid-deserving country as both democratic and committed to economic liberalism were so strong that it is hard to see how any party campaigning on an anti-adjustment basis could have had any chance of attracting sufficient financial assistance after an election. Given that inter-national aid frequently accounts for between 10 and 15 per cent of the GNP in African countries, it is not surprising that election campaigns seem to have been fought with a keen eye to the international constituency, with parties often even adopting the discourse of the good governance agenda. In many cases, external actors seem to have had a clear influence on the election campaign, sending clear and unambiguous signals as to their preferences.

In Zambia one of the most striking differences between the opposition party and the ruling UNIP was precisely their attitude and relationship to donors and creditors, as well as other external actors in the democratisation process. The MMD openly endorsed free market policies and promised future cooperation and accommodation with the Bretton Woods institutions. UNIP, on the other hand, had a long and troubled relationship with the international finance community, and this was to worsen dramatically during the transition process. Soon after agreeing to multi-party elections, the government abandoned further efforts at economic adjustment. It will be recalled that the food riots in June 1990 were sparked by a doubling of the price of maize meal, but the IMF and the World Bank were soon demanding further reductions in food subsidies. President Kaunda refused to comply with these conditions, arguing that yet another price increase would almost certainly lose UNIP the election. The official price on maize meal was therefore kept constant from the announcement of the election in August 1990 until polling day over a year later. Because of high inflation, this meant that customers actually experienced a fall in the price of maize meal relative to other commodities (Bratton 1994b).

As a result of the government's lack of financial restraint, Zambia again ran into arrears with the IMF and the World Bank, and when in September the country defaulted on its loan payments the two institutions suspended all further aid. Several bilateral donors followed suit, and the UNIP government was thus cut off from vital economic resources only weeks before election day.[8] Kaunda accused the Bretton Woods institutions of seeking to influence the election by causing economic hardship that the general public would blame on the sitting government. In sharp contrast to the MMD, which was busy wooing international support, UNIP in a full-page advertisement in the *Times of Zambia* launched an angry attack on international actors alleging 'a big imperialist plot' against the party.[9] This plot, the party argued, included not only donors and creditors, but also international and domestic election observers.

The Zambian democratisation process was the first in anglophone Africa and attracted worldwide attention. More than one hundred international observers in nine delegations were present during the elections, but Kaunda had only very reluctantly and after considerable pressure from the opposition agreed to accept the presence of external monitoring teams. UNIP's resentment of the teams resurfaced a week before the election, when the party in the same advertisement claimed that the various domestic and international observer groups were not actual election monitors, but that their assignment was 'to facilitate the removal of the UNIP Government and replace it with a puppet one like has happened in many parts of the world'. According to the advertisement, the various domestic civic groups that participated in the election monitoring were all MMD supporters and part of the 'big imperialist plot'. The advertisement further argued that it was well known that the UNIP government had not been acceptable to the Americans, and that like 'the Sandinistas in Nicaragua, the UNIP leadership had been targeted for removal'. Zambians were warned that there were 'powerful foreign forces behind certain parties which were being portrayed as saviours of this country' and that the central issue of the election was the 'preservation of national sovereignty and independence'. Even more ominous, if the imperialist strategy failed and UNIP won the election, the international observer groups would declare that the elections were not free and fair and the MMD would receive international backing for a violent resurgence against the government. The result would be 'bloodshed', and while foreign countries would evacuate their nationals 'Zambians will be left to butcher each other'.

The claims of an imperialist plot and the parallel to Nicaragua were of course far-fetched, and President Kaunda later dissociated himself from the allegations. But the advertisement is interesting because it reveals the extent of UNIP's feeling of abandonment by the international community. Although the observer teams cannot be accused of partisanship,[10] there is little doubt that the MMD was the 'darling' of the international community. Unlike the old-fashioned and interventionist UNIP, MMD represented the new world order. It had embraced democracy and economic liberalism and encapsulated the mood of change of the early 1990s. Its economic policy as set out in the *Manifesto* was a straight endorsement of the restructuring package of the Bretton Woods institutions; the party had even adopted the World Bank's favourite catch-phrase 'an enabling environment' (MMD 1991). The MMD stated its commitment to a 'balanced structural adjustment programme' and declared that the 'current economic role of government as a central participant in business undertakings shall cease'. Instead the party promised to implement 'suitable monetary and fiscal policies; create a positive system of administering investment schemes; abolish monopolies and provide a free market system; ensure free collective bargaining; institute market determined allocation policies; stimulate positive growth-oriented international trade policies; mobilise domestic savings and develop a capital market; and rationalise government regulatory measures' (ibid.).

This rather hackneyed list of economic policy measures could have been taken from almost any World Bank document, and after years of Kaunda's resistance and ambivalence to liberalisation the MMD *Manifesto* cannot have failed to please Zambia's creditors. It provided hope of trouble-free adjustment, with full cooperation on policy implementation as well as repayment of debts. The MMD's strong commitment to both economic liberalism and democracy also made Zambia look like one of the few countries in sub-Saharan Africa where the neo-liberal dream could come to fruition, a potential success story of structural adjustment policies. Against Chiluba and the MMD, Kaunda and UNIP looked distinctively like representatives of the old order, the likes of Ceauşescu and Eastern European communist parties. There was also little belief among international observers in Kaunda's commitment to democracy or the party's ability and willingness to change its autocratic ways after twenty-seven years in power.

The impression of foreign support for the MMD was reinforced by both Chiluba's and his deputy Arthur Wina's visits overseas during the election campaign. In April 1991 Chiluba travelled to the USA, where he had discussions at the State Department and with the Foreign Affairs Committee of the Senate. He also met officials from the National Endowment for Democracy (NED), which later sponsored the biggest election monitoring team to Zambia. In Britain, Chiluba was the guest of Minister for Overseas Aid Lynda Chalker, while Wina was received by the IMF and the World Bank. The fact that both Chiluba and Wina left the country in the heat of the campaign signals the importance of international support for the MMD, and perhaps also the eagerness of external actors like the Bretton Woods institutions to influence the policy of what looked increasingly likely to become Zambia's next ruling party. The symbolic value of the MMD's foreign endorsement should not be underestimated. The reception of the opposition leaders by state officials and international institutions helped legitimise the MMD and gave it an aura of respectability and importance at home. It is of course impossible to determine whether or not such external recognition influenced the election result, but it definitely reinforced the impression of international support for political change. It also added to UNIP's feeling of isolation and abandonment: at the same time as the government was castigated for its economic mismanagement and cut off from financial assistance, the main opposition party walked the corridors of power around the world. A clearer indication of political support and preference is hard to imagine.

In Ghana the situation was quite different. While Kaunda had been among the most reluctant clients of the Bretton Woods institutions, President Rawlings had been the most enthusiastic and loyal follower of their advice. The international community was therefore keen not to interrupt or jeopardise Ghana's path to economic liberalism, and the country accordingly presented donors and creditors with a certain dilemma. On the one hand, Western donors, and especially the USA, pressed for the reinstitution of political pluralism, while on the other they were reluctant to see a less reform-friendly government voted into power. This fear among donors was expressed by the *Financial Times*, which reported that Western donors felt that at the very least a defeat of Rawlings would cause a period of economic policy instability (in Haynes 1995). It is hard to imagine that Ghana's determined and prolonged pursuit of economic adjustment could have been maintained under democratic rule, and with electoral competition back on the agenda future austerity measures could be threatened by democracy's temptation towards populist policies. An added concern was that, despite the relative success of Ghana's adjustment programme in macro-economic terms, foreign investment had been fairly slow in materialising. Political, social and economic upheaval caused by a transfer of power was considered potentially detrimental to further foreign investment, and the opposition's call for an investigation of human rights abuses under Rawlings' tenure raised the spectre of political turmoil and instability, and was therefore not an attractive proposition from the point of view of the international finance institutions.

Rawlings could thus preside over the transition to multi-party democracy assured that he had the support of Ghana's donors and creditors. Again, the symbolic value of this should not be overlooked. While Kaunda was castigated by the international donor community for his failure to take control of the economy, Rawlings' domestic legitimacy was enhanced by his continued international backing. Conversely, continued external support for Rawlings did little to further the chances of the already fragmented opposition, which despite their commitment to adjustment must have appeared to donors and creditors as a less secure option. Continuity, rather than change (as in Zambia) accordingly became the mantra of Rawlings' electoral campaign. This emphasis on continuity was helped by Rawlings' ability to prevent an exodus of senior and middle-ranking government figures to rival parties (perhaps partly because of his external support), and he could thus rightfully claim superior experience and a few macro-economic successes in managing the country compared to the opposition (Haynes 1995). In this way, Rawlings' slogan 'Unity, Stability and

Development' is likely to have appealed to domestic as well as external constituencies.

In Côte d'Ivoire the external influences were different yet again. The country had maintained closed links with its former colonial master, but at the end of the Cold War France changed its attitude towards its African allies. Increasingly, these states were regarded as an economic liability, and there was growing frustration with the inefficient structures of the one-party states. Accordingly, France joined the other Western states in calling for political liberalisation on the African continent, as signalled at the Franco-African summit meeting of La Baule in June 1990 when President Mitterrand stressed that 'French aid [to Africa] will be lukewarm toward authoritarian regimes and more enthusiastic for those initiating a demo-cratic transition' (in Martin 1995: 180). This change of attitude was also evident in May 1990, when France declined to send troops to assist the beleaguered President Houphouet-Boigny in his quest to quell widespread protests and put down the army mutiny at the airport. Although Houphouet-Boigny was by now no favourite of the international donor community, he and his ruling party represented a known entity, whose conservative policies had ensured an economic setting friendly to foreign business and investment. What is more, all the opposition parties in Côte d'Ivoire campaigned on a vaguely leftist, social-democratic platform that was not particularly appealing to donors and creditors. Houphouet-Boigny, by contrast, seemed to play more to the tune of the international donor community and appeared to court its support. The most obvious move designed to reassure donors and creditors was his appointment in April 1990 of Allasane Ouattara, a former director of the IMF's Africa Depart-ment, as chair of an inter-ministerial committee charged with rescuing the failing economy. Ouattara's proposed programme included measures to cut public-sector jobs, reduce the cost of the civil service, and privatise state-owned companies, and the programme went some way towards reassuring donors and creditors that the 'right' economic route would be followed (Crook 1995). As such the appointment is yet another example of how election campaigns were conducted with one eye to the donor com-munity.

In Kenya direct and concerted pressure by donors and creditors was needed before President Moi, who referred to democracy campaigners as 'unpatriotic people with borrowed brains', conceded to multi-party elec-tions (Riley 1992: 545). In November 1991 donors suspended aid worth about $1 billion to Moi's regime, and in early December the president accepted the reintroduction of democratic elections (Robinson 1993). But as the above discussion shows, direct pressure and threats to withhold aid are far from the only ways in which donors and creditors have influenced the transition processes in Africa. In the post-Cold War era, the power to define democracy resided with donors, and in this respect, development discourse had a major impact. Through the good governance discourse, democracy came to be associated primarily with elections and economic liberalism, while conceptualisations that included a more just and equitable distribution of wealth were marginalised. Politicians vying for power in African countries soon adopted this definition of democracy. Although many leaders and members of the elite were at the outset opposed to political competition, they had in the end less to lose from this form of democracy than from responding to the demands of their own impoverished domestic constituencies. The form of democracy demanded by donors and creditors thus offered incumbents and elites the possibility of holding on to or capturing power, without giving in to any of the demands for social welfare and redistribution at home. What is more, a democratically elected government could expect renewed international legitimacy, and the prospect of a more generous treatment by donors. In this way, the political and economic elite would again be able to enjoy the lifestyles they were accustomed to. In this sense, a *de facto* alliance occurred between the elites in many African countries and the continent's donors and creditors, in that they shared a broadly similar conceptualisation of democracy that centred on political rights and a continued economic liberalism.

Conclusion

The return of democracy to Africa was undoubtedly a proud and important moment in the continent's modern history. It offered hope of a better future and an end to repression for millions, as well as the prospect of the continent's re-admittance into the international arena as an equal political and economic actor, not merely a humanitarian concern. But democracy in Africa has largely failed to deliver on its promise of greater welfare and justice for all, and the above discussion points to some important factors in explaining why this is so. The democracy movements in Africa were not undifferentiated movements, a unified civil society united against the oppressive state, nor was there only one vision of democracy among the parties and their followers. Instead they contained very different conceptualisations of democracy, and the end result needs to be investigated with this in mind. In short, we need to ask: whose victory? whose movement? and what kind of democracy? The answer is that in many

African countries democratisation was a victory for the liberal conceptual-isation of democracy and those who had most to gain from continued economic liberalisation – the elite and the middle classes, as well as donors and creditors. Their vision of democracy prevailed, and assured the con-tinuation of elite lifestyles while shielding them from domestic demands for redistribution and increased provision of social welfare. For donors and creditors in turn, democracy provided development aid with a post-Cold War rationale and secured the continued repayment of debts, as well as the continuation and deepening of global economic liberalism. For the impoverished majority in many African countries, democratisation meant at best more of the same, at worst renewed enthusiasm for economic liberalisation, and by implication further suffering and hardship. Competing visions of democracy and alternative social policies were defeated and appear to have been marginalised within political debates. The result is a form of democracy characterised by an inability to respond to popular demands for socio-economic reforms and an inability to incorporate popular sectors into the political process in any meaningful way. As the next chapter will show, this is a key factor in explaining the social unrest and instability that has plagued so many of the new democracies in sub-Saharan Africa.

Notes

1. The voter turn-out was 55 per cent, down 10 per cent from 1983, and the presid-ential 'Yes' vote was 95.5 per cent, 2.5 per cent higher than in the previous election (Callaghy 1990).

2. The Cedi was devalued from 2.75 to 30 to the US dollar in 1983, followed by a further devaluation to Cedi 50 to the dollar in 1984 and 60 at the end of 1985. The next year the Cedi was devalued to 90 to the dollar, before the introduction of an auctioning system that by the end of 1986 had reduced the value of the local currency to 150 per dollar (Green 1988: 9).

3. A partial exception to this was the position of many ruling parties, as incumbents such as Kaunda and Moi sought to blame external actors, rather than their own in-competence and mismanagement, for the economic malaise of their countries. At the same time they needed external support, and the result was an ambivalent attitude to continued adjustment.

4. The Zambian coup was put down within hours, and the premature celebrations were brutally repressed by the security forces. According to some reports, as many as fifty people were killed (Baylies and Szeftel 1992).

5. The MMD's Frederick Chiluba won 76 per cent of the votes in the presidential election, against Kaunda's 24 per cent. In the parliamentary election, the MMD won 75 per cent, or 125 of the 150 seats (Carter Center 1992).

6. In the parliamentary election KANU won 100 of the 188 seats. In Ghana,

President Rawlings was elected with nearly 60 per cent of the vote, while his party won virtually all seats in the parliamentary election, which was boycotted by the opposition because of alleged fraud in the presidential contest.

7. Houphouet-Boigny won 82 per cent of the votes in the presidential election, while the PDCI secured 72 per cent, or 163 of the 175 seats in the parliamentary contest.

8. As an illustration of the pervasiveness of the 'Washington consensus', it can be mentioned that even the Scandinavian countries, commonly perceived to have a more humanitarian approach to development, turned their back on Kaunda and followed the Bretton Woods institutions in withholding financial assistance. In his effort to avoid further cuts in the maize subsidy, President Kaunda wrote personally to the Swedish and Norwegian prime ministers appealing for support for his decision to postpone further price hikes until after the elections. Kaunda argued that the removal of the subsidy would jeopardise stability and the transition process, but neither government defended Kaunda's right to postpone the restructuring programme (*Klassekampen*, 15 November 1991).

9. The advertisement appeared on 25 and 26 October 1991 and is reprinted in Carter Center 1992: 138–42.

10. It should, however, be noted that fears and reservations about intervening too aggressively in Zambia's internal political affairs were also expressed by some Lusakan diplomats and even some members of the observer groups (see Björnlund et al. 1992: 427). These reservations seem to have concerned in particular the extensive involvement of the Z-Vote team and President Carter.

6

Economic Liberalisation and Democratic Erosion

Celebrations of 'Africa's second independence' were short-lived. Only a few years after the much-praised return of political pluralism, the democratic credentials of numerous countries lay in ruins. The euphoria and optimism of the transition period have been replaced by disillusionment and discontent as democracy's promise of prosperity has failed to materialise, and in the face of domestic unrest and instability, the fragility of Africa's democracies has become all too apparent. In many countries, post-transition elections have been a far cry from 'free and fair', opposition parties have been subjected to increasing intimidation and harassment, the media have been silenced, and political and civil rights have gradually been eroded. On occasions the military has tried, and in some cases even succeeded, in putting an end to democratic politics altogether.

This chapter seeks to explain the rapid deterioration of democratic standards in many African countries by focusing on the relationship between external demands for continued economic adjustment and domestic political instability and unrest. The central argument is that economic adjustment has impeded rather than facilitated the institutionalisation of democratic principles and procedures. While liberalisation may have earned democratically elected governments international acclaim and financial support, at least in the initial stages of their terms in office, it simultaneously undermined their domestic support base. Adjustment imposed new hardships on a public that eagerly looked to democratic leaders to bring a reprieve from hunger and deprivation, and the resulting disappointment stimulated pervasive social unrest, widespread industrial strikes and fierce political opposition. Faced with such hostile conditions, democratic procedures and principles have been diluted or abandoned as governments have reverted to the tried and tested methods of the one-party state in order to contain civil disorder and silence critics. In most cases, the formal trappings of multi-party democracy (elections, constitutions, parliaments etc.) have survived, while the content of civil and political rights has been eroded.

This chapter contends that the importance of international financial assistance for state survival in Africa is a crucial factor in this situation: a total collapse of democratic structures and procedures would almost certainly bring international isolation and a suspension or termination of aid flows. The effect of external pressures for simultaneous economic and political liberalisation in Africa is thus slightly paradoxical in that it has contributed both to the maintenance of (an imperfect) political pluralism and to the persistence of social and political unrest, which continues to pose a permanent threat to the survival of pluralism. Moreover, the promotion of democracy and economic liberalism as two sides of the same coin has prevented the process of democratisation from progressing beyond the electoral stage, as it effectively rules out social reforms towards a more equitable distribution of wealth. In this way, the good governance discourse presides over the creation of what can be termed *exclusionary democracies*, that is, democracies that cannot incorporate the majority of the population and their demands in any meaningful way.

No More 'Cruel Choices'

The perception of democracy and economic growth as mutually re-inforcing is today so commonplace that it is worth recalling that until fairly recently the conventional wisdom of development discourse presented political pluralism and growth in starkly dichotomous terms, as competing values that could not be achieved simultaneously. As noted earlier, there was, according to this view, a 'cruel choice' to be made between development and participation, or to put it more bluntly between consumption today and growth tomorrow. Launching a society into economic growth, such accounts asserted, required substantial sacrifices on behalf of the population, as it necessitated huge investments in factories, technology, infrastructure, education, and so on. Democratic governments were regarded as unable or unlikely to survive the risks this involved in terms of loss of votes and support: 'Governments must resort to strong measures and they must enforce them with an iron hand in order to marshal the surpluses needed for investment. If such measures were put to a popular vote, they would surely be defeated' (Rao 1984/85: 75). Fear of losing votes would accordingly prevent democratic governments from embarking on long-term investment schemes, as the electorate was seen as unwilling to accept the required reduction in public services and restraints on wages and consumption (Hewlett 1979). In a system where approval is sought from the electorate 'the politician cannot afford ... to follow any policies which will not produce tangible benefits for the electorate by the time the next election comes around' (Nehru 1979: 57). Democratic regimes, in other words, were regarded as inherently prone to populist, expansionist policies and preoccupied with issues of distribution rather than accumulation. In order to be re-elected, they would have to appease powerful interest groups like trade unions, urban consumers and domestic industrialists, and their hands would therefore be tied in terms of economic policies. Authoritarian regimes, on the other hand, were seen to be more insulated from vested interests and independent of popular support and electoral cycles. In particular, authoritarian rulers could ignore organised labour and maintain low wages in the interests of accumulation, and their greater capacity for coercion was seen to strengthen further their ability to enforce unpopular policies in order to maximise long-term economic gain.[1]

The 'cruel choice' doctrine embodied a perception of an optimal development path where reforms were introduced gradually and in a particular order (Huntington 1968). First, a country had to deal with the challenge of nation-building and a vast array of other development problems, and this was seen to justify the suspension or postponement of civil and political rights (see Huntington and Nelson 1976; Hewlett 1979; Kohli 1986). Political participation was thought to jeopardise stability by overburdening the fragile institutions of developing countries, and democracy would come only when a country was 'ready' for it, and when it would no longer hamper economic development. As Almond and Powell put it, 'state building and economy building are logically prior to political participation and material distribution, since power sharing and welfare sharing are dependent on there being power and welfare to share' (1966: 363).

By the early 1990s the perception of a trade-off between democracy and growth had become an outdated and unfashionable view, largely because of the obvious failure of authoritarian rule in both the former Communist bloc and vast areas of the South. An influential body of opinion now holds that pro-authoritarian studies are rooted in a particular time period, and that recent research demonstrates that democracies are much more robust and capable economic managers than previously assumed (Maravall 1995; Geddes 1995; Remmer 1990). The perception of a positive synergy between democracy and capitalism is a key characteristic of contemporary scholarship, and it is frequently argued that economic growth depends on open competition and predictability that can only be found in societies organised according to democratic principles (Goodell and

Powelson 1982). Democracy is regarded as the political equivalent of the free market, in the sense that competition between individuals in the political arena parallels the interaction of free market forces. Unlike authoritarian centralisation, which is said to extinguish entrepreneurial initiatives and stifle informal-sector activities, democratic rights are seen to safeguard property and contractual rights, which in turn create the security and incentives necessary for economic growth. Basically, citizens who are not subjected to arbitrary extractions and confiscations of property are more likely to invest in productive enterprises. A democratic system is also regarded as more favourable to growth because of its superiority when it comes to generating information and public debate (Maravall 1995; Healey and Robinson 1992; van de Walle 1995). Free and vigorous media and a vocal political opposition will encourage dialogue with those affected by economic policies and stimulate a more open debate about policy alternatives. Active and informed legislative assemblies are also expected to be a positive force for economic growth, primarily because they can scrutinise public expenditure and discourage corruption and rent seeking (Healey and Robinson 1992).

According to much contemporary scholarship, then, democracy and economic growth are perfectly compatible, and the claim that democratic regimes easily become hostage to interest groups politics and forced to adopt costly distributive policies is rejected. On the contrary, it is argued that elections act as the ultimate check on governments by punishing bad policies and encouraging prudent and beneficial economic management. In line with this argument, *The Economist* commented that 'far from inhibiting growth, democracy promotes it' because governments are forced to worry about their citizens' prospects (1994b: 17). Democracies are also regarded as more flexible than authoritarian regimes. While authoritarian regimes often depend on a narrow elite for their support and are locked into inappropriate patterns of expenditure and investment, democracies represent wider public interests and are therefore able to consider a broader range of policies. They are seen to adapt to changing conditions with greater ease, because policies that hurt some will benefit others and accordingly prevent the alienation of the entire electorate.

It is nevertheless recognised that winning popular support for economic reforms will be difficult, and some scholars accordingly advocate a 'sequencing' of reforms that has some similarities with the 'cruel choice' position. In the manner of the East Asian 'Tiger' models it has for example been suggested that authoritarian regimes that launch economic adjustment prior to political liberalisation stand the greatest chance of consolidating both sets of reforms in the longer term (e.g. Haggard and Kaufman 1992). A successful economic reform programme may create the conditions for democratisation, and with this in mind Robinson has argued that 'advocates of rapid political liberalization should consider the implications of forcing the pace of political reform at a time when pragmatic authoritarian regimes are in the process of consolidating economic reforms, and should concentrate their efforts on the latter until such time as a democratic transition can be successfully negotiated and sustained' (1996: 116).

For most African countries, however, 'sequencing' is not on the menu of policy options. Donors and creditors demand simultaneous adjustment, although there is a token recognition that this may at times be a difficult path to follow. The World Bank, for example, notes that 'the process of political transition may initially slow down the process of economic reform, as the new system settles down, and there is the danger that competing interests may lead to a stalemate in some areas' (1994a).[2] But this is regarded as only a temporary and passing situation, before the mutually reinforcing effects of the two transition processes come into play. According to the Bank, 'greater political openness will lead to the opening of national dialogue and debate over reforms. This serves both to educate the public and contribute to a national sense of ownership of the reform process' (ibid.). What is more, 'coalitions empowered by political liberalization may contribute ... to the emergence of good governance – that is the practice by political leadership of accountability, transparency, openness, predictability, and the rule of law' (ibid.). In practice, then, donors and creditors leave African countries with few options but simultaneous adjustment. Authoritarianism is not only seen as a violation of human rights, and therefore as intolerable, but it has also proved disastrous for development and growth. And although the ideological fervour with which neo-liberalism was promoted in the 1980s has faded somewhat, economic liberalism is still regarded by the donor community as the only route to future prosperity. Free markets, current development orthodoxy holds, will maximise growth and welfare more than any other known economic strategy, and ultimately wealth will trickle down and all sections of the population will benefit. In the meantime, it is often expected that poor people will be willing to sacrifice rapid economic improvements in return for political and civil rights, and that democratic governments will enjoy a 'honeymoon' period with high levels of legitimacy when economic reforms can be implemented with a minimum of resistance (see e.g. Maravall 1995; Remmer 1995; Whitehead 1993b). This does not seem to have been the case in sub-Saharan Africa. By contrast, as this chapter will show, the post-transition period in many countries has been plagued by persistent unrest and protest against economic austerity.

It appears that in the same way as the 'cruel choice' doctrine posed the contradiction between democracy and development far too sharply and dogmatically, the contemporary insistence on compatibility is similarly overdrawn and exaggerated. Authoritarianism is clearly not a desirable alternative to democracy, but a rigid link between democracy and economic liberalism creates tensions and conflicts that may ultimately threaten the survival and viability of both. Indeed, African countries are asked to pursue economic policies with such severe social consequences that it is questionable whether even established democracies in the West would be able to survive them without considerable turmoil and loss of office for the ruling party. This is not to say that democracy cannot work in poor countries or that economic hardship is the only threat to the consolidation of new democracies. While the emergence of democracy is not conditional on a particular level of economic prosperity, once established the survival of pluralism is undoubtedly made easier if it succeeds in generating and distributing wealth and welfare (see Przeworski and Limongi 1997). This is particularly the case in countries with a long history of authoritarian and patrimonial state practices, where most politicians are trained within the one-party tradition and may be easily tempted to resort to past habits to deal with the conflicts of democratic politics. Unfortunately, it is precisely the generation and distribution of wealth and welfare that the pursuit of economic adjustment makes so elusive in contemporary Africa.

Two Irreconcilable Constituencies

It can be argued that upon taking office, most elected African governments had two irreconcilable constituencies: the domestic majority and external donors and creditors. While crucially dependent on both, for their re-election and financial survival respectively, governments found that to satisfy the two at the same time was virtually impossible. External sponsors demanded continued economic liberalisation, which was sure to create domestic dissatisfaction and invite unpopularity at the polls. Responding to popular demands for social improvements, on the other hand, was likely to result in a loss of vital financial assistance. In principle this could lead to difficult balancing acts, complicated political choices and delicate compromises. In practice this has only partially been the case. While elected governments have frequently tried to avoid, postpone, manipulate and dilute economic adjustment programmes, their dependence on continued financial assistance has generally led them to fall into line with the demands of their external constituency. The African political elite, as argued in the previous chapter, also holds a vision of democracy that has much in common with the form of pluralism promoted by the North. Taken together, aid dependency and elite visions of democracy go a long way towards explaining why, since the return of democracy, the wishes of external supporters appear to have taken clear precedence over the needs and demands of domestic constituencies.

Zambia serves as a good illustration here. As we have seen, the MMD's entire election campaign was conducted with an eye to the international arena, as the party was painfully aware that it would inherit a near bankrupt economy in desperate need of aid. When the MMD took office in November 1991, inflation was running at nearly 400 per cent, the budget deficit was 7.5 per cent of GDP, and the US$7.5 billion foreign debt equalled more than 160 per cent of GNP and repayments consumed some 60 per cent of meagre export earnings, making Zambia one of the most debt-stressed economies in the world.[3] The country had been cut off from vital financial assistance from the Bretton Woods institutions and several bilateral donors as a result of President Kaunda's refusal to comply with IMF demands in the run-up to the election, and without the reinstatement of generous foreign aid, Zambia was doomed to further decline. President Chiluba made no secret of this in his opening speech to Parliament, declaring that 'only our donors and patient creditors stand between us and calamity' (Chiluba 1993: 9). By necessity, therefore, the MMD's main priority was to restore cordial relations with donors and creditors.

The key to improved donor relations was economic policy, and the government's first major undertaking was to launch one of Africa's most ambitious programmes to convert the state-run economy into a free market. Incorporating all the usual elements of the structural adjustment package, the MMD aimed for a rapid transformation of the Zambian economy.[4] In an effort to attract foreign investors, a 'one-step investment centre' was set up to cut red tape and the 1993 budget allowed for 100 per cent repatriation of after-tax profits, with no restrictions and no bureaucratic screening (Kasonde 1993: 127). Yet the most radical element of the liberalisation programme was the drive to privatise Zambia's many parastatals, which accounted for 80 per cent of the country's economic activity. With the help of donor finance, the Zambia Privatisation Agency (ZPA) was set up in June 1992 and Zambia became, in effect, a country for sale at discount prices. 'We will privatize everything', President Chiluba said, 'from a toothbrush to a car assembly plant' (in Ham 1992: 41). Numerous high-profile manufacturing concerns, such as Zambia Breweries, Zambia Sugar Company, the National Tobacco Corporation, and several milling companies were sold, and public utilities – electricity, water and the railways – similarly went under the hammer. In the space of a few years, Zambia's economy was fundamentally changed and by the end of 1998, 90 per cent of the 275 state-owned companies were expected to have been privatised, many of them sold to multinational investors like Tate & Lyle, Lonrho and Unilever.[5]

Initially donors and creditors were impressed with the MMD's sincere commitment to economic restructuring. President Chiluba urged the international community to support the liberalisation effort, reminding donors that '*nothing less than the survival of Zambia as a democratic nation is at stake*' (Chiluba 1993: 15, italics in original). Soon aid was pouring in. Total development assistance nearly doubled from US$482 million in 1990 to $880 million in 1991, and reached a record $1 billion in 1992. The reform effort also enabled the government to negotiate a substantial debt relief package with the Paris Club of official donors, which in July 1992 reduced debt-servicing obligations by over $900 million. This generosity placed Zambia among Africa's top aid receivers, with a full 124 aid dollars per head of population in 1992 (World Bank 1994c and 1995).

Domestically, however, the adjustment programme was far from popular. During the election campaign Chiluba had presented himself as a 'man of the people', a trade unionist who knew the troubles and pains of ordinary workers. The MMD's slogan 'The Hour Has Come!' had also infused many with the optimistic belief that the party's leadership would usher in a new social order and rapidly improving standards of living. Repeated attempts by the government to dampen expectations by arguing that the Kaunda years had left the state coffers completely empty and that recovery would take time had little effect, and such appeals for patience failed to silence public criticism (see e.g. Chiluba 1993: 7–14). Instead popular disappointment with the MMD soon manifested itself in widespread social and industrial unrest. The first eight months of 1992, for example, saw over fifty strikes as just about every occupational group struck for a living wage. In August 1992 some three hundred wives of miners in Ndola were arrested during a protest against the low salaries paid to their husbands, and in mid-1993 strike action among civil servants and teachers paralysed government departments and schools across the country. Civil and industrial unrest continued more or less unabated during the MMD's first term in office, providing a clear indication of the government's growing unpopularity among those who had been its main supporters – workers and the urban masses.[6]

In this situation, the government became gradually more hesitant in its pursuit of economic adjustment. Donors and creditors, however, continued to press for further privatisation and rapid reform, thus threatening to undermine the government's domestic support even further. The MMD's difficulties in trying to juggle the competing demands of its two constituencies are clearly evident in the prolonged wranglings over the privatisation of the copper mines. Export of copper was the backbone of Zambia's post-independence economy, but falling production due to ageing capital equipment, shortages of skilled labour, poor maintenance and inadequate investment led donors and creditors to make financial assistance conditional on the privatisation of Zambia Consolidated Copper Mines (ZCCM). Despite its unreserved commitment to privatisation in its party *Manifesto*, the government was dragging its feet over the sale of the mines, fearing the political consequences that would result from the sale of the country's main employer. The political calculations were complicated by the fact that the mines are situated in the Copperbelt, the heartland of the MMD's support in the 1991 elections. As many as 20,000 jobs in the mining industry were at risk from privatisation, and for Chiluba – a former trade unionist and a Bemba-speaker – the sale of the ZCCM looked like political suicide. The government was already confronted with massive social discontent as a result of the various austerity measures, and any increase in unemployment among the politically vocal mining constituencies was almost certain to lose the MMD support in the impending local and general elections.

Zambia's external sponsors, however, were reluctant to recognise such political obstacles and grew increasingly frustrated with the MMD's foot-dragging and delaying tactics. In December 1994 the Paris meeting of donors made aid pledges of US$2 billion conditional on the privatisation of the ZCCM (*Africa Confidential*, 28 April 1995). Further attempts by President Chiluba to convince donors that the economic reforms could jeopardise his political survival similarly failed to soften external pressures, and when it became apparent that the government intended to postpone privatisation until after the 1996 elections, the IMF declined to extend a much-needed credit line until the adjustment programme was re-established. Only when the government eventually returned to the negotiating table and began preparations for privatisation was financial assistance resumed. The actual process of selling the mining conglomerate nevertheless took several years, due to both domestic opposition and various governmental delaying tactics, but by now ownership of the country's main asset has largely passed to various foreign companies, such as the

South African mining giant Anglo American Corporation. Thousands of Zambians lost their jobs and their livelihoods in the process.

In the case of the privatisation of the copper mines, the Zambian government managed to stall and delay the demands of its external constituency in order not to provoke undue domestic resentment prior to the all-important 1996 presidential and general election. Eventually, however, the government agreed to privatisation, and overall there can be little doubt that faced with the difficult task of juggling the often conflicting demands of its external and internal constituencies, the MMD has been more responsive to its international financial sponsors than to its electorate. In trying to satisfy both its external and domestic constituencies, the government was trapped in a situation where political logic contradicted economic logic. Measures that were economically prudent in terms of attracting foreign assistance – for example, privatising the copper mines – were at the same time nothing short of political folly in terms of the government's electoral strategy. The MMD's main domestic constituencies were precisely the sections of the population hardest hit by economic adjustment, namely workers and the urban poor. The continuation of these policies could potentially lose the MMD the next election, as the disaffected urban population increasingly looked to the opposition for protection of their interests. The MMD was caught between a rock and a hard place: compelled by their aid dependency to implement adjustment measures, they were inevitably courting unpopularity and potentially defeat at the polls.

'Kill Me Now'

The situation in Zambia is by no means unique. Across the continent newly elected governments were faced with similar choices that pitted domestic expectations of welfare improvements against external demands for economic reform. And in most countries, external demands have been heeded over domestic preferences. This choice of policy direction, which is of course not only due to aid dependency, but also owes a great deal to the African elite's conceptualisation of democracy, has proved destabilising in most countries. As governments responded to external demands, while ignoring or attempting to stall and defer the wishes and requirements of their domestic constituencies, protest and instability became almost permanent features of many new democracies. In this way, a main effect of structural adjustment in Africa has been the alienation of domestic constituencies, making the conditions for the survival of democracy uncertain and volatile.

Only a few years after the return of political pluralism, the situation in many countries was strikingly similar to the immediate pre-transition period, with numerous strikes, large-scale protests and demonstrations. As it became increasingly clear that democracy was not bringing an end to poverty and deprivation, people again took to the streets to vent their anger. In Kenya, for example, public anger at the rising cost of living has been openly expressed on several occasions since the return of multi-partyism. One of the largest displays of discontent occurred after the government in March 1998 put up personal income tax, value added tax and excise duty on gas and petrol, which caused the cost of food and transport to rise dramatically. In protest, bank workers immediately went on strike, and on 14 March over five thousand people attended a rally to protest against austerity measures and corruption. Similar rallies have taken place across the continent, and in the 'model adjuster', Ghana, civil and industrial unrest has been an almost permanent feature as adjustment has continued unabated after the transition to democracy. While Ghana's rural population has benefited from increased producer prices and investment in welfare services, the urban population has become progressively poorer and in 1999 the UNDP estimated that 12 million Ghanaians live below the poverty line (*Ghanaian Chronicle*, 19 January 2000). The trade unions have been vociferously opposed to the government's adjustment programmes, and strikes have erupted in most sectors of the economy, including the all-important Ashanti Goldfields. Disagreements over civil service reforms have also threatened widespread disruption, while students have voiced their continued opposition and recently called for a campaign of demon-strations and disturbances.

The largest show of public discontent in Ghana came in May 1995, when more than fifty thousand people marched through Accra in protests against the imposition of value added tax at 20 per cent in accordance with demands from the Bretton Woods institutions. Summing up the effect of years of austerity policies, the VAT demonstration was named *Kume Preko* – 'You may as well kill me'. The new tax had pressed up prices on virtually everything, and impoverished Ghanaians were expressing their anger by calling for Rawlings' resignation. Five people were killed in the demonstra-tion, allegedly by government-inspired violence (*Africa Confidential* 36 (11) 1995). *Kume Preko* was organised by a broad opposition grouping called the Alliance for Change, and posed a serious threat to the government. Elections were only a year away, and the Alliance, which included most political parties in the country, seemed at this point to be able to deprive Rawlings if not of his presidency, then at the very least of his parliamentary majority. Despite such domestic political worries, the Bretton Woods institutions insisted that Rawlings persist with the austerity programme, indicating that lending would be cut by over $300 million over the next year if Ghana failed to meet public spending cuts (ibid.).

On this occasion, the domestic constituencies emerged victorious, as the dreaded tax was abolished. But the reprieve was only temporary. President Rawlings and his party were re-elected in 1996, in a free and fair election, and VAT was soon reintroduced at the lower rate of 10 per cent. It is important to note, however, that in the 1996 elections, the opposition parties won in all the major towns, indicating the depth of urban resentment towards economic austerity (see *Africa Confidential* 36 (25) 1996). The opposition's ability to capitalise on rising urban discontent has persisted during Rawlings' second term in office, and strikes and popular unrest have been no less frequent. The economy has remained at the centre of political debate, and in November 1999 the opposition organised a peaceful march in protest against the continuation of austerity policies. Between five thousand and ten thousand supporters took part in the rally, and speaker after speaker attacked the government's economic mismanagement, official corruption and plans to sack more state employees. Significantly, the rally took place only two days after a donor meeting chaired by the World Bank, and was a pointed reminder of President Rawlings' difficulty in satisfying his two constituencies. While donors and creditors wanted to see a more rapid reform process and were urging the government to speed up the sale of state companies and the reduction of the public-sector wage bill, Ghana's citizens were calling for an end to adjustment.

In Zambia, too, unrest grew fast as the effects of the MMD's dramatic liberalisation measures began to be felt and rapidly undermined people's already precarious livelihoods. In the first full MMD budget year, GDP fell by 2.8 per cent and at the end of 1992 prices were 207 per cent higher than in December 1991 (Kasonde 1993: 114). Shortly after taking office, the government removed food subsidies and the cost of maize meal alone leapt by 500 per cent (*The Economist*, 20 February 1993). The welfare state, which was never very well developed, suffered severe attacks and spending on social services declined from 7.4 per cent of GDP in 1991 to just 0.4 per cent in 1993. User fees were introduced, so that for the first time since independence state hospitals and clinics charged for treatment and patients paid for their own drugs. Unemployment rose dramatically as a result of the various adjustment measures, and in the first two years of MMD rule, 40,000 jobs – more than one in ten – in the formal economy were lost. Since then the number of job losses have doubled, as a result of privatisation and retrenchment in the public sector. De-industrialisation has emerged as a trend, and small-scale industries have gone bankrupt at an alarming rate. Over 70 per cent of the installed capacity in the clothing sector ceased production in 1992, due to imports of second-hand garments from South Africa and Zimbabwe. In 1995 alone, 30 state-owned firms and 120 private companies closed down. The former collapsed due to the withdrawal of state subsidies, while the latter were unable to compete with cheap imports following the dismantling of trade barriers. Foreign investment and privatisation have not been sufficient to divert the trend towards de-industrialisation, and manufacturing production declined by 9 per cent in 1994 and by a further 4.5 per cent in 1995.[7]

Not surprisingly, such drastic measures have been the cause of civil and industrial protest in post-transition Zambia, and the open display of popular dissatisfaction provided the political opposition with ample ammunition. The opposition parties, led by UNIP, repeatedly attacked the government's rigid enforcement of structural adjustment policies and argued that the economic liberalisation programme amounted to a 'recolonisation' of the Zambian economy. The government was also accused of inflicting unnecessary suffering on the population, and in July 1993 UNIP and two other newly formed parties joined forces to advocate the first of a series of civil disobedience campaigns against the government's economic policy.

In Côte d'Ivoire as well, the imposition of adjustment policies has caused turmoil and provided the opposition with plenty of political capital. Following the elections in 1990, the political situation in West Africa's traditionally most stable country has been volatile and uncertain. When Houphouet-Boigny died in 1993, the presidency passed to Henri Konan Bedie, then president of the National Assembly. The modernising prime minister, Allasane Ouattara, who had effectively ruled the country during the last months of Houphouet-Boigny's term in office, resigned along with his government, and a new government was formed. Although an increase in commodity prices caused a small economic boom in the post-election period, conditions for the majority of people have failed to improve. By contrast, the number of people living below the poverty line is increasing, especially in the urban slums. Nevertheless, the government continued with the austerity programme, and as a result economic protest and political unrest have been frequent. Schools and universities were affected by strikes and violence all through the late 1990s. The civil service has been plagued by strikes over pay and deteriorating working conditions, and at times the government's financial problems led to the late payment and even nonpayment of salaries to public sector workers, fuelling further discontent and providing the opposition with popular support.

In many of Africa's new democracies, then, the pursuit of simultaneous economic and political liberalisation caused widespread unrest, to the point where countries appeared ungovernable and elected leaders began to fear that they would suffer humiliating defeats in impending elections. To a large extent, political unrest and social discontent stemmed from external demands for continued economic adjustment, and when elected governments could no longer satisfy both their domestic and their external constituencies, they began, as the next section will show, to chip away at democratic principles and procedures in order to secure their own political survival.

Withering Democracy?

While the emergence of a critical press, vocal civil society organisations and an active political opposition can be seen as the essential characteristics of a healthy democratic polity, it soon became apparent that many newly elected governments lacked the capacity or the willingness to tackle criticism, dissent and economically motivated protest without resorting to the authoritarian measures of the past. Particularly as elections drew nearer and the possibility of defeat loomed on the horizon, Africa's hard-won civil rights and political liberties were gradually eroded and abandoned. In country after country, the press has again been censored or silenced, the opposition and individual critics harassed, while democratic procedures and principles have increasingly given way to more autocratic methods.

One of the more dramatic collapses of democracy occurred in Côte d'Ivoire, when on Christmas Eve 1999 the country experienced its first ever successful military coup. The coup must be seen against the background of deteriorating economic conditions, which had caused social discontent and prolonged political turmoil. President Bedie's response to this situation had been a gradual restriction of political freedoms and increased harassment of the opposition and government critics. As a result, the elections in 1995 took place amidst violence, mass demonstrations, boycotts and allegations of fraud and vote rigging. At the heart of the violence was a redrafting of the constitution, deliberately designed to prevent former Prime Minister Ouattara from contesting the election. Ouattara, who has spent most of the time since his resignation as deputy managing director of the IMF in Washington, had a proven record of administrative capability, as well as friends in high places, and he was therefore regarded as the main threat to the government's re-election. But by amending the constitution so that anyone who had a parent born abroad was banned from standing for office, the government succeeded in excluding Ouattara from the contest. The government alleged that Ouattara was not fully Ivoirien, but from neighbouring Burkina Faso, and despite his protestations the election went ahead without Ouattara and Bedie won 95 per cent of the vote, with his party securing an overwhelming majority in the National Assembly. The president has since then pushed through several other, undemocratic constitutional changes, and extended the presidential term from five to seven years. The persecution of Ouattara also continued, as the government seemed determined to keep him out of the political arena and to prevent him from running for the presidency in 2000. As the election drew nearer, political tensions in Côte d'Ivoire increased. President Bedie continued to insist that Ouattara was a foreigner, and when Ouattara eventually obtained a certificate to prove his Ivoirian identity, the Ministry of Justice annulled it on the grounds that it was issued on a Sunday. In September 1999 a political rally at which Ouattara was due to address his supporters was banned because it was regarded as a threat to law and order, and a few days later security forces using armoured vehicles arrested nearly four hundred opposition supporters in front of Ouattara's residence. The clash followed the issuing of a warrant for Ouattara's arrest, allegedly for having acquired his nationality documents in a fraudulent manner. A couple of days later, riot police fired teargas near the opposition leader's house and sent armoured personnel carriers with mounted machine-guns to disperse hundreds of supporters just released from two days of police detention. Other opposition leaders were given lengthy prison sentences for alleged involvement in violent public order offences during demonstrations. Ethnic tensions also mounted under President Bedie, as a result of his deliberate politicisation of a doctrine of 'Ivoirité'. The traditionally peaceful coexistence of various ethnic, immigrant and religious groups was thus under threat, as Bedie's policies inspired clashes between Ivoirians and the large immigrant population, and incensed the Muslim population in the North from which Ouattara drew much of his support.

The military coup of 24 December 1999 must be seen against the deteriorating political situation and the economic travails of the country. The coup started on the 23rd, with disgruntled soldiers rampaging through Abidjan, looting shops and forcing customers to lie on the floor as they emptied the supermarket tills. Initially the affair seems to have been merely a demand for unpaid bonuses and better living conditions by dissatisfied soldiers, some of whom claimed that they had served with the UN peace-keeping force in the Central African Republic for more than a year without pay (*Mail & Guardian*, 24 December 1999). This was also the initial reaction by the government, which maintained that it was not threatened by the mutiny (ibid.). By Christmas Eve, however, it had turned into a full-scale military intervention and General Robert Guei announced that the army had taken control of the country. Among Ivoirians, who had suffered under President Bedie's economic mismanagement, the coup seems to have aroused little protest.[8] Within a few days of the coup, all the opposition parties had joined the general's government, with Ouattara's party holding the three important ministries of finance, economy and construction. The general has promised the restoration of 'genuine democracy' after a 'transitional period', and the general election is now due to take place before 31 October 2000, although no specific timetable has been given.

The military intervention in one of Africa's traditionally most stable countries is a poignant reminder of the fragility of democracy in Africa and of the need for elected leaders to appease the armed forces. Rumours and fear of military intervention exist in most countries, and in Côte d'Ivoire talk of alleged coup plans started soon after the 1995 election. General Guei himself is a long-term foe of former President Bedie, who sacked him from the position of army chief of staff shortly before the elections. The dismissal followed Guei's refusal to send his troops into the streets in order to suppress the escalating violence without a written order from the president. The disaffected military continued to pose a threat to Bedie's rule, and as the economic and political situation deteriorated the conditions for an intervention were increasingly in place. This is not to say that economic adjustment was the only reason for the coup, but it underscores the difficulty of maintaining a sphere of political freedom and tolerance in conditions of economic decline and popular protest. The temptation towards authoritarian methods when popular support is waning is strong, and as political unrest increases the military may find it necessary to intervene to restore 'law and order'.

In Zambia, the deterioration of democratic standards was less dramatic, but arguably equally fundamental and certainly more rapid. The first serious breach of democratic procedure in Zambia occurred in early March 1993, when a state of emergency was declared in response to the so-called Zero Option Plan. The plan, allegedly written by members of UNIP, aimed to 'wrestle power from the MMD government in order to form a government responsive to people's needs ... before the 1996 elections' (in

Ihonvbere 1996: 229–30). Echoing themes from UNIP's election campaign, the MMD was described as a creation of the West and its leaders were accused of corruption, self-enrichment and neglect of the country's social infrastructure. In order to overthrown the government, the Zero Option document outlined a campaign of civil disobedience, which according to the plan's authors could be mobilised without difficulty as the population was already 'disgruntled with the government' (ibid.: 229). When excerpts from the Zero Option Plan were published in the *Times of Zambia*, President Chiluba warned that Zambia's democracy was threatened, and as emergency rule was imposed a total of twenty-three UNIP members were arrested and detained without charges (see Ham 1993). The state of emergency remained effective for a full twelve weeks, after which those UNIP members who were still in detention were released but soon re-arrested for similar offences.

The government's reaction to the alleged plot seems to have been excessive, especially as UNIP's leadership immediately after the publication of the plan made it abundantly clear that Zero Option was not party policy. In other words, the document was a testimony to the deep divisions within UNIP between its younger, more radical members and its moderate leadership. As such, the Zero Option Plan was potentially far more threatening to the survival of UNIP as a viable opposition party than it was to the stability and survival of the government. By the same token, the imposition of emergency rule was arguably more damaging to political freedom and democracy than the plan itself.

The period of emergency rule was the first sign of things to come in Zambia. As the opposition parties and the media became more active and vocal, the government displayed an increasing intolerance towards opposition and criticism. In July 1993 UNIP and two other opposition parties launched the first of a series of civil disobedience campaigns against the government's economic restructuring package, and argued for a more gradual approach to adjustment, better safety-nets for the poor and better protection for domestic industries. The opposition parties had already made significant inroads into MMD's support base in several local and by-elections, and these advances, coupled with social discontent, and allegations of high-level corruption and involvement in drug smuggling, unnerved the MMD.[9] In the two years prior to the 1996 elections harassment and intimidation of the opposition and independent critics escalated rapidly, and during this period political rights and civil liberties were severely curtailed to the extent that it can be argued that the MMD effectively engineered its own election victory.

Harassment of the opposition became manifestly more brutal and relentless after July 1994, when former President Kaunda announced his formal return to active politics. Despite the formation of numerous new parties, mostly by disaffected MMD politicians, Kaunda was still perceived as the only major political force outside the ruling party. With his lifelong political experience, his standing as 'father of the nation' and his ability to inspire people, Kaunda made UNIP appear a potential victor in the impending elections. Kaunda's leading role in the civil disobedience campaigns against structural adjustment also appealed to the vast majority of the voters, who despite their overwhelming display of disdain for Kaunda in the 1991 election had now realised that they were even worse off under democracy than during the one-party era.

Were it not for their serious consequences for the future of Zambia's democracy, the MMD's attempts to prevent Kaunda from returning to politics and contesting the presidential election could be described as almost ridiculous in their ingenuity and obstinacy. Instead, the affair has undertones of tragedy. Immediately after Kaunda's announcement of his 'comeback', the home affairs minister alleged that Kaunda had received foreign backing for his bid to return to power and that he had therefore been placed under surveillance 'in the interest of national security'. About a year later it was announced that Kaunda was to be deported to Malawi, because 'the government is satisfied that the former President is not a Zambian' (in Human Rights Watch/Africa 1996: 34). Kaunda's parents were both born in Malawi, the then British colony of Nyasaland, which until 1963 was part of the Federation of Central Africa. The government claimed that Kaunda had not officially relinquished his Malawian citizenship until 1970, and that he had ruled the country illegally for six years. The planned deportation was abandoned only following intense international and domestic pressures and fears that such action would cause social unrest.[10]

This was not, however, the end of the MMD's harassment of the former president. In yet another echo from the one-party era, the government turned to constitutional revision in order to limit the electoral chances of the opposition, and particularly of UNIP. The new constitution stipulated not only that a presidential candidate must be a Zambian citizen, but also that his or her parents must have been born in Zambia. The amendment seemed to be exclusively designed to prevent Kaunda from contesting the 1996 election. In addition, Kaunda was banned by a clause that limited the number of presidential terms to two, while UNIP's vice-president, Senior Chief Inyambo Yeta, was disqualified by a new rule that prohibited traditional chiefs from contesting presidential elections. The MMD's constitutional tampering thus excluded the two leaders of the main opposition party from the electoral competition.

International observers were quick to condemn the proposed changes as a breach of good governance, and the opposition demanded that the government abandon the draft constitution and enter negotiations on electoral reform. But the government refused to rethink its position, and as the elections scheduled for 18 November 1996 drew nearer, Zambian politics threatened to spiral out of control. Following a series of bombings and bomb threats, UNIP's vice-president and seven other senior party members were arrested and charged with treason, with the government alleging that they were connected to a clandestine anti-government organisation known as 'Black Mamba'.[11] In October, Kaunda announced that his party would boycott the elections, and the party embarked upon yet another civil disobedience campaign. By early November seven other parties had joined the election boycott and the disobedience campaign. Nevertheless, the elections went ahead as planned, and not surprisingly resulted in another landslide victory for the MMD. Chiluba won 73 per cent of the votes in the presidential contest and his party secured 131 of the 150 parliamentary seats, thus increasing its majority. The massive victory, however, conferred little legitimacy on the government, and by the time President Chiluba started his second term in office all illusions of Zambia as a pioneer of democracy had been shattered. Not only had the constitution skewed the election results, but the press had also been subjected to increasing intimidation and censorship during the election campaign. Unlike in 1991, when international observers flocked to Zambia, they unilaterally declined invitations to observe the 1996 election fearing that their mere presence would grant legitimacy to what was from the outset a flawed process. The opposition parties refused to recognise the election results, and since the election the political situation in Zambia has become progressively worse. Surveillance and harassment of government critics has increased. In August 1997 both Kaunda and another opposition leader were shot and wounded during an opposition rally, and Kaunda later claimed that the incident was an assassination attempt by the government. A few months later, a failed military coup provided further proof of the MMD's rising unpopularity and the fragility of the country's democratic institutions. More than ninety soldiers, businessmen and politicians were arrested and while Kaunda and several others were later released, fifty-nine soldiers have been sentenced to death for their involvement in the coup. All in all, it is fair to say that by the end of the 1996 elections Zambia was a democracy in name only.

In Ghana, democracy has fared comparatively better. The elections in 1996 were not only keenly contested, but also free and fair according to both domestic and international observers (see Gyimah-Boadi 1999). The anticipated violence failed to materialise, and although President Rawlings and the National Democratic Congress (NDC) won a solid victory, the opposition's representation rose from eleven to sixty-six of the two hundred seats in Parliament. Despite this comparatively good record, there are reasons for concern in Ghana. Political tension is mounting in preparation for the elections in 2000, when President Rawlings, having served the two terms permitted by the constitution, will have to step down. The government's reaction to opposition and discontent has become visibly more brutal, and as economically motivated protest has become commonplace repression has escalated. According to *Africa Confidential* (39 (2) 1998), the police now practise a version of 'zero tolerance' policing and officers sent to deal with demonstrations are given AK47 assault rifles as standard issue. There have been a succession of deaths and injuries from police shootings, and the opposition alleges that behind the veil of 'zero tolerance' the government is chipping away at constitutional rule, making the conditions for the opposition and its supporters ever more precarious. There has also been sharp criticism of President Rawlings' autocratic leadership style, and the political culture of patrimonialism seems unchanged. In 1998 a reform movement emerged within the NDC, attacking the lack of internal democracy and calling for an end to corruption and sycophancy. The movement has since split with the NDC and registered as a separate political party, the National Reform Party, and its members have reportedly been subjected to continual harassment and threats of arrest and detention by the security forces (*Africa Confidential* 40 (11) 1999). In brief, while democracy in Ghana persists in the form of free and fair elections, civil liberties and political rights are far from secure and seem to be shrinking.

In Kenya, by contrast, President Moi has continued to show a more or less blatant disregard for the democratic practices forced upon him by donors and creditors. In a telling show of his profound distaste for democratic politics, he suspended the first elected multi-party Parliament after it had sat for only one day. Although it was reinstated, little has changed in 'democratic' Kenya. The country's democratic experiment seems to have been a continual battle of the wills between Moi and his donors and creditors, with the president promising economic reform and improvements on human rights only to renege on these once aid has been released. Economically motivated protests have been brutally repressed, as in the Saba Saba demonstrations in 1997 when fourteen people were shot dead.

President Moi has also ruthlessly manipulated ethnic tensions to his own advantage, and there are continued speculations and allegations that the government is behind ethnic violence in the Rift Valley. The 1997 election, like the one in 1992, was again marred by allegations of malpractice, but Moi succeeded in winning a second term in office – if only by a whisker. Large-scale corruption is as prevalent as ever, and it remains to be seen whether the recently announced recovery strategy and the appointment of the long-term government critic Dr Richard Leakey as head of the Civil Service will succeed in improving public service efficiency and root out corruption. Despite having all the formal trappings of democracy, it would at present be overly generous to describe Kenya as anything but a highly undemocratic country.

Exclusionary Democracies

Contemporary development discourse, as discussed in Chapter 3, constructs structural adjustment programmes as a democratic venture, a way of empowering the 'people' and putting them back in 'charge of their own lives'. The majority of poor Africans, however, have experienced adjustment as anything but empowering, and the imposition of such programmes has served to dilute the democratic content of Africa's new pluralist political structures. Governments have pursued policies aimed at satisfying their external constituencies, while the demands of domestic constituencies have been put on hold indefinitely. African governments have tried, mostly in vain, to sell adjustment to their citizens and to convince them that ultimately everyone will benefit from the reforms. In a clear echo of World Bank thinking, for example, the Zambian government attempted to represent its economic policies as an intrinsic part of the process of democratisation. Most notably, the radical privatisation was presented as a way of giving the nation's wealth back to the 'people'. Turning conventional understandings of ownership on its head, Chiluba argued that nationalised companies had been the property of the privileged few, whereas privatisation would give even 'ordinary people ... a chance to own a share in a business of their choice' (Chiluba 1993: 60). Privatisation means that 'you and only you will have control of what happens to your money and no one will use it without your consent'. Privatisation was, in other words, a way of 'putting you back in control of your own life' (ibid.: 60–1). Needless to say, for the millions of Zambians who can afford only one meal a day privatisation has more frequently entailed unemployment than their elevation to the status of shareholders.

President Chiluba's efforts to justify and legitimise the liberalisation programme also contained echoes of the favoured World Bank theme of self-help, perhaps with an added touch of Thatcherism. At the celebration of the MMD's first year in power, Chiluba expressed his concern for all those who have suffered under the economic programme: 'I feel for those people who have to cope with higher prices, with inflation and are un-employed. My heart bleeds for the poor.' Then, hinting at his own humble background and reputation as a 'self-made man', he continued, 'of all people I know how difficult it is to pull yourself up by your own bootstraps when you don't even have shoes' (Chiluba 1993: 61). But despite these concessions to the plight of the poor, the implication is clear: in a market democracy everyone is free to make their own success or failure and people should not expect the state to provide for them. On the contrary, the aim is to provide an 'enabling environment' where people can prosper and do business, not to cater for their every need (ibid.: 70). Accordingly, Chiluba declared in an interview that his greatest achievement as president had not been to liberalise the economy, but to end the dependency culture in Zambian society. Zambian people, he claimed with pride, no longer looked to the state to provide for their livelihood (*The Times*, 7 March 1997).

It is certainly the case that across Africa people have come to expect less and less from the state in terms of welfare and security, and the return of democracy has done little to reverse this trend. Instead economic liberalisation and the reduction in the provision of public services continue, and people have been increasingly forced to rely on community, family and kinship organisations for their welfare and everyday survival. In this respect democracy has been a disappointment, as elected leaders have proved as socially insensitive as their authoritarian predecessors. Various religious and welfare groups have voiced their concern over the continued suffering of the poor majority. In Zambia, for example, the Catholic bishops warned in a public letter that the MMD's policies were leading to 'economic apartheid', while newspaper columnists have nicknamed the MMD 'the Movement for Moneyed Democrats' (in Burnell 1994: 28). In Ghana, in a play on President Rawlings' initials and nickname JJ, the feeling of betrayal has been captured in such slogans as 'From Junior Jesus to Junior Judas'. For the majority of Africans, then, the return of multi-party politics has brought little change. Although democracy may, at least initially, have expanded the room for political expression, particularly in terms of a more critical press and opportunities for social and industrial protest, the political influence of Africa's newly enfranchised citizens has been highly limited. In particular, demands for socio-economic improvements by the poorer sections of the population have been effectively ruled out *a priori* by economic liberalisation programmes. In this sense, these are exclusionary democracies: they allow for political parties and elections but cannot respond to the demands of the majority or incorporate the masses in any meaningful way.[12]

The linkage of democracy to continued economic liberalisation has narrowed the policy agenda in African countries, and the influence of citizens has been severely curtailed by the power of the international financial institutions and Africa's dependence on continued development assistance. In fact, it could be asked whether multi-party democracy has any meaning at all in polities where aid dependency defines the boundaries within which domestic economic policy can be formulated. Numerous opposition parties may criticise the adverse social effects of structural adjustment, but were they to gain power the dependency on foreign assistance would only enable these parties to make minor alterations to economic policy. Newly enfranchised Africans may have multiple parties to choose from when they go to the polls, but genuine political choice nevertheless remains severely constrained. In effect, there is only one political-economic model available to the African continent: economic liberalism in the form of structural adjustment programmes designed by the IMF and the World Bank. This is a form of democracy characterised by external control and local political emasculation.

The degree of control exerted over many new democracies by donors and creditors, and especially the Bretton Woods institutions, by virtue of Africa's need for development aid runs contrary to key aspects of democracy such as national sovereignty and self-government. Accordingly, the donor community has been keen to resist any accusation of undue influence over domestic policy choices, and has eagerly promoted the notion of national 'ownership' of structural adjustment programmes. 'Ownership' implies that the Bretton Woods institutions no longer impose policies on African countries, but merely put their superior economic knowledge and planning skills at the disposal of governments, who then make an autonomous and independent decision to adopt the suggested policy measures. 'Ownership' is not only supposed to avoid violations of democracy and sovereignty, but is also expected to increase the efficacy of structural adjustment as governments feel more responsible for the success of programmes they themselves have chosen. Most African governments see the issue differently, however. In the words of one Mozambican government official, for example, the only change after the talk of 'ownership' became part of the development terminology is that 'the World Bank now tells us that we must say it is our policy – and we do. We need World Bank money and aid is conditional on World Bank approval; we know we won't get that money if we tell the truth' (*Africa Confidential* 37 (25) 1996). Without World Bank/IMF tutelage, assistance will not be forthcoming from the vast majority of bilateral sources, but without the power to determine economic policy and domestic spending, national democracy and self-determination remain highly circumscribed.

Conclusion

How, then, do the democratic experiences discussed in this chapter compare to the postulates of contemporary development discourse? International donors and creditors have demanded simultaneous economic and political liberalisation across the continent, and have punished lack of progress in terms of democracy and human rights by suspending or terminating aid. It seems, however, that the demand for continued economic adjustment has in itself contributed to the erosion of democratic standards and in this way donors and creditors have added to the difficulties of consolidating democracy. The popular demand for political change in most countries was first and foremost a demand for socio-economic change, and although political rights and civil liberties may be highly valued, the transition to democracy was simultaneously expected to restore mass prosperity. As this chapter has shown, the public reaction to the continuation of austerity policies under democratic regimes has been widespread social unrest and a record number of industrial strikes, which provided fertile ground for the growth of political opposition and which in turn have often been met by governmental repression. The result in most countries has been a highly precarious political situation.

There are few signs of a mutually reinforcing relationship between democracy and economic liberalism in Africa's new democracies. From the point of view of elected governments, the demands of their two main constituencies appeared opposing and irreconcilable. Economic and political logic seemed contradictory, so that economic prudence spelt political danger. Frequently the choice was between continued economic adjustment and defiance of donor conditionality, between cutting the civil service, selling state companies, bringing in more donor funds and a populist strategy of increased public spending. The first carried the risk of electoral defeat, while the latter might secure domestic popularity but would almost certainly result in a loss of vital financial assistance. As we have seen, the first casualty of this dilemma was often the democratic process itself, as democratic practices and principles were gradually eroded or abandoned all together.

The rapid deterioration of democratic standards in many countries has in large part, but by no means exclusively, been caused by the pressures arising from the continuation of structural adjustment. These programmes threaten the consolidation of democracy by exacerbating social conflict and differentiation, while at the same time undermining the state's capacity to respond to domestic demands. Given that many of these governments consisted of politicians schooled within the one-party tradition and with little ideological or principled commitment to democracy, the turn to authoritarian measures in times of political turmoil is perhaps not all that surprising. The demand for simultaneous economic and political liberalisation has continually forced elected governments to adopt potentially destabilising policies, and the donor community has been largely unwilling to take account of domestic political obstacles to economic adjustment.

A more politically sensitive approach towards new democracies would have entailed a more gradual implementation of economic austerity measures, in order to prevent people's standards of living from plummeting to depths that were sure to erode the support of governments and cause widespread social unrest. Donor insistence on continued economic liberalisation has, however, ruled out a more gradual approach to adjustment as well as reforms to create a more just and equitable social order. Herein lies the central contradiction of current development policy: without such socio-economic reforms, Africa's new democracies are unable to respond to demands for improved living standards and to incorporate the masses in any meaningful way. Such exclusionary democracies seem almost doomed to persistent unrest and instability, which in turn may induce authoritarian responses by beleaguered governments. In this way it can be argued that although external pressure may have secured the survival of certain structures and procedures of democracy in Africa, the demand for economic liberalisation has at the same time impeded the consolidation of democracy. Instead of consolidation, the result has been a fragile democracy, often little more than a facade, and this seems an almost inevitable outcome of the pursuit of simultaneous economic and political liberalisation in conditions of poverty and underdevelopment.

Notes

1. A parallel debate existed concerning the relative advantage of military over civilian rule. Many maintained that military rule was more conducive to economic growth than

civilian rule, and authors such as Pye (1966), Shils (1964) and Levy (1966) argued that the military in developing countries was a progressive force, able to combine modernisation with maximum levels of stability and control. Others, such as Bienen (1971) and Nordlinger (1970), regarded the military as too obsessed with the maintenance of order to act as an effective modernising agent. Sirowy and Inkeles (1990) concluded after a review of the literature that military regimes appear to perform worse than civilian governments in terms of improving the basic quality of life of the masses and improving access to health facilities and schools.

2. Note that the World Bank's main concern here appears to be how to avoid jeopardising the economic reform programme, rather than how to protect democracy.

3. See Chiluba (1993); World Bank (1995); *Africa Review* (1993/94). The inflation figure is an unofficial estimate of average inflation in October 1991 (*Africa South of the Sahara* 1994: 977). Inflation for the year as a whole stood at 92.6 per cent (*Africa Review* 1997).

4. Structural adjustment programmes were discussed in more detail in Chapter 2.

5. The figures are provided by the chief executive of the ZPA in a special supplement to *The Times* (7 March 1997).

6. See Ham (1992); *Times of Zambia* (4 August 1992); Ihonvbere (1996: 191–2) for discussions of civil and industrial unrest during the MMD's first period in power.

7. The figures in this section are collected from *The Economist* (20 November 1993); *Africa Confidential* (38 (4) 1997 and 36 (10) 1995); Burnell (1994); *Africa South of the Sahara* (1998: 1111).

8. Not only had the continuation of structural adjustment caused widespread suffering in Côte d'Ivoire, but large-scale corruption also seems to have continued unabated. In 1999 the EU suspended aid because of serious irregularities in accounting practices, and government officials were suspected of having embezzled aid to the value of at least $29 million (*Africa Confidential* 40 (14) 1999).

9. It should be mentioned that voter turn-out was extremely low in both local and parliamentary by-elections, signalling a general disillusionment with politics, not only with the MMD. In the first local elections in November 1992 fewer than 10 per cent of registered voters went to the polls, while in Parliamentary by-elections voter turn-out was generally below 20 per cent. By contrast, voter participation in the independence election in 1964 was a full 94.8 per cent, while in 1992 voter participation fell to 45 per cent.

10. The government applied the same method of harassment to numerous other members of the opposition, and several independent critics and politicians had their citizenship scrutinised and were threatened with deportation. In a few cases deportation was actually carried out.

11. 'Black Mamba' was Kaunda's nickname during the independence struggle. The trial of the eight UNIP members failed to link them to 'Black Mamba' or any other violent conspiracy against the government, and it remains unclear whether or not the organisation actually existed.

12. The term exclusionary democracy has also been used by Remmer (1985/86).

7

The Success of the Good Governance Discourse

This study does not as such constitute an argument against the promotion of democracy on the African continent, nor has it been my concern to devise a more 'correct' development theory. Instead the mode of analysis is one that seeks to make visible the political consequences of adopting one representation of social reality rather than another. It seeks, in other words, to draw attention to the relations of power implicated in development discourse, the identities that are constructed and perpetuated by its practices, and the meaning assigned to democracy within the discourse. Although the study concludes that contemporary development discourse has been largely unsuccessful in its declared aim to establish stable multi-party democracies in Africa, this does not mean that the development effort has failed. Foucault, when speaking of the prison, suggested that focusing on its perceived 'failure' might be to pursue the wrong line of inquiry. Perhaps instead, he proposed,

> one should reverse the problem and ask oneself what is served by the failure of the prison; what is the use of these different phenomena that are continually being criticized; the maintenance of delinquency, the encouragement of recidivism, the transformation of the occasional offender into a habitual delinquent, the organisation of a closed milieu of delinquency. (1991: 272)

Like the penal system, development is commonly perceived both by its practitioners and by its critics to have failed in achieving its stated aims and objectives, and has reproduced poverty and encouraged aid dependency. Nevertheless, the development effort continues and is constantly reinvented and reformulated in order finally to arrive at a solution to the problems of underdevelopment. Applied to development, Foucault's suggestion encourages an analysis that focuses not on development's declared goals, but instead on what development as a practice actually does and what interests are served by these practices. The analysis thus shifts from a focus on what development is, or ought to be, to an exploration of the social and political implications of these ideas and representations.

The good governance discourse, despite the efforts of its proponents to present it as radically different from past development doctrines, reproduces the hierarchies and relationships that have been the hallmarks of development ever since its inception in the post-war period. As a 'regime of truth', development discourse has produced a form of knowledge about the third world that still informs and underpins contemporary North–South relations. Although the subjects and categories produced by development have by no means been static or monolithic, or immune to renegotiations by the third world itself, the discourse remains embedded within specific experiences and relations of power and cannot be separated from the political and social setting in which it was produced. The construction of subjects as underdeveloped and developed, and the placing of these in a hierarchical and unequal relationship to each other, was not some neutral or accurate transcription of reality, but served to legitimise and normalise the right of the North to intervene in order to develop the South. The present narration of development as an absence of democracy and good governance is a reaffirmation of this right, and a key effect of the discourse is the renewed entitlement of the North to define the choices and policies of the South. More specifically, it sanctions the promotion of a particular form of democracy, while de-legitimising others.

This study has accordingly given special attention to the meaning attached to democracy and good governance within contemporary development discourse. Essentially, the discourse blurs the distinction between democratisation and the retreat of the state from the social and economic field. Democracy is tacked on to the promotion of economic liberalism, which is accorded primacy in discourse and practice. Democracy emerges as the necessary political framework for successful economic reforms, as there is concern that the latter will be 'wasted if the political context is not favourable' (World Bank 1989: 192). Within the discourse, democracy and economic liberalism are conceptually linked in the one concept of 'good governance', and by implication more interventionist economic policies become 'bad governance' and incompatible with democracy. In this way, a new legitimacy is constructed for the Bretton Woods institutions' heavily criticised structural adjustment programmes, which now become a force for democracy and a way of freeing civil society from the oppressive powers of the state. This representation thus gives structural adjustment programmes a 'democratic face', and the demand for further economic liberalisation by donors and creditors appears as a quest for good governance and democracy.

One of the political consequences of constructing democracy and good governance in this way has been the emergence of unstable, exclusionary democracies. The pursuit of simultaneous economic and political liberalisation has presented elected governments with complex and intractable dilemmas, where economic and political logic have often appeared contradictory and conflicting. On the one hand is the demand for further economic adjustment, on the other the expectation that social improvements will follow in the wake of democracy. While one choice invites popular discontent and electoral rejection, the other spells the reduction of international financial assistance. As we have seen, the first casualty of this dilemma has frequently been democracy itself, as elected leaders in country after country have returned to the authoritarian practices of the past in order to suppress political criticism and economically motivated unrest.

It is difficult to divorce the fragility of these new democracies from their pursuit of simultaneous economic and political liberalisation and their concomitant inability to incorporate the majority of the population into the political process in any meaningful way, let alone respond to their expectations of improved welfare. Nevertheless, the good governance discourse and much contemporary scholarship show a clear convergence towards procedural or minimalist conceptions of democracy, where democracy is conceived as a political system separate and apart from socio-economic conditions and structures. While in development discourse democracy is wedded to structural adjustment, the dominant position among scholars is that democracy cannot entail any *a priori* commitment to particular values such as social justice and equality, as this would in effect be to prejudge the preferences of voters. The superiority of democracy as a system of governance is thus seen to arise not from its ability to produce equality, but from its capacity to affect a peaceful and bloodless change from one government to another. In the words of Przeworski, an ardent defender of minimalist conceptions of democracy,

> the miracle of democracy is that conflicting political forces obey the result of voting. People who have guns obey those without them. Incumbents risk their control of governmental offices by holding elections. Losers wait for their chance to win office. Conflicts are regulated, processed according to rules, and thus limited. This is not consensus, yet not mayhem either. Just limited conflict; conflict without killing. (1999: 49)

In many African countries, however, such a situation seems a long way off. Instability persists and the likelihood that losers or incumbents may reach for their guns remains high. The 'miracle of democracy', in other words, does not seem to have worked in Africa, and the economic predicament of the continent is of importance in this context. Endorsing Lipset's dictum that the 'more well-to-do a country, the greater the chance that it will sustain democracy' (1960: 31), Przeworski argues that poverty can prevent the democratic miracle from materialising. His predictions for the survival chances of democratic structures in poor countries do not make for optimism. According to his calculations, the expected life of democracy in a country with a per capita income under $1,000 is about eight years, while countries with a per capita income of between $1,001 and $2,000 can expect to sustain democracy for eighteen years (1999: 49). Such statistically based arguments should not lead to deterministic conclusions, nor do they necessarily point to a causal relationship between democratic breakdown and poverty. It is nevertheless a sobering realisation that the vast majority of countries in Africa fall within these income brackets (World Bank 1999/ 2000).

One of the reasons why pluralism is so difficult to maintain in countries with a low per capita income is the high degree of social and economic inequality that characterises many of these societies. Conflicts in deeply differentiated societies are frequently more intense and harder to solve, as the stakes are higher for the actors involved. The elite has more reasons to fear the distributional demands of the poorer sections of the population, and the temptation to close down or restrict democratic political channels accordingly remains strong. Approached from this perspective, it seems that a minimalist approach to democracy in poor countries is counterproductive, and more specifically that to link the promotion of democracy to continued structural adjustment in Africa is making consolidation difficult. In order to get to the point where democracy will be valued and respected for its procedures and its ability to effect a peaceful change of government, it must first have ameliorated the intensity of social conflicts and delivered tangible benefits. A genuine concern for democracy in Africa would accordingly concentrate efforts around the question of how to craft an economic policy that would facilitate consolidation. This in turn would entail a more politically sensitive approach to adjustment and most likely a more gradual implementation of economic austerity measures, in order to protect people's living standards from plummeting to depths that are almost guaranteed to erode government legitimacy and cause widespread social and political protest and unrest. It is precisely these kinds of policies and reforms that are rendered difficult, if not impossible, by the fusion of democracy and economic liberalism. The contemporary meaning assigned to good governance rules out reforms towards a more just and equitable social order, and makes it difficult for African countries to reach the conditions where actual or potential losers in the democratic game will look to the next election to settle their grievances, rather than to take to the streets in protest or reach for their arsenal of weapons. In this sense, the very heart of contemporary development discourse can be seen as internally contradictory, as its proposed economic reforms threaten to undermine and erode the suggested political reforms.

The hegemonic status of the 'Washington consensus', however, is such that no alternative to simultaneous liberalisation is perceived to exist for African countries. The view from Washington concerning economic policy has not only been accepted by virtually all bilateral donors, so that very little disagreement exists over the major issues of economic policy, but has also been internalised by African elites. Political leaders, incumbents as well as those in opposition, have come to understand that without acceptance of the neo-liberal paradigm, no international financial assistance will be forthcoming. In this way, alternative economic policies have become marginalised or come to be regarded as unfeasible, and an influential body of opinion now holds that although the imposition of structural adjustment programmes has caused widespread suffering and might jeopardise the survival chances of democracy, African countries have in reality no other option.[1] Conditions on the continent, this view contends, are such that no other economic path could have produced any better results, and the corollary of this view is that without structural adjustment programmes things would have been much worse, especially for the poorer sections of the population. This is because adjustment, although stipulating the reduction of state expenditure, also releases new donor funds to countries that comply with these demands. Without these donor funds the provision of services to the poor would have deteriorated even further or collapsed altogether. While there may be some truth to this argument, there is now evidence to suggest that poor countries committed to adjustment policies do not necessarily get the increased aid that they have been led to expect. Some countries – for example, Uganda and Mozambique – are finding that the conditions applied by the IMF to control money supply and reduce government deficits prevent them from using additional assistance to fund recurrent costs, including social development expenditures. The effect is that if extra funds are forthcoming from donors, the rules require these to be channelled into uses other than enhancing and expanding services for the poor (Riddell 1999: 326; see also Hanlon 1996). It is not necessarily the case, therefore, that conditions would have been worse without adjustment, nor do arguments to this effect constitute a rigorous defence of economic liberalism or the pursuit of simultaneous liberalisation.

Instead of seeking to explain donor insistence on simultaneous liberalisation as a consequence of the actual successes and achievements of this approach, this study suggests that the good governance agenda is best understood as a discursive formation – that is, as a historically contingent form of knowledge intimately connected to prevailing structures and relations of power at the time of its formation. The analysis has shown how the conditions of possibility of the discourse were provided primarily by the end of the Cold War and the collapse of Communism, when the perceived worldwide victory of liberal values rendered possible the institution of governance and democracy as the prime goals of development. Ironically, however, the triumph of the capitalist development model coincided with a growing recognition of the failure of economic liberalisation on the African continent. After more than a decade of structural adjustment, not a single convincing success could be credited to these programmes. But the neo-liberal development paradigm could hardly be abandoned at the moment of capitalism's global victory over Marxism-Leninism, and in the good governance agenda the failure of adjustment policies was blamed on the 'poor governance' of African governments. Economic liberalisation, it was argued, would work only if accompanied by political reforms towards greater pluralism and freedom, and in this way Western triumphalism and the need to construct a new legitimacy for the IMF's and the World Bank's severely criticised structural adjustment programmes coalesced in the formation of the good governance discourse.

Given its embeddedness in particular relations of power, it is not surprising that the good governance discourse's claim to 'empower ordinary people' has been shown frequently to ring hollow. The term empowerment in the good governance discourse is largely deprived of its more radical, political implications, and no longer signifies a capacity of the excluded to challenge prevailing structures and hierarchies of power. Instead the term is emasculated, primarily by linking empowerment to economic liberalism. Analysed within the overall setting of the good governance discourse, empowerment becomes a highly instrumental term, indicating mainly that people should 'pull their weight' and make development projects more cost-efficient. It signifies the expectation that people will be more responsible for their own welfare and development, more willing to contribute to community projects and pay user fees for state services. A term more commonly found in radical political contexts is thus applied to describe a shifting of responsibility for welfare and security from the state to unpaid local labour, and serves to garner support for policies that have been severely criticised for their negative social effects on poor people and for overburdening women in particular. As such, the use of empowerment by the good governance discourse can be seen as a prime illustration of what Rist (1997) has referred to as the 'seductiveness of development'.

The choice of the term empowerment is nevertheless interesting considering the efforts of the donor community, and the World Bank in particular, to represent the good governance discourse as apolitical and value-neutral. The discourse narrates the proposed restructuring of African societies as commonsensical and technical, rather than contested and political. Disagreement and conflicts over social goals are absent from the analysis, and development emerges as a neutral project guided by 'technical considerations of economy and efficiency, rather than ideological and political preferences' (Shihata 1991: 95). This denial of politics and the political is a key characteristic of development discourse and it is also one of its key practical effects.[2] By depoliticising its own interventions and dispelling existing political realities from vision, development discourse has the effect of portraying even the most sensitive political operations as somehow neutral and commonsensical. Not only is poverty reduced to a technical problem, but the radical transformation of Africa's economies and the transitions to multi-party democracy also take on a primarily technical character. The good governance agenda proposes democratisation and empowerment without addressing issues of power and politics, the unequal nature of African societies, divisions between rich and poor, or conflict along gender or ethnic lines. This suspension of politics and the construction of democracy as a political form separate and apart from social and economic structures serve to bestow legitimacy on the existing social order, including the marginalisation of large sections of the population. By making redistribution of resources towards the underprivileged and marginalised sections of society close to impossible, the governance discourse serves to maintain the status quo and the existing balance of forces within African countries. Needless to say, keeping things more or less as they are is also a political preference, not a neutral and objective position. A key practical effect of the good governance discourse is thus that it allows for the continuation of oligarchy under a different name.

Rather than judging the good governance discourse on the extent to which it achieves its stated objective of 'empowering ordinary people', the arguments in this study suggest that development should be seen as part of the multiple technologies and mechanisms of power employed in global politics, and as one of the ways in which the North maintains its dominance and influence over the South. The good governance discourse produces democracies that are exclusionary both in the sense that they cannot incorporate the poor majority in any meaningful way, and to the extent that this is a form of democracy where the power and influence of external constituencies is extraordinarily high. The degree of control exerted by donors and creditors, and especially the Bretton Woods institutions, in these new democracies poses a challenge to key features of liberal democracy as commonly conceived in political theory, in that it threatens to erode the right to national self-determination and self-government. In fact, it could be asked whether multi-party democracy has any but the most limited meaning in polities where dependency on external financial assistance defines the boundaries within which domestic policy is formulated.

In the majority of African countries today, newly enfranchised populations may have dozens of political parties to choose from when they go to the polls. Genuine political choice nevertheless remains severely constrained, and in effect there is only one model available to Africa – economic liberalism in the form of structural adjustment programmes designed by the World Bank and the IMF. Opposition parties may criticise the effects of adjustment, but should they attain political office they would have to fall into line with the 'Washington consensus' in order to attract vital foreign funds. This is a form of democracy characterised by external control and local political emasculation, where fine-tuning of externally directed policies is the best that can be hoped for and where the voices of the poor majority are persistently overruled by governments' accountability to financial sponsors and the need to attain continued assistance. The consensus among donors on the desirability of economic adjustment ensures that countries that do not comply with the conditions set by the Bretton Woods institutions not only lose access to their financial packages, but also find that most bilateral donors tighten their purse-strings. In this way, policy-making in many African countries has become subservient to the need to maintain international financial assistance, and their domestic policy choices are hence severely restricted. The result is what Mkandawire (1999) has termed 'choiceless democracies', democracies where pronouncements in favour of economic liberalism are the only political route available.

It seems an undeniable paradox that the return of national liberal democracy to the African continent has been paralleled by an increasing transfer of power and influence over policy matters to international actors. Arguably this increased importance of international bodies in domestic affairs can be observed everywhere, as globalisation – defined here simply as the intensification of global interconnectedness – poses severe challenges to the status of the nation-state as an autonomous and independent actor. As economic, political, social and cultural relations across borders have intensified, considerable power has been vested in various international organisations, transnational companies and finance institutions, and although the state remains an important locus of power in the international system its sovereignty and autonomy is constrained by recent processes of globalisation. This interconnectedness challenges the very notion of democratic sovereignty as conventionally defined in political theory. Liberal democracy, as observed by Held (1991, 1995), McGrew (1997) and others, was premised on the sovereignty of nation-states and assumed that the state had control over its own fate, subject only to limits and compromises imposed upon it by actors, agencies and forces operating within its territorial boundaries. Historically, democratic theory assumed an essential correspondence between the democratic community and the territorially defined nation-state, and the 'demos' was traditionally perceived to be contained exclusively within these boundaries. In the face of globalisation, this perception of a correspondence between the political community and the nation-state becomes largely obsolete, as issues of vital importance to domestic constituencies are frequently decided by centres of power located outside the nation-state and by organisations and agencies that are not subject to democratic control by citizens.

These issues are of relevance to democracies everywhere, but they have a particular salience for African countries. The 'autonomous sovereign state' of conventional political and democratic theory may be nowhere to be found as an actual existing state, but the concept is even more problematic when applied to the African context. For most African states autonomy and sovereignty have always been a virtual illusion, constrained both by their low status in the international system and by their relationships to their domestic societies. So weak is the autonomy of many of these states that they have been termed 'quasi-states', possessing only a feeble sovereignty and surviving primarily by virtue of their external legal recognition rather than their domestic support and legitimacy (Jackson 1990). In the light of the already precarious existence of the 'autonomous sovereign state', globalisation seems to pose particularly severe challenges for Africa's new democracies. One of the main articulations of globalisation on the continent has been the imposition of structural adjustment programmes to manage the economic crisis and enable the repayment of debts. The continent's strategic and economic marginalisation in the new world order and its dependency on foreign assistance have facilitated intervention and governance by international institutions and organisations, to the extent that more and more of the decisions that determine the life and well-being of Africa's peoples are today made outside the continent, in the Washington offices of the Bretton Woods institutions. Power, in other words, is increasingly located outside the political community as conventionally defined by democratic theory, and outside the reach of the democratic control of Africa's citizens.

The good governance discourse helps legitimise this world order. By constructing African countries as undemocratic and lacking in good governance, the right of the democratic countries of the North to intervene and set conditions for development aid to Africa is reconfirmed. The countries of the North are treated as implicitly democratic, serving as models to be emulated by the South, and shielded from the democratic scrutiny that African countries are subjected to. More importantly, the good governance agenda constructs democracy as relevant only *within* countries, and not within international institutions and relations. Domestic politics must be democratised, but international relations are left untouched and protected from the reach of the good governance discourse. In this way contemporary development discourse can be said to be part of the global governance of the African continent, one of the ways in which present international structures and relations of power are maintained and reproduced. Accordingly, one of the main effects of the good governance discourse, despite all its proclamations in favour of democracy, is to help reproduce and maintain a world order that is essentially undemocratic.

Notes

1. See for example Young (1991).

2. This effect of development is also conveyed by the title of Ferguson's incisive study of development aid in Lesotho, *The Anti-Politics Machine* (1994), which argues that one of the main effects of development is the pre-eminently political operation of expanding bureaucratic state power.

References

Abrahamsen, R. 1997 'The Victory of Popular Forces or Passive Revolution? A Neo-Gramscian Perspective on Democratisation', *Journal of Modern African Studies* 35 (1): 129–52.

Africa Leadership Forum 1990 *Conference on Security, Stability, Development and Co-operation in Africa*, 17–18 November, Addis Ababa.

Africa Recovery 1990 *Commentary: Eastern Europe, Africa's Needs and the UN*, April–June: 15–17.

Akwetey, E. O. 1994 *Trade Unions and Democratisation. A Comparative Study of Zambia and Ghana*, University of Stockholm, Stockholm.

Alagiah, G. 1987 'In and Out of Touch', *South*, February: 19–20.

Albrow, M. 1996 *The Global Age: State and Society Beyond Modernity*, Polity Press, Cambridge.

Almond, G. A. 1970 *Political Development: Essays in Heuristic Theory*, Little, Brown and Company, Boston, MA.

Almond, G. A. and J. S. Coleman (eds) 1960 *The Politics of the Developing Areas*, Princeton University Press, Princeton, NJ.

Almond, G. A. and G. B. Powell 1966 *Comparative Politics: A Developmental Approach*, Little, Brown and Company, Boston, MA.

Almond, G. A. and S. Verba 1963 *The Civic Culture: Political Attitudes and Democracy in Five Nations*, Princeton University Press, Princeton, NJ.

Apter, D. E. 1965 *The Politics of Modernization*, University of Chicago Press, Chicago and London.

Augelli, E. and C. Murphy 1988 *America's Quest for Supremacy and the Third World*, Pinter, London.

Ayoade, J. A. A. 1988 'States without Citizens: An Emerging African Phenomenon', in D. Rothchild and N. Chazan (eds) *The Precarious Balance: State and Society in Africa*, Westview Press, Boulder, CO and London.

Bangura, Y. 1986 'Structural Adjustment and the Political Question', *Review of African Political Economy* No. 37: 24–37.

Bangura, Y. and P. Gibbon 1992 'Adjustment, Authoritarianism and Democracy in Sub-Saharan Africa: An Introduction to Some Conceptual and Empirical Issues', in P. Gibbon, Y. Bangura and A. Ofstad (eds) *Authoritarianism, Democracy and Adjustment. The Politics of Economic Reform in Africa*, Nordiska Afrikainstitutet, Uppsala.

Barya, J.-J. B. 1993 'The New Political Conditionalities of Aid: An Independent View from Africa', *IDS Bulletin* 42 (1): 16–23.

Bayart, J.-F. 1986 'Civil Society in Africa', in P. Chabal (ed.) *Political Domination in Africa: Reflections on the Limits of Power*, Cambridge University Press, Cambridge.

— 1993 *The State in Africa: The Politics of the Belly*, Longman, London.

Baylies, C. and M. Szeftel 1992 'The Fall and Rise of Multi-Party Politics in Zambia', *Review of African Political Economy* No. 54: 75–91.

Beckman, B. 1992 'Empowerment or Repression? The World Bank and the Politics of Adjustment', in P. Gibbon, Y. Bangura and A. Ofstad (eds) *Authoritarianism, Democracy and Adjustment. The Politics of Economic Reform in Africa*, Nordiska Afrikainstitutet, Uppsala.

Beetham, D. 1992 'Liberal Democracy and the Limits of Democratization', *Political Studies* XL: 40–53.

— 1994 'Conditions for Democratic Consolidation', *Review of African Political Economy* No. 60: 157–72.

Benney, M., A. P. Gray and R. H. Pear 1956 *How People Vote*, Routledge & Kegan Paul, London.

Berelson, B. R. 1956 'Democratic Theory and Public Opinion', in H. Eulau, J. G. Eldersveld and M. Janowitz (eds) *Political Behaviour, A Reader in Theory and Research*, The Free Press, Glencoe.

Berelson, B. R., P. F. Lazarsfeld and W. N. McPhee 1954 *Voting*, University of Chicago Press, Chicago.

Bernstein, H. 1979 'Modernization Theory and the Sociological Study of Development', in D. Lehmann (ed.) *Development Theory: Four Critical Studies*, Frank Cass, London.

Bhabha, H. 1990 'The Other Question: Difference, Discrimination, and the Discourse of Colonialism', in R. Ferguson et al. (eds) *Out There: Marginalization and Contemporary Cultures*, MIT Press, Cambridge, MA.

Bienen, H. 1971 *The Military and Modernization*, University of Chicago Press, Chicago.

Björnlund, E., M. Bratton and C. Gibson 1992 'Observing Multiparty Elections in Africa: Lessons from Zambia', *African Affairs* 91 (364): 405–31.

Booth, D. 1985 'Marxism and Development Sociology: Interpreting the Impasse', *World Development* 13 (7): 761–87.

Bratton, M. 1989 'Beyond the State. Civil Society and Associational Life in Africa', *World Politics* XLI (3): 407–30.

— 1994a 'International versus Domestic Pressures for "Democratization" in Africa', paper presented at the conference 'The End of the Cold War: Effects and Prospects for Asia and Africa', School of Oriental and African Studies, UCL, London.

— 1994b 'Economic Crisis and Political Realignment in Zambia', in J. A. Widner (ed.) *Economic Change and Political Liberalization in Sub-Saharan Africa*, Johns Hopkins University Press, Baltimore, MD and London.

Bratton, M. and D. Rothchild 1992 'The Institutional Bases of Governance in Africa', in G. Hyden and M. Bratton (eds) *Governance and Politics in Africa*, Lynne Rienner, Boulder, CO and London.

Bratton, M. and N. van de Walle 1992 'Popular Protest and Political Reform in Africa', *Comparative Politics* 24: 419–42.

Braudel, F. 1985 *Civilization and Capitalism. Volume 2: The Perspective of the World*, Collins, London.

Brown, S. 1983 *The Faces of Power: Constancy and Change in United States Foreign Policy from Truman to Reagan*, Columbia University Press, New York.

Burnell, P. 1994 'Zambia at the Crossroads', *World Affairs* 157 (1): 19–28.

Calhoun, C. 1993 'Civil Society and the Public Sphere', *Public Culture* 5: 267–80.

Callaghy, T. M. 1990 'Lost Between State and Market: The Politics of Economic Adjustment in Ghana, Zambia, and Nigeria', in J. M. Nelson (ed.) *Economic Crisis and Policy Choice: The Politics of Adjustment in the Third World*, Princeton University Press, Princeton, NJ.

— 1994 'Africa: Falling off the Map?', *Current History*, January: 31–6.

Campbell, H. et al. 1960 *The American Voter*, John Wiley, New York.

Carter Center of Emory University and National Democratic Institute of International Affairs 1992 *The October 31 1991 National Elections in Zambia*, Washington, DC.

Caufield, C. 1997 *Masters of Illusion: The World Bank and the Poverty of Nations*, Macmillan, London.

Chabal, P. 1986 'Introduction: Thinking about Politics in Africa', in P. Chabal (ed.) *Political Domination in Africa: Reflections on the Limits of Power*, Cambridge University Press, Cambridge.

— 1994 *Power in Africa: An Essay in Political Interpretation*, Macmillan, London.

Chalker, L. 1991 *Good Government and the Aid Programme*, speech by the Minister for Overseas Development at the Royal Institute of International Affairs, 25 June, Overseas Development Administration, London.

Chazan, N. 1982 'The New Politics of Participation in Tropical Africa', *Comparative Politics* 14 (2): 169–98.

— 1988a 'Ghana: Problems of Governance and the Emergence of Civil Society', in L. Diamond, J. J. Linz and S. M. Lipset (eds) *Democracy in Developing Countries. Volume 2: Africa*, Adamantine Press, London.

— 1988b 'Patterns of State-Society Incorporation and Disengagement in Africa', in D. Rothchild and N. Chazan (eds) *The Precarious Balance: State and Society in Africa*, Westview Press, Boulder, CO and London.

— 1992 'Liberalization, Governance and Political Space in Ghana', in G. Hyden and M. Bratton (eds) *Governance and Politics in Africa*, Lynne Rienner, Boulder, CO.

— 1993 'Between Liberalism and Statism: African Political Cultures and Democracy', in L. Diamond (ed.) *Political Culture and Democracy in Developing Countries*, Lynne Rienner, Boulder, CO.

Chege, M. 1992 'Remembering Africa', *Foreign Affairs* 71 (1): 146–63.

Cheru, F. 1989 *The Silent Revolution in Africa: Debt, Development, and Democracy*, Zed Books, London.

Chiluba, F. J. T. 1993 *Democracy in Zambia: Key Speeches of President Chiluba 1991/92* (ed. D. Chanda), Africa Press Trust, Lusaka.

Chomsky, N. 1992 *Deterring Democracy*, Vintage Books, London.

Chossudovsky, M. 1997 *The Globalization of Poverty: Impacts of IMF and World Bank Reforms*, Zed Books, London.

Clapham, C. 1993 'Democratization in Africa: Obstacles and Prospects', *Third World Quarterly* 14 (3): 432–8.

Clough, M. 1992 *Free at Last? US Policy Toward Africa and the End of the Cold War*, Council on Foreign Relations Press, New York.

Cohen, H. L. 1995 'Political and Military Security', in J. W. Harbeson and D. Rothchild (eds) *Africa in World Politics: Post-Cold War Challenges*, Westview Press, Boulder, CO.

Cohen, J. L. and A. Arato 1992 *Civil Society and Political Theory*, MIT Press, Cambridge, MA and London.

Coleman, J. S. (ed.) 1965 *Education and Political Development*, Princeton University Press, Princeton, NJ.

Cook, R. 1997a *British Foreign Policy*, speech at the launch of the Foreign Office Mission Statement, 12 May, Locarno Suite, FCO, London.

— 1997b *Britain's New Approach to the World*, speech to the Labour Party Conference, 2 October, Brighton.

— 1998 *Human Rights: Making the Difference*, speech to the Amnesty International Human Rights Festival, 16 October, London.

Corbo, V., S. Fischer and S. B. Webb 1992 *Adjustment Lending Revisited*, World Bank Symposium, World Bank, Washington, DC.

Cornia, G. A. 1991 *Is Structural Adjustment Conducive to Long-Term Development? The Case of Africa in the 1980s*, Queen Elizabeth House/Centro Studi Luea d'Agliano, Development Studies Working Papers No. 42, Oxford.

Cornia, G.A., R. Jolly and F. Stewart (eds) 1987 *Adjustment with a Human Face: Protecting the Vulnerable and Promoting Growth*, Oxford University Press, Oxford.

Cowen, M. and R. Shenton 1995 'The Invention of Development', in J. Crush (ed.) *Power of Development*, Routledge, London and New York.

— 1996 *Doctrines of Development*, Routledge, London.

Cox, R. W. 1986 'Social Forces, States and World Orders: Beyond International Relations Theory', *Millennium* 12 (2): 162–75.

— 1987 *Production, Power and World Order: Social Forces in the Making of History*, Columbia University Press, New York.

Crook, R. C. 1990 'Politics, the Cocoa Crisis, and Administration in Côte d'Ivoire', *Journal of Modern African Studies* 29 (4): 649–69.

— 1995 'Côte d'Ivoire: Multi-Party Democracy and Political Change: Surviving the Crisis', in J. A. Wiseman (ed.) *Democracy and Political Change in Sub-Saharan Africa*, Routledge, London.

Crush, J. 1995 (ed.) *Power of Development*, Routledge, London and New York.

Cullen, D. 1992–93 'Human Rights Quandary', *Foreign Affairs* 75 (2): 79–88.

Curtis, M. 1998 *The Great Deception: Anglo-American Power and World Order*, Pluto Press, London.

Dahl, R. 1979 'Procedural Democracy', in P. Laslett & J. Fishkin (eds) *Philosophy, Politics and Society*, Yale University Press, New Haven, CT.

Dahl, R. A. 1956 A *Preface to Democratic Theory*, University of Chicago Press, Chicago and London.

Davis, L. 1995 'Opening Political Space in Cameroon: The Ambiguous Response of the Mbororo', *Review of African Political Economy* 22 (64): 213–28.

Decalo, S. 1992 'The Process, Prospects and Constraints of Democratization in Africa', *African Affairs* 91 (362): 7–35.

Diamond, L. 1988a 'Introduction: Roots of Failure, Seeds of Hope', in L. Diamond, J. J. Linz and S. M. Lipset (eds) *Democracy in Developing Countries. Volume 2: Africa*, Adamantine Press, London.

— 1988b 'Nigeria: Pluralism, Statism and the Struggle for Democracy', in L. Diamond, J. J. Linz and S. M. Lipset (eds) *Democracy in Developing Countries. Volume 2: Africa*, Adamantine Press, London.

— 1989 'Beyond Authoritarianism and Totalitarianism: Strategies for Democratization', *Washington Quarterly* 12 (1): 141–63.

Diamond, L., J. J. Linz and S. M. Lipset 1988 (eds) *Democracy in Developing Countries. Volume 2: Africa*, Adamantine Press, London.

Di Palma, G. 1990 *To Craft Democracies: An Essay on Democratic Transitions*, University of California Press, Berkeley.

Doty, R. L. 1996 *Imperial Encounters*, University of Minnesota Press, Minneapolis.

Doyle, M. W. 1983a 'Kant, Liberal Legacies and Foreign Affairs', *Philosophy and Public Affairs* 12 (3): 205–35.

— 1983b 'Kant, Liberal Legacies and Foreign Affairs, Part 2', *Philosophy and Public Affairs* 12 (4): 323–54.

— 1997 *Ways of War and Peace*, W. W. Norton & Company, New York.

Dreze, J. and A. Sen 1989 *Hunger and Public Action*, Clarendon Press, Oxford.

Ekeh, P. P. 1992 'The Constitution of Civil Society in African History and Politics', in B. Caron, A. Gboyega and E. Osaghae (eds) *Democratic Transitions in Africa*, Credu, Ibadan.

Elson, D. 1991 'Structural Adjustment: Its Effects on Women', in T. Wallace and C. March (eds) *Changing Perceptions, Writings on Gender and Development*, Oxfam, Oxford.

Emerson, R. 1971 'The Prospects for Democracy in Africa', in M. F. Lofchie (ed.) *The State of the Nations: Constraints on Development in Independent Africa*, University of California Press, Berkeley, CA.

Escobar, A. 1984–85 'Discourse and Power in Development: Michel Foucault and the Relevance of his Work to the Third World', *Alternatives* 19 (3): 377–400.

— 1988 'Power and Visibility: Development and the Invention and Management of the Third World', *Cultural Anthropology* 3 (4): 428–43.

— 1995 *Encountering Development. The Making and Unmaking of the Third World*, Princeton University Press, Princeton, NJ.

Esteva, G. 1992 'Development', in W. Sachs (ed.) *The Development Dictionary: A Guide to Knowledge as Power*, Zed Books, London.

Fanon, F. 1986 *Black Skin, White Masks*, Pluto Press, London.

Fatton, R. Jr. 1995 'Africa in the Age of Democratization: The Civic Limitations of Civil Society', *African Studies Review* 38 (2): 67–99.

Ferguson, J. 1994 *The Anti-Politics Machine: 'Development', Depoliticization and Bureaucratic Power in Lesotho*, University of Minnesota Press, Minneapolis.

Foucault, M. 1970 *The Order of Things: An Archaeology of the Human Sciences*, Tavistock, London.

— 1972 *The Archaeology of Knowledge*, Routledge, London.

— 1980 *Power/Knowledge: Selected Interviews and Other Writings 1972– 1977* (ed. Colin Gordon), Harvester Press, Brighton.

— 1986 *The Uses of Pleasure*, Pantheon Books, New York.

— 1991 *Discipline and Punish: The Birth of the Prison*, Penguin, London.

Friedman, M. 1962 *Capitalism and Freedom*, University of Chicago Press, Chicago.

Fukuyama, F. 1989 'The End of History?', *The National Interest*, 16: 3–5, 8–15.

— 1992 *The End of History and the Last Man*, Hamish Hamilton, London.

Galli, R. 1990 'Liberalization is not Enough: Structural Adjustment and Peasants in Guinea-Bissau', *Review of African Political Economy* 49: 52–68.

Gallie, W. B. 1955–56 'Essentially Contested Concepts', *Proceedings of the Aristotelian Society* 56: 167–98.

Gamble, G. 1988 *The Free Economy and the Strong State*, Macmillan, London.

Gann, L. H. 1988 'The Berlin Conference and the Humanitarian Conscience', in S. Forster, W. J. Mommsen and R. Robinson (eds) *Bismarck, Europe and Africa*, Oxford University Press, Oxford.

Geddes, B. 1995 'Challenging the Conventional Wisdom', in L. Diamond and M. F. Plattner (eds) *Economic Reform and Democracy*, Johns Hopkins University Press, Baltimore, MD and London.

Geisler, G. 1993 'Fair? What has Fairness Got to Do with It? Vagaries of Election Observations and Democratic Standards', *Journal of Modern African Studies* 31 (4): 613–37.

Gendzier, I. L. 1985 *Managing Political Change. Social Scientists and the Third World*, Westview Press, Boulder, CO and London.

Gertzel, C. (ed.) 1984 *The Dynamics of the One-Party State in Zambia*, Manchester University Press, Manchester.

Gibbon, P. 1992 'Structural Adjustment and Pressures toward Multi-partyism in Sub-Saharan Africa', in P. Gibbon, Y. Bangura and A. Ofstad (eds) *Authoritarianism, Democracy and Adjustment: The Politics of Economic Reform in Africa*, Nordiska Afrikainstitutet, Uppsala

— 1993 'The World Bank and the New Politics of Aid', *European Journal of Development Research* 5 (1): 35–62.

Gill, S. (ed.) 1997 *Globalisation, Democratisation and Multilateralism*, Macmillan, London.

Gladwin, C. H. (ed.) 1991 *Structural Adjustment and African Women Farmers*, University of Florida Press, Gainesville.

Goodell, G. and J. P. Powelson 1982 'The Democratic Prerequisties of Development', in R. Gastil (ed.) *Freedom in the World: Political Rights and Civil Liberties*, Freedom House, New York.

Gordon, C. 1991 'Governmental Rationality: An Introduction', in G. Burchell, C. Gordon and P. Miller (eds) *The Foucault Effect: Studies in Governmentality*, University of Chicago Press, Chicago.

Gourevitch, P. 1978 'The Second Image Reversed: the International Sources of Domestic Politics', *International Organization* 32 (4): 881–912.

Griffith-Jones, S. and R. van der Hoeven 1990 *Debt – The Unwanted Heritage of Today's Children*, IDS Discussion Paper No. 280, Institute of Development Studies, Sussex.

Green, R. H. 1988 'Ghana: Progress, Problematics and Limitations of the Success Story', *IDS Bulletin* 19 (1): 7–15.

Gyimah-Boadi, E. 1999 'Ghana: the Challenges of Consolidating Democracy', in R. Joseph (ed.) *State, Conflict and Democracy in Africa*, Lynne Rienner, Boulder, CO.

Hadenius, A. 1992 *Democracy and Development*, Cambridge University Press, Cambridge.

Haggard, S. and R. R. Kaufman 1992 'Economic Adjustment and the Prospects for Democracy', in S. Haggard and R. R. Kaufman (eds) *The Politics of Economic Adjustment*, Princeton University Press, Princeton, NJ.

Hall, J. A. 1995 'In Search of Civil Society', in J. A. Hall (ed.) *Civil Society: Theory, History, Comparison*, Polity Press, Cambridge.

Halliday, F. 1987 'State and Society in International Relations', *Millennium* 16 (2): 215–29.

— 1989 *Cold War, Third World*, Hutchinson Radius, London.

Ham, M. 1992 'Luring Investment', *Africa Report* September/October: 39–41.

Hanlon, J. 1996 *Peace Without Profit: How the IMF Blocks Development in Mozambique*, James Currey, Oxford.

Harbeson, J., D. Rothchild and N. Chazan 1994 (eds) *Civil Society and the State in Africa*, Lynne Rienner, Boulder, CO.

Hawthorn, G. 1993 'Liberalization and "Modern Liberty": Four Southern States', *World Development* 21 (8): 1299–1312.

Haynes, J. 1995 'Ghana: From Personalist to Democratic Rule', in J. Wiseman (ed.) *Democracy and Political Change in Sub-Saharan Africa*, Routledge, London.

Healey, J. and M. Robinson 1992 *Democracy, Governance and Economic Policy: Sub-Saharan Africa in Comparative Perspective*, Overseas Development Institute, London.

Held, D. 1987 *Models of Democracy*, Polity Press, Cambridge.

— 1991 'Democracy and Globalization', *Alternatives* 16: 201–8.

— 1995 *Democracy and the Global Order*, Polity Press, Cambridge.

Herbst, J. 1993 *The Politics of Reform in Ghana, 1982–91*, University of California Press, Berkeley.

Hewlett, S. A. 1979 'Human Rights and Economic Realities: Tradeoffs in Historical Perspective', *Political Science Quarterly* 94 (3): 453–73.

Hibou, B. 1999 'The "Social Capital" of the State as an Agent of Deception', in J.-F. Bayart, S. Ellis and B. Hibou *The Criminalization of the State in Africa*, James Currey, Oxford.

Hippler, J. 1995 'Democratisation of the Third World After the End of the Cold War', in J. Hippler (ed.) *The Democratisation of Disempowerment: The Problem of Democracy in the Third World*, Pluto Press, London.

Hodder, B. W. 1978 *Africa Today: A Short Introduction to African Affairs*, Methuen, London.

Hoffman, J. 1991 'Capitalist Democracies and Democratic States: Oxymorons or Coherent Concepts?', *Political Studies* xxxix: 342–9.

Holm, H.-H. and G. Sørensen 1995 (eds) *Whose World Order? Uneven Globalization and the End of the Cold War*, Westview Press, Boulder, CO and Oxford.

Holmquist, F. W., F. S. Weaver and M. D. Ford 1994 'The Structural Development of Kenya's Political Economy', *African Studies Review* 37 (1): 69–105.

Hoogvelt, A. 1997 *Globalisation and the Postcolonial World: The New Political Economy of Development*, Macmillan, London.

Hoselitz, B. 1965 'Investment in Education and its Political Impact', in J. S. Coleman (ed.) *Education and Political Development*, Princeton University Press, Princeton, NJ.

Human Rights Watch/Africa 1996 *Zambia: Elections and Human Rights in the Third Republic*, Human Rights Watch/Africa, New York.

Huntington, S. P. 1968 *Political Order in Changing Societies*, Yale University Press, New Haven, CT.

— 1984 'Will More Countries Become Democratic?', *Political Science Quarterly* 99 (2): 193–218.

— 1991 *The Third Wave: Democratization in the Late Twentieth Century*, University of Oklahoma Press, Norman and London.

Huntington, S. P. and J. Nelson 1976 *No Easy Choice: Political Participation in Developing Societies*, Harvard University Press, Cambridge, MA.

Hurd, D. 1990 'Promoting Good Government', *Crossbow* Autumn: 4–5.

IDS Bulletin 1993 'The Emergence of the "Good Government" Agenda: Some Milestones', *IDS Bulletin* 24 (1): 7–8.

Ihonvbere, J. O. 1996 *Economic Crisis, Civil Society and Democratization: The Case of Zambia*, Africa World Press, Trenton, NJ and Asmara.

ILO 1981 *Zambia: Basic Needs in an Economy under Pressure*, International Labour Organisation, Addis Ababa.

IMF 1965 *Direction of Trade Statistics. Yearbook*, International Monetary Fund, Washington, DC.

— 1992 *Direction of Trade Statistics. Yearbook*, International Monetary Fund, Washington, DC.

Jackson, R. H. 1990 *Quasi-States: Sovereignty, International Relations, and the Third World*, Cambridge University Press, Cambridge.

Jebuni, C. D. and A. D. Oduro 1998 'Structural Adjustment and the Transition to Democracy', in K. A. Ninsin (ed.) *Ghana: Transition to Democracy*, Codesria Book Series, Dakar.

Jesperson, E. 1993 'External Shocks, Adjustment Policies and Economic and Social Performance', in G. Cornia, R. van der Hoeven and P. Mkandwire (eds) *Africa's Recovery in the 1990s: From Stagnation and Adjustment to Human Development*, St. Martin's Press, New York.

Joseph, R. 1992 'Zambia: A Model for Democratic Change', *Current History*, May: 199–201.

Kant, I. 1983 *Perpetual Peace and Other Essays* (trans. T. Humphrey) Hackett Publishing, Cambridge.

Karl, T. L. 1990 'Dilemmas of Democratization in Latin America', *Comparative Politics* 23 (1): 1–21.

Kasonde, E. 1993 'Budget Speech by the Honourable E. G. Kasonde, MP, Minister of Finance, 29 January 1992', in F. J. T. Chiluba *Democracy in Zambia. Key Speeches of President Chiluba 1991/92* (ed. Donald Chanda), Africa Press Trust, Lusaka.

Keane, J. 1988 *Democracy and Civil Society*, Verso, London.

Kesselman, M. 1973 'Order or Movement? The Literature of Political Development as Ideology', *World Politics* 26 (1): 139–54.

Kegley, C. and E. Wittkopf 1987 *American Foreign Policy: Patterns and Process*, St. Martin's Press, New York and London.

Kipling, R. 1995 *The Complete Verse*, Kyle Cathie, London.

Kohli, A. 1986 'Democracy and Development', in J. Lewis and V. Kallab (eds) *Development Strategies Reconsidered*, Transaction Books, New Brunswick, NJ.

Konadu-Agyemang, K. 1998 'Structural Adjustment Programs and the Perpetuating of Poverty and Underdevelopment in Africa: Ghana's Experience Revisited', *Scandinavian Journal of Development* 17 (2–3): 127–44.

Kraus, J. 1991 'The Political Economy of Stabilization and Structural Adjustment in Ghana', in D. Rothchild (ed.) *Ghana: The Political Economy of Recovery*, Lynne Rienner, Boulder, CO.

Lal, D. 1983 *The Poverty of 'Development Economics'*, Hobart Paperback 16, IEA, London.

Lancaster, C. 1993 'Governance and Development: The Views from Washington', *IDS Bulletin* 24 (1): 9–15.

Landell-Mills, P. 1992 'Governance, Cultural Change and Empowerment', *Journal of Modern African Studies* 30 (4): 543–67.

Landell-Mills, P. and I. Serageldin 1991 'Governance and the External Factor', *Proceedings of the World Bank Annual Conference on Development Economics 1991*, Washington, DC.

Latham, R. 1993 'Democracy and War-Making: Locating the International Liberal Context', *Millennium* 22 (2): 139–64.

Leftwich, A. 1993 'Governance, Democracy and Development in the Third World', *Third World Quarterly* 14 (3): 605–24.

Levy, M. 1966 *Modernization and the Structures of Society*, Princeton University Press, Princeton, NJ.

Light, M. 1991 'Soviet Policy in the Third World', *International Affairs* 67 (2): 263–80.

— 1992 'Moscow's Retreat from Africa', *Journal of Communist Studies* 8 (2): 21–40.

Linz, J. J. 1990 'Transitions to Democracy', *Washington Quarterly* 13 (3): 143–64.

Lipset, S. M. 1960 *Political Man: The Social Basis of Politics*, Heinemann, London.

Lockwood, M. 1992 *Engendering Adjustment or Adjusting Gender? Some New Approaches to Women and Development in Africa*, IDS Discussion Paper 315, Institute of Development Studies, Sussex.

Lowenthal, A. F. (ed.) 1991 *Exporting Democracy: The United States and Latin America*, Johns Hopkins University Press, Baltimore, MD and London.

Macpherson, C. B. 1977 *The Life and Times of Liberal Democracy*, Oxford University Press, Oxford.

McCleary, W. A. 1989 'Policy Implementation under Adjustment Lending', *Finance and Development*, March.

McGrew, A. (ed.) 1997 *The Transformation of Democracy*, Polity Press, Cambridge.

Mamdani, M. 1995 'Democratization and Marketization', in K. Mengisteab and B. I. Logan (eds) *Beyond Economic Liberalization in Africa: Structural Adjustment and the Alternatives*, Zed Books, London.

Manor, J. (ed.) 1991 *Rethinking Third World Politics*, Longman, London.

Manzo, K. 1991 'Modernist Discourse and the Crisis of Development Theory', *Studies in Comparative International Development* 26 (2): 3–36.

Manzo, K. 1995 'Black Consciousness and the Quest for a Counter-Modernist Development', in J. Crush (ed.) *Power of Development*, Routledge, London.

Maravall, J. M. 1995 'The Myth of the Authoritarian Advantage', in L. Diamond and M. F. Plattner (eds) *Economic Reform and Democracy*, Johns Hopkins Univeristy Press, Baltimore, MD and London.

Martin, G. 1995 'Francophone Africa in the Context of Franco-African Relations', in J. W. Habeson and D. Rothchild (eds) *Africa in World Politics: Post-Cold War Challenges*, Westview Press, Boulder, CO.

Marx, K. 1963 *The 18th Brumaire of Louis Bonaparte*, International Publishers, New York.

Memmi, A. 1967 *The Coloniser and the Colonised*, Beacon Press, Boston, MA.

Mengisteab, K. 1995 'A Partnership of the State and the Market in African Development: What is the Appropriate Strategy Mix?', in K. Mengisteab and B. I. Logan (eds) *Beyond Economic Liberalization in Africa: Structural Adjustment and the Alternatives*, Zed Books, London.

Miliband, R. 1992 'Fukuyama and the Socialist Alternative', *New Left Review* No. 193, May/June: 108–13.

Mill, J. S. 1976 'Considerations on Representative Government', in H. B. Acton (ed.) *Utilitarianism, On Liberty, and Considerations on Representative Government*, Dent & Sons, London.

MIT 1968 *The Role of Popular Participation in Development*, Massachusetts Institute of Technology, Report 17, Report of the Conference on the Implementation of the Title IX of the Foreign Assistance Act, 24 June–2 August, MIT Press, Cambridge, MA.

Mkandawire, T. 1999 'Crisis Management and the Making of "Choiceless Democracies"', in R. Joseph (ed.) *State, Conflict, and Democracy in Africa*, Lynne Rienner, Boulder, CO.

MMD 1991 *The MMD Campaign Manifesto*, in F. J. T. Chiluba (1993) *Democracy in Zambia. Key Speeches of President Chiluba 1991/92* (ed. D. Chanda), Africa Press Trust, Lusaka.

Moore, B. Jr. 1991 *The Social Origins of Dictatorship and Democracy* (first published 1966), Penguin Books, London.

Moore, M. 1993 'Declining to Learn from the East? The World Bank on "Governance and Development"', *IDS Bulletin* 24 (1): 39–50.

Morris-Jones, W. H. 1954 'In Defense of Apathy', *Political Studies* 2: 25–37.

Moser, C. O. N. 1991 'Gender Planning in the Third World: Meeting Practical and Strategic Gender Needs', in T. Wallace and C. March (eds) *Changing Perceptions: Writings on Gender and Development*, Oxfam, Oxford.

Mosely, P., J. Harrigan and J. Toye 1991 *Aid and Power: The World Bank and Policy Based Lending*, Volume 1, Routledge, London.

Mosely, P. and J. Weeks 1993 'Has Recovery Begun? Africa's Adjustment in the 1980s Revisited', *World Development* 21 (10): 1583–606.

Moss, T. J. 1995 'US Policy and Democratisation in Africa: The Limits of Liberal Universalism', *Journal of Modern African Studies* 33 (2): 189–209.

Müller, E. N. 1985 'Dependent Economic Development, Aid Dependence on the United States, and Democratic Breakdown in the Third World', *International Studies Quarterly* 29: 445–69.

Mwanza, A. M. (ed.) 1992 *The Structural Adjustment Programme in Zambia: Lessons from Experience*, SAPES Books, Harare.

Nandy, A. 1983 *The Intimate Enemy: Loss and Recovery of Self under Colonialism*, Oxford University Press, Delhi.

Ncube, P. D., M. Sakala and M. Ndulo 1987 'The International Monetary Fund and the Zambian Economy – A Case Study', in K. J. Havnevik (ed.) *The IMF and the World Bank in Africa: Conditionality, Impact and Alternatives*, Scandinavian Institute of African Affairs, Uppsala.

Nehru, B. K. 1979 'Western Democracy and the Third World', *Third World Quarterly* 1 (2): 223–35.

Norgaard, R. B. 1994 *Development Betrayed: The End of Progress and a Coevolutionary Revisioning of the Future*, Routledge, London.

Nordlinger, E. 1970 'Soldiers in Mufti: The Political Impact of Military Rule upon Economic and Social Change in Non-Western States', *American Political Science Review* 64: 1131–48.

Novichi, M. A. 1992 'Zambia: A Lesson in Democracy', *Africa Report*, November/December: 13–17.

Nyerere, J. 1968 *Freedom and Socialism*, Oxford University Press, Dar Es Salaam.

O'Brien, D. C. 1979 'Modernization, Order and the Erosion of a Democratic Ideal: American Political Science 1960–70', in D. Lehmann (ed.) *Development Theory: Four Critical Studies*, Frank Cass, London.

O'Donnell, G. and P. Schmitter 1986 *Transitions from Authoritarian Rule. Volume 4: Tentative Conclusions about Uncertain Democracies*, Johns Hopkins University Press, Baltimore, MD and London.

O' Donnell, G., P. Schmitter and L. Whitehead (eds) 1986 *Transitions from Authoritarian Rule: Prospects for Democracy. Volumes 1–4*, Johns Hopkins University Press, Baltimore, MD and London.

O'Neill, K. and B. Munslow 1995 'Angola: Ending the Cold War in Southern Africa', in O. Furley (ed.) *Conflict in Africa*, I.B.Tauris, London and New York.

Onimode, B. (ed.) 1989 *The IMF, the World Bank and the African Debt. Volume 2: The Social and Political Impact*, Zed Books, London.

ODA 1993 *Taking Account of Good Government*, Overseas Development Agency Technical Note No. 10, Government and Institutions Dept, ODA, London.

ODI 1992 *Aid and Political Reform*, Briefing Paper, January, Overseas Development Institute, London.

Owusu, M. 1992 'Democracy and Africa – A View from the Village', *Journal of Modern African Studies* 30 (3): 369–96.

Packenham, R. A. 1966 'Political-Development Doctrines in the American Foreign Aid Program', *World Politics* 18 (2): 194–235.

Pateman, C. 1970 *Participation and Democratic Theory*, Cambridge University Press, Cambridge.

Ponte, S. 1994 'The World Bank and Adjustment in Africa', *Review of African Political Economy* 66: 539–58.

Pool, I. de Sola (ed.) 1967 *Contemporary Political Science: Towards Empirical Theory*, McGraw-Hill, New York.

Proccacci, G. 1991 'Social Economy and the Government of Poverty', in G. Burchell, C. Gordon and P. Miller (eds) *The Foucault Effect: Studies in Governmentality*, University of Chicago Press, Chicago.

Przeworski, A. 1991 *Democracy and the Market: Political and Economic Reforms in Eastern Europe and Latin America*, Cambridge University Press, Cambridge.

— 1999 'Minimalist Conception of Democracy: A Defense', in I. Shapiro and C. Hacker-Cordon (eds) *Democracy's Value*, Cambridge University Press, Cambridge.

Przeworski, A. and F. Limongi 1997 'Development and Democracy', in A. Hadenius (ed.) *Democracy's Victory and Crisis*, Cambridge University Press, Cambridge.

Pye, L. 1966 *Aspects of Political Development*, Little, Brown, Boston, MA.

Rao, V. 1984/85 'Democracy and Economic Development', *Studies in Comparative International Development* 19 (4): 67–81.

Remmer, K. L. 1985/86 'Exclusionary Democracy', *Studies in Comparative International Development* 20 (4): 64–85.

— 1990 'Democracy and Economic Crisis: The Latin American Experience', *World Politics* 42 (3): 315–35.

— 1995 'New Theoretical Perspectives on Democratization', *Comparative Politics* 28 (1): 103–22.

Reno, W. 1998 *Warlord Politics and African States,* Lynne Rienner, Boulder, CO.

Riddell, R. C. 1999 'The End of Foreign Aid to Africa? Concerns about Donor Policies', *African Affairs* 98 (392): 309–35.

Riley, S. P. 1992 'Political Adjustment or Domestic Pressure: Democratic Politics and Political Choice in Africa', *Third World Quarterly* 13 (3): 539–51.

Rist, G. 1997 *The History of Development: From Western Origin to Global Faith,* Zed Books, London.

Robertson, A. F. 1984 *People and the State: An Anthropology of Planned Development,* Cambridge University Press, New York.

Robinson, M. 1993 'Will Political Conditionality Work?', *IDS Bulletin* 24 (1): 58–66.

— 1994 'Governance, Democracy and Conditionality: NGOs and the New Policy Agenda', in A. Clayton (ed.) *Governance, Democracy and Conditionality: What Role for NGOs?,* INTRAC, Oxford.

— 1996 'Economic Reform and the Transition to Democracy', in R. Luckham and G. White (eds) *Democratization in the South: The Jagged Wave,* Manchester University Press, Manchester and New York.

Rostow, W. W. 1960 *The Stages of Ecomomic Growth: A Non-Communist Manifesto,* Cambridge University Press, Cambridge.

Rousseau, J.-J. 1968 *The Social Contract,* Penguin, London.

Roy, A. 1999 *The Cost of Living,* Flamingo, London.

Rueschemeyer, D., E. H. Stephens and J. D. Stephens 1992 *Capitalist Development and Democracy,* Polity Press, Cambridge.

Russett, B. 1993 *Grasping the Democratic Peace: Principles for a Post-Cold War World,* Princeton University Press, Princeton, NJ.

Rustow, D. A. 1970 'Transitions to Democracy: Toward a Dynamic Model', *Comparative Politics* 2 (3): 337–63.

Sachs, W. (ed.) 1992 *The Development Dictionary: A Guide to Knowledge and Power,* Zed Books, London.

Said, E. 1979 *Orientalism,* Vintage Books, New York.

Saine, A. S. M. 1995 'Democracy in Africa: Constraints and Prospects', in K. Mengisteab and B. I. Logan (eds) *Beyond Economic Liberalization in Africa: Structural Adjustment and the Alternatives,* Zed Books, London.

Sandbrook, R. 1988 'Liberal Democracy in Africa: A Socialist-Revisionist Perspective', *Canadian Journal of African Studies* 22 (2): 240–67.

Sartori, G. 1962 *Democratic Theory,* Wayne State University Press, Detroit.

Schatz, S. P. 1994 'Structural Adjustment in Africa: A Failing Grade So Far', *Journal of Modern African Studies* 32 (4): 679–92.

Schatz, S. P. 1996 'The World Bank's Fundamental Misconception in Africa', *Journal of Modern African Studies* 34 (2): 239–47.

Schraeder, P. J. 1995 'Political Elites in the Process of Democratisation in Africa', in J. Hippler (ed.) *The Democratisation of Disempowerment. The Problem of Democracy in the Third World*, Pluto Press, London.

Schumpeter, J. A. 1976 *Capitalism, Socialism and Democracy*, Allen & Unwin, London.

Shearman, P. 1987 'Gorbachev and the Third World: An Era of Reform?', *Third World Quarterly* 9 (4): 1083–117.

Shihata, I. F. I. 1991 *The World Bank in a Changing World: Selected Essays*, Martinus Nijhoff, Dordrecht.

Shils, E. 1964 'The Military in the Development of New States', in J. Johnson (ed.) *The Military and Society in Latin America*, Stanford University Press, Palo Alto, CA.

Short, C. 1999 *Speech by the Rt Hon. Clare Short to the Labour Party Conference*, 30 September, Bournemouth.

Shrestha, N. 1995 'Becoming a Development Category', in J. Crush (ed.) *Power of Development*, Routledge, London.

Shuurman, F. J. (ed.) 1993 *Beyond the Impasse: New Directions in Development Theory*, Zed Books, London.

Sirowy, L. and A. Inkeles 1990 'The Effects of Democracy on Economic Growth and Inequality: A Review', *Studies in Comparative International Development* 25 (1): 126–57.

Skinner, Q. 1973 'The Empirical Theorists of Democracy and Their Critics: A Plague on Both Their Houses', *Political Theory* 1 (3): 287–306.

Stewart, F. 1991 'The Many Faces of Adjustment', *World Development* 19 (12): 1847–64.

Sørensen, G. 1993a 'Introduction', in G. Sørensen (ed.) 'Political Conditionality', *European Journal of Development Research* 5 (1): 1–5.

— 1993b *Democracy and Democratization. Processes and Prospects in a Changing World*, Westview Press, Boulder, CO and Oxford.

Tarp, F. 1993 *Stabilization and Structural Adjustment: Macroeconomic Frameworks for Analysing the Crisis in Sub-Saharan Africa*, Routledge, London and New York.

Taylor, C. 1990 'Models of Civil Society', *Public Culture* 3 (1): 95–118.

Therborn, G. 1983 'The Rule of Capital and the Rise of Democracy', in D. Held et al. (eds) *States and Societies*, Basil Blackwell, Oxford.

Thomas, B. P. 1988 'State Formation, Development and the Politics of Self-Help in Kenya', *Studies in Comparative International Development* 23 (3): 3–27.

Thornton, J. 1992 *Africa and the Africans in the Formation of the Atlantic World, 1400–1680*, Cambridge University Press, Cambridge.

Toye, J. 1987 *Dilemmas of Development: Reflections on the Counter-Revolution in Development Theory*, Basil Blackwell, Oxford.

— 1992 'Interest Group Politics and the Implementation of Adjustment Policies in Sub-Saharan Africa', in P. Gibbon, Y. Bangura and A. Ofstad (eds) *Authoritarianism, Democracy and Adjustment: The Politics of Economic Reform in Africa*, Nordiska Afrika Institutet, Uppsala.

Truman, H. 1949 *Public Papers of the President*, 20 January, United States Government Printing Office, Washington, DC.

UN 1995 *Our Global Neighbourhood*, The Report of The Commission on Global Govern-ance, Oxford University Press, Oxford.

UNECA 1989a *African Alternative Framework to Structural Adjustment Programmes for Socio-Economic Recovery and Transformation (AAF–SAP)*, United Nations Economic Commission for Africa, Addis Ababa.

— 1989b *Statistics and Policies: Preliminary Observations on the World Bank Report 'Africa's Adjustment and Growth in the 1980s'*, United Nations Economic Commission for Africa, Addis Ababa.

USAID 1990 *The Democracy Initiative*, USAID Strategy Papers, US Agency for Inter-national Development, Washington, DC.

Uvin, P. 1993 '"Do as I Say, Not as I Do": The Limits of Political Conditionality', *European Journal of Development Research* 5 (1): 63–84.

van de Walle, N. 1994 'Neopatrimonialism and Democracy in Africa, with an Illustration from Cameroon', in J. A. Widner (ed.) *Economic Change and Political Liberalization in Sub-Saharan Africa*, Johns Hopkins University Press, Baltimore, MD.

— 1995 Crisis and Opportunity in Africa, in L. Diamond and M. F. Plattner (eds) *Economic Reform and Democracy*, Johns Hopkins University Press, Baltimore, MD and London.

Walzer, M. 1991 'The Idea of Civil Society', *Dissent* (Spring): 293–304.

Wank, D. L. 1995 'Civil Society in Communist China? Private Business and Political Alliance', in J. A. Hall (ed.) *Civil Society: Theory, History, Comparison*, Polity Press, Cambridge.

Watkins, K. 1995 'Aid Under Threat', *Review of African Political Economy* 66: 517–23.

Weber, M. 1970 'Politics as Vocation', in H. H. Gerth and C. W. Mills (eds) *From Max Weber*, Routledge & Kegan Paul, London.

White, G. 1994 'Civil Society, Democratization and Development (I): Clearing the Ana-lytical Ground', *Democratization* 1 (3): 375–90.

— 1995 'Civil Society, Democratization and Development (II): Two Country Cases', *Democratization* 2 (2): 56–84.

Whitehead, L. 1986 'International Aspects of Democratization', in G. O'Donnell, P. C. Schmitter and L. Whitehead *Transitions From Authoritarian Rule: Prospects for Demo-cracy. Volume 3*, Johns Hopkins University Press, Baltimore, MD and London.

— 1993a 'Introduction: Some Insights from Western Social Theory', *World Development* 21 (8): 1245–61.

Whitehead, L. 1993b 'On "Reform of the State" and "Regulation of the Market"', *World Development* 21 (8): 1371–93.

Widner, J. A. (ed.) 1994 *Economic Change and Political Liberalization in Sub-Saharan Africa*, Johns Hopkins University Press, Baltimore, MD and London.

Williams, D. and T. Young 1994 'Governance, the World Bank and Liberal Theory', *Political Studies* XLII: 84–100.

Williamson, J. 1993 'Democracy and the "Washington Consensus"', *World Development* 21 (8): 1329–36.

Wiseman, J. A. 1993 'Democracy and the New Political Pluralism in Africa: Causes, Consequences and Significance', *Third World Quarterly* 14 (93): 439–49.

— 1995 'Introduction: The Movement Towards Democracy. Global, Continental and State Perspectives', in J. A. Wiseman (ed.) *Democracy and Political Change in Sub-Saharan Africa*, Routledge, London and New York.

World Bank 1989 *Sub-Saharan Africa: From Crisis to Sustainable Growth*, World Bank, Washington, DC.

— 1992a *Governance and Development*, World Bank, Washington, DC.

— 1992b *World Development Report*, Oxford University Press, Oxford.

— 1993 *Zambia: Prospects for Sustainable and Equitable Growth*, Country Operations Division, World Bank, Washington, DC.

— 1994a *Adjustment in Africa: Reforms, Results and the Road Ahead*, World Bank Policy Research Unit, Washington, DC.

— 1994b *Governance: The World Bank's Experience*, World Bank, Washington, DC.

— 1994c *World Development Report*, Oxford University Press, Oxford.

— 1995 *World Development Report*, Oxford University Press, Oxford.

— 1998/1999 *World Development Report*, World Bank, Washington, DC.

— 1999/2000 *World Development Repor*, World Bank, Washington, DC.

World Bank/UNDP 1989 *Africa's Adjustment in the 1980s*, World Bank, Washington, DC.

Yeebo, Z. 1991 *Ghana: The Struggle for Popular Power*, New Beacon Books, London.

Young, C. 1991 'Democratization and Structural Adjustment: A Political Overview', in L. Deng, M. Kostner and C. Young (eds) *Democratization and Structural Adjustment in Africa in the 1990s*, African Studies Program, University of Wisconsin, Madison.

Zack-Williams, A. B. 1990 'Sierra Leone: Crisis and Despair', *Review of African Political Economy* 49: 22–33.

Zartman, I. W. (ed.) 1995 *Collapsed States: The Disintegration and Restoration of Legitimate Authority*, Lynne Rienner, Boulder, CO.

Zolberg, A. 1966 *Creating Political Order: The Party States of West Africa*, Rand McNally, Chicago.

Periodicals and Newspapers

Africa Confidential, 1985–2000.

Africa Review, 1985–1999.

Africa South of the Sahara, 1990–1999.

The Economist, 1993a 'Kenya: Shocked, Shocked – A Little', 9 January: 47.

— 1993b 'Zambia: The Miseries of Modeldom', 20 February: 68.

— 1993c 'Zambia: Blame the IMF', 20 November: 73.

— 1994a 'Africa: A Flicker of Light', 5 March: 21–22.

— 1994b 'Why Voting Is Good For You', 27 August: 17.

— 1997 'An African Success Story', 14 June: 77.

Keesings Record of World Events, 1990–1998.

Southern Africa Political and Economic Monthly, 1992.

Eagle Express, 31 October 1991, Lusaka.

Financial Times, 4 March 1997, London.

Ghana Chronicle various (Africa News Online).

Guardian, 17 June 1995, London.

Klassekampen, 15 November 1991, Oslo.
The Mail & Guardian, various, South Africa.
The Times, 7 March 1997, London.
Times of Zambia, various, Lusaka.
Weekly Post, various, Lusaka.
The Post, various, Lusaka.
Zambia Daily Mail, various, Lusaka.

Index

Africa: crisis in, 10; disengagement from, 33; dispensability of, 34; integration into world capitalism, 7; social power structures in, 56

aid: conditionality of, 3, 32, 103, 109, 134, 135 (applied by IMF, 142); dependency on, 98, 118; to Africa, 113 (decline in, 34) *see also* donors of aid

Anglo American Corporation, 121

Angola, disengagement from, 33

apathy, value of, 70–2

austerity, 99, 123; protests against, 117, 122, 124, 135

authoritarian regimes, 116, 117; economic performance of, 2–3

Bandung Conference, 21

Bayart, J.-F., 63

Bedie, Henri Konan, 124, 125, 126

Benin, 5, 98

Berlin Conference, 36

Bhabha, Homi, 22

Black Mamba organisation (Zambia), 130

bourgeoisie: as agent of democracy, 62–4; as inherently democratic, 65; in Africa, 62; property rights of, 80

Boutros-Ghali, Boutros, 35

Bretton Woods institutions, 11, 12, 29, 37, 38, 39, 83, 88, 92, 94, 98, 104, 105, 107, 118, 122, 123, 134, 139, 145, 147 *see also* World Bank *and* International Monetary Fund

business community, strengthening of, 61–2

capitalism: and democracy, 76–7; as integral to African culture, 50; indigenous democratic, 47–52; state-, 49

censorship of the press, 125

Central African Republic, 29

Chad, 29, 33

Chalker, Lynda, 11, 106

change, external and internal factors of, xi, 1, 3, 5, 6, 7, 8, 9

Chile, amnesty from prosecution, 79

Chiluba, Frederick, 5, 89, 106, 118, 120, 128, 130, 132–3

China, 4

Chinese, as entrepreneurial class, 64

civil and political rights, xv

civil services, cutting of, 135

civil society, 54, 65, 76; as countervailing power of state, 52; emergence of, 86; in Africa, 55; in the West, 62; in World Bank discourse, 53; liberating of, 52–6; relation to democratisation, 55–6; segmented nature of, 55; viewed as homogeneous, 56

Clinton, Bill, 35

Cold War, x, xii, 2, 8, 19, 27, 28, 29, 70, 103, 108; end of, 3, 26, 32–6, 37, 44, 143; hostilities in Africa, 32

colonialism, 7, 11, 22, 36

communism, 17; collapse of, 2, 3, 4, 26, 32, 34, 43, 143; containment of, 36; fear of, 19

community responsibility, 59

Congo, 33

Constant, Benjamin, 76

Cook, Robin, 51

corruption, 3, 41, 91, 97, 115, 126, 131, 132

cost recovery, 56–9

cost-sharing, 65

Côte d'Ivoire, xi, xiii, 33, 86, 87, 96–7, 103, 108, 124; austerity in, 96; military coup in, 125–7
cultural sensitivity, xii

Dahl, Robert, 71
de-industrialisation, 124
debt, 96, 110; relief of, 119
democracy, 12, 13, 23, 25, 34–5, 36, 45, 52, 64, 72, 98, 99–100, 103, 106, 107, 131, 139; and avoidance of catastrophes, 78; arriving from top-down, 80; as characteristic political form of capitalism, 76; as contested concept, 67, 68; capitalist, 77; changing face of, 26–32; choiceless, 145; definitions of, 68, 69, 72, 74, 109; deterioration of, xiv, 112–37; dissociated from economic structures, 74; establishment of, 63; exclusionary, xiv, 113, 132–5, 140; failure of, in Africa, 109; fragility of, 82, 127, 136; left theories of, 75; liberal, x, xiii, 26, 29, 30, 70, 110, 146; of lowered expectations, 79; poverty as obstacle to, 141; relationship with economic growth, 113–15; relationship with structural adjustment, 141; rise of, in the West, 62; robustness of, 114; theory of, xii, 68–76; transition to, 22; uncertainty of, 75, 78; universal suffrage, 69; within development discourse, 29, 30
democratic demands, economic roots of, 87–98
democratic diffusion, 4, 9
democratic elitism, 69, 71, 118
democratic pacts, 79–80
democratic revival in Africa, explanation of, 2–6
democratic wave, metaphor of, 4
democratisation, ix, xi, x, xiii, 1–24, 51, 55, 104, 132; causes of, 9; donor pressure for, 3
dependency, 7; culture of, 133
devaluation: of Cedi (Ghana), 92, 93, 95; of Kwacha (Zambia), 88, 89
development: alternative forms of, 21; anti-communist function of, 19; as

contested terrain, ix; as way of accessing third world, 20; belief in, 47; broadening of, 31; hierarchies of, 19; institutionalisation of, 16; invention of, 13–22; problematisation of, 19
development discourse, 1–24; achieves status of truth, 21, 22; new, 25–46; non-neutrality of, 2; seductiveness of, 144
development industry, ix
Djibouti, 29
domino effect, 4
donors of aid, 4; aid withheld, 90; power of, xiv

economic liberalism and liberalisation, x, xiv, 51, 52, 57, 61, 63, 64, 65, 76, 77, 79, 83, 84, 89, 109, 110, 112–37, 145; failure of, 143; relationship with democratisation, 56, 86, 139
education, 100; cuts in, 93; danger of, 28
elections, 83; as check on governments, 115; fairness of, 81
elites, formation of, 7
empowerment, 64, 65, 132, 144; of 'ordinary people', 143; through cost recovery, 56–9
'enabling environment', 105
Escobar, A., 14, 21
Ethiopia, 28, 33
Eurocentrism, 6
European Council, 31
exclusionary democracy see democracy, exclusionary

fascism, 70
fear, as category, 17
food riots see riots, over food
Forum for the Restoration of Democracy (FORD), 101–2 (Kenya)
Foucault, Michel, 14, 138
France, 33, 108; aid policy of, 31, 108
Friedman, Milton, 76
Fukuyama, Francis, 36, 76

Gabon, 33
Ghana, xi, xiii, 39, 86, 87, 91–6, 98,

102, 103, 107–8, 122–3, 130–1;
Economic Recovery Programme
(ERP), 92; growth record of, 92
Ghana Trade Union Congress (TUC),
94–5
globalisation, 8, 9, 145, 146
good governance and its agenda, ix, x,
xi, xii, 11, 12, 22, 23, 25, 28, 31, 36,
37, 40, 41, 42, 44, 51, 56, 57, 86,
104, 113, 116; analysis of, xii; as
constructed by World Bank, 48; as
discursive formation, 26; as
modernisation theory, 59–64;
criticism of, 34; emergence of, 1, 32;
lack of success of, xiv; seductiveness
of, 47–66; success of discourse,
138–47 *see also* governance *and*
World Bank
Gorbachev, Mikhail, 32–3
governance: crisis of, 30, 41; emergence
of term, 71; poor, 43
growth, economic, 25, 27, 31, 40, 42,
43; stages of, 18
Guei, General Robert, 127

Harambee movement, Kenya, 57
health care, reduction of, 93
home-grown solutions, need for, 60
Houphouet-Boigny, Félix, 96, 103, 108,
124
human rights, 29, 31; abuses of, 3
Huntington, S.P., 4, 28, 68, 73, 79, 80
Hurd, Douglas, 31, 36, 51

India, democratic politics in, 78
industrialisation, 48
informal sector, 50
International Monetary Fund (IMF),
xii, 8, 10, 11, 12, 30, 37, 44, 88, 90,
95, 96, 99, 104, 106, 118, 120, 125,
134, 135, 145
International Relations, 7
Islam, 126

Kant, Immanuel, *Perpetual Peace*, 35
Kaunda, Kenneth, 87, 89, 91, 99, 104,
105, 106, 107, 118, 119, 129, 130;
citizenship of, 129
Kenya, xi, xiii, 28, 29, 33, 86, 87, 98,
101–3, 108, 122, 131–2; elections in,
4

Keynes, John Maynard, 12
Keynesianism, retreat from, 29
Kume Preko movement (Ghana), 122

land, communal ownership of, 61
land titling, 61
Leakey, Dr Richard, 132
liberalisation, political, 116
Liberia, 28, 33, 55
Lipset, S.M., 68, 70, 141

Mandela, Nelson, 5
Marx, Karl, 15
Massachusetts Institute of Technology,
report, 28
Mill, John Stuart, 70, 73
Mine Workers' Union (Zambia), 91
Mitterrand, François, 31, 108
modernisation, xii, 28, 61; dash for, 48,
49, 50; theory, 2, 59–64
modernity, 26
Moi, Daniel Arap, 4, 101, 102, 108,
131–2
Moore, Barrington, 62
Movement for Freedom and Justice
(MFJ) (Ghana), 102
Movement for Multiparty Democracy
(MMD) (Zambia), 100–1, 104, 105,
106, 118–21, 123–4, 128–30, 133
Mozambique, 33, 142
multi-party politics *see* political
pluralism

Namibia, 5; independence of, 33
nation states, sovereignty of, 146
National Democratic Congress (NDC)
(Ghana), 131
National Endowment for Democracy
(NED) (USA), 106
National Reform Party (Ghana), 131
National Tobacco Company (Zambia),
119
National Union of Ghana Students, 95
neo-liberalism, 9, 29, 30, 37, 39, 42, 43,
142
New Economic Recovery Programme
(Zambia), 90
New World Order, 25–46
Nicaragua, 105
Non-Aligned Movement, 21

North–South relations, xi, 2, 14, 17, 21, 22, 23, 139, 144, 147
Notre Dame de la Paix (Côte d'Ivoire), 97
Nyerere, Julius, 5

O'Donnell, G.P., 5–6, 79, 80–1
Odinga, Jaranogi Oginga, 101
one-party government, 4, 5
Organisation for Economic Cooperation and Development (OECD), 31
Orientalism, as systematic discipline, 15
Ouattara, Allasane, 108, 124, 125–7

parallel markets, emergence of, 54
Parsons, Talcott, 26
participation, 67, 71, 72, 73; associated with extremism, 70
pluralism, 4, 31
political, definitions of, 75
political legitimacy, 51
political pluralism, ix, xi, xiii, 1, 91, 107, 112, 113, 117, 122, 133, 141, 143, 145
politics, denial of, 144
poor people, 133, 141, 142; assistance for, 17–18; in Ghana, 91; in Zambia, 89; incorporation into political process, xiii; political parties of, marginalised, 82
population, problem of, 20
poverty, xiv, 14, 20, 47, 78, 99, 100, 102, 116, 122, 124; as breeding-ground for communism, 19; democratisation of, 67–85; growth of, 91; in Ghana, 93; increased by structural adjustment programmes, 40; obstacle to democracy, 141; reduced to technical problem, 144 *see also* poor people
power, exclusive to the state, 54, 56, 57
power–knowledge nexus, 13, 25, 26, 42; and invention of development, 13–22
private enterprise, 62
privatisation, 10, 93, 118–19, 120, 121, 124, 132
pro-democracy movements, 10, 44, 84, 86, 109; composition of, 100; emergence of, 3

Programme of Action to Mitigate the Social Costs of Adjustment (PAMSCAD) (Ghana), 94
progress, belief in, 15
Provisional National Defence Council (PNDC) (Ghana), 91–2, 94, 95
Przeworski, A., 140–1
public sector, job losses, 93–4
public services, cuts in, 88, 133

Rawlings, Flight Lieutenant Jerry, 91–2, 95, 96, 107–8, 131, 133; call for resignation of, 122
regime of truth, 13
riots; in Côte d'Ivoire, 97; over food, 91, 99, 100, 104
Rostow, W.W., 18
Rousseau, J.-J., 70; *The Social Contract*, 73
Rwanda, 55

Saba Saba, Kenya, demonstrations in, 131
Said, Edward, *Orientalism*, 13–15
structural adjustment programmes, xii, xiii, xiv, 9–13, 30, 51, 52, 53, 56, 58, 63, 86, 89, 105, 107, 112, 116, 117, 120, 121, 123, 125, 132, 134, 136, 139, 140, 142, 143, 145, 146; demonstrations against, 10; failure of, 26, 32, 37–42; 'ownership' of, 134; relationship with democratisation, 86; rioting against, 91, 97; role in increasing poverty, 40; support for, 98–109; types of, 37
Schmitter, P., 79, 80–1
Schumpeter, Joseph, xii, 69, 71, 74
Somalia, 28, 33, 55
soullessness of the masses, 69, 72
South Africa, 124
state: African, poor performance of, 50; as foreign invention, 49; autonomous sovereign, 146; distrust of, 55; dominance of, 52; interdependence with society, 8; post-colonial, 48; quasi-, 146; reduction of, 38, 41, 42, 50, 53, 54, 55, 58, 59, 84; rhizome form of, 63; role of, 8; seen as oppressive, 67
status quo, maintenance of, 76–82

strikes, 97, 119, 122, 123, 135; in Côte d'Ivoire, 124; in Ghana, 95; in Zambia, 91
students, 97, 122; protests in Gabon, 98; protests in Kenya, 98
subsidies, removal of, 88, 89, 123, 124
Sudan, 28

Tanzania, 5
third world, 21, 22, 27, 28, 36; as object of intervention, 6; as subject of development, 20; construction of, 15 (as underdeveloped, xi, 1); denial of effective agency of, 6; viewed as homogeneous, 18; Western hegemony over, 42–3
trade unions, 3, 5, 100, 114
tradition, 61; of family and ethnic ties, 60
traditional society, 26; strengths of, 48–9
Truman, Harry, inaugural address, 15, 16, 17, 18, 20

Uganda, 142
underdevelopment, 14, 16, 20, 21, 139; as absences and deficiencies, 18, 32; invention of, 15
UNICEF, *Adjustment with a Human Face*, 40
Union of Soviet Socialist Republics (USSR), 92; foreign policy of, 32–3
United National Independence Party (UNIP) (Zambia), 90, 91, 100, 101, 104, 105, 106, 124, 127, 128, 129, 130
United Kingdom (UK): closure of embassies, 33; view of aid, 31
United Nations Development Programme (UNDP), 20
United Nations Economic Commission for Africa (UNECA), 38
United States of America (USA), 33, 43, 105, 107; aid to Africa, 28, 31, 35, 36; foreign policy of, 35; pre-eminence of, 16, 20; view of aid, 142
universalism, liberal, 35
University of Ghana, closure of, 95
urbanisation, 27
US Agency for International Development (USAID), 31
user charges introduced, 58, 91; for hospitals, 93

value added tax, imposed in Ghana, 122–3
voluntary organisations, 59; emergence of, 54; growth of, 53

Washington consensus, x, 142, 145
Weber, Max, xii, 69, 71, 72
welfare rights, 79
Wina, Arthur, 106
women: make up shortfall in public services, 58; participation of, 58
World Bank, xii, 10, 11, 12–13, 20, 25, 30, 32, 37, 38, 40, 44, 51, 52, 53, 58, 61, 88, 90, 95, 96, 99, 104, 105, 106, 116, 123, 132, 134, 135, 144, 145; *Adjustment in Africa …*, 38–9, 42; Articles of Agreement, 11–12; focus on governance, 25, 48; *Governance and Development*, 47–8, 60; *Governance: The World Bank Experience*, 48, 54; study of developing countries, 41; *Sub-Saharan Africa …*, 30–1, 41, 47
World Food Programme, 20
World Health Organization, 20

Yeta, Senior Chief Inyambo, 129

Zaire, 28, 33
Zambia, xi, xiii, 5, 86, 87–91, 98, 99, 100–1, 102, 104–6, 107, 118–21, 123–4, 127–30, 133; agreements with IMF and World Bank, 88 (abandoned, 90); business community in, 64; debt of, 88; decline of, 87; growth of political protest in, 90
Zambia Breweries, 119
Zambia Congress of Trade Unions (ZCTU), 89, 100
Zambia Consolidated Copper Mines (ZCCM), 120
Zambia Privatisation Agency (ZPA), 118
Zambia Sugar Company, 119
Zero Option Plan (Zambia), 127–30
Zimbabwe, 124

Studies in African Politics, Society and Development:
Recent Zed Books titles

Hans Abrahamsson and Anders Nilsson, Mozambique, *The Troubled Transition: From Socialist Construction to Free Market Capitalism*

Adebayo Adedeji (ed.), *South Africa and Africa: Within or Apart?*

Adebayo Adedeji (ed.), *Comprehending and Mastering African Conflicts: The Search for Sustainable Peace and Good Governance*

Adebayo Adedeji (ed.), *Nigeria: Renewal from the Roots? The Struggle for Democratic Development*

A. Adepoju (ed.), *Family, Population and Development in Africa*

Ifi Amadiume, *Re-inventing Africa: Matriarchy, Religion and Culture*

Ifi Amadiume, *Daughters of the Goddess, Daughters of Imperialism: African Women, Culture, Power and Democracy*

Oliver Barlet, *African Cinemas: Decolonizing the Gaze*

Jeff Haynes, *Religion and Politics in Africa*

Charles Larson, *The Ordeal of the African Writer*

Juma, Mugabe and Kameri-Mbote (eds), *Coming to Life: Biotechnology in African Economic Recovery*

Hein Marais, *South Africa: Limits to Change – The Political Economy of Transition*

J. May (ed.), *Poverty and Inequality in South Africa: Meeting the Challenge*

Linda Melvern, *A People Betrayed: The Role of the West in Rwanda's Genocide*

K. Mengisteab and B. I. Logan (eds), *Beyond Economic Liberalization in Africa: Structural Adjustment and the Alternatives*

John Mihevc, *The Market Tells Them So: The World Bank and Economic Fundamentalism in Africa*

William Minter, *Apartheid's Contras: An Inquiry into the Roots of War in Angola and Mozambique*

Robert Morrell (ed.), *Changing Masculinities in a Changing Society: Men and Gender in Southern Africa*

Stephanie Newell (ed.) *Writing African Women: Gender, Popular Culture and Literature in West Africa*

O. Ojo (ed.), *Africa and Europe: The Changing Economic Relationship*

Helen Pankhurst, *Gender, Development and Identity: An Ethiopian Study*

Ian Scoones et al., *Hazards and Opportunities: Farming Livelihoods in Dryland Africa*

Anika Rahman and Nahid Toubia, *Female Genital Mutilation: A Guide to Laws and Policies Worldwide*

Richard Sandbrook, *Closing the Circle: Democratization and Development in Africa*

Meredith Turshen and Clotilde Twagiramariya (eds), *What Women do in War Time: Gender and Conflict in Africa*

Charles Villa-Vicencio and Wilhelm (eds), *Looking Back, Raching Forward: Reflections on the Truth and Reconciliation Commission of South Africa*

Richard Werbner and Terence Ranger (eds), *Postcolonial Identities in Africa*

Richard Werbner (ed.), *Memory and the Postcolony: African Anthropology and the Critique of Power*

Francis Wilson, Nazneen Kanji and Einar Braathen (eds), *The Role of the State in Poverty Alleviation: Southern Africa in Focus*

For full details of this list and Zed's other subject and general catalogues, please write to: The Marketing Department, Zed Books, 7 Cynthia Street, London NI 9JF, UK or e-mail: sales@zedbooks.demon.co.uk

Visit our website at: http//www.zedbooks.demon.co.uk